Words of Life 2014

Daily Wisdom from Women Monastics

Edited by **Sr. Jean Marie Dwyer, OP**

NOVALIS

© 2013 Novalis Publishing Inc.

Cover design: Martin Gould
Cover photo by Amerie78/iStockphoto
Interior photos: p. 5 and p. 375 (Plaisted)
Layout: Audrey Wells

Published by Novalis

Publishing Office
10 Lower Spadina Avenue, Suite 400
Toronto, Ontario, Canada
M5V 2Z2

Head Office
4475 Frontenac Street
Montréal, Québec, Canada
H2H 2S2

www.novalis.ca

ISBN: 978-2-89646-581-1

Printed in Canada.

We acknowledge the financial support of the Government of Canada through the Canada Book Fund for business development activities.

5 4 3 2 1   17   16   15   14   13

Introduction

R eading and pondering Scripture are powerful tools for transforming our Christian life. In *Words of Life 2014*, monastic women of two traditions, the sisters of the Precious Blood monasteries and the Dominican Nuns, share the fruits of their daily reading, praying with, and meditating on the word of God.

Sacred reading is a daily practice in our monastic lives. We take a line or short passage from the Scripture and pray with it, silencing our minds and hearts to hear God speak through God's inspired word. Sitting in silence with the Scripture and pondering one sentence—even one word—can be life-changing. For example, in Scripture the word "freedom" means so much more than "to be without responsibilities."

In a busy, noisy world, sacred reading offers an effective way to quiet ourselves and reconnect with God. The reflections in this issue of *Words of Life* grow out of a prayerful reading of the Bible, and also offer practical ways to apply the text in daily life. Our private life with God always flows forth into our public life as we become fully present to others and to all the events and circumstances of each day.

Sharing this project with each other and sharing with you from the silence and rhythm of our communal and individual prayer have been a joy and a privilege to all of us who contributed. Sixty years of monastic living underlie our reflections and our witness: God is faithful, a merciful and loving God.

Sr. Jean Marie Dwyer, OP

Numbers 6.22-27 • Psalm 67 • Galatians 4.4-7 • Luke 2.16-21

So they went with haste and found Mary and Joseph, and the child lying in the manger. When they saw this, they made known what had been told them about this child; and all who heard it were amazed at what the shepherds told them.

Luke 2.16-17

One like us

The shepherds went with haste to see Jesus and they found him in a manger. Poor and living on the fringe of society, the shepherds came to see the Saviour announced by the angels, and found one like them. Jesus, the king, the Son of God, came not in pomp or splendour but in the image of the poor and forsaken.

Let us go with urgency and expectation to find the Lord in the faces of all we meet each day.

Where do we go from here?

On this feast of the Mother of God, take Mary's response to God's glory and make it your own. Seek out times and places where you can help others to see God at work in their lives, and like the shepherds, to announce to them that today is the day of God's favour.

Help me to see your presence in unexpected places and people, and let me share the Good News of your love with joy.

1 John 2.22-28 • Psalm 98 • John 1.19-28

M ake a joyful noise to the Lord, all the earth;
break forth into joyous song and praises. ...
Let the sea roar, and all that fills it;
the world and those who live in it.

Psalm 98. 3-4, 7

....

God is here

Psalm 98 is jubilant in praise! Why? Because the psalmist is overwhelmed by God's marvellous presence in his life. He sees God everywhere: in the seas, in the mountains and hills, and in God's people. He shouts, "Make a joyful noise! God does not forget us! His faithful and steadfast love accompanies us through life in sorrow and in joy!"

In the gospel, John the Baptist declares, "Among you stands one whom you do not know." But the psalmist calls out to us: You *do* know him! Let us look for him everywhere, in the most unlikely places and in every friend and stranger. God is here.

Where do we go from here?

Service to others often draws attention to ourselves as much as it does to others. Today is the day to do a service that no one will know. What can we do to help someone in need? Today is the commemoration of the Holy Name of Jesus. If we are homebound, we can use the awesome power of prayer to name someone for whom we normally do not pray.

Dear God, help me to recognize and make a joyful noise in your presence, to give thanks for your faithful love and marvellous deeds.

I John 2.29; 3.1-6 • Psalm 98 • John 1.29-34

The next day he saw Jesus coming toward him and declared, "Here is the Lamb of God who takes away the sin of the world! ... And I myself have seen and have testified that this is the Son of God."

John 1.29, 34

To serve in love

John the Baptist saw his whole mission as one of serving and giving witness to the one who was to come. He did not focus on himself but only on the one who was greater than he, Jesus, God's Son.

To be a person who serves is the primary vocation of the followers of Jesus. Jesus said of himself, "I have come to serve, not to be served." Can we define ourselves as the one who serves? Great deeds often elude us. But what about small deeds of giving? Our gift can be something as simple as a smile, a loving touch, a word of encouragement, patience with the kids or a loved one—all bestowed freely on those who pass through our lives each day.

Let us carry the needs of others in our heart, interceding for them and living as gifts to the world around us.

Where do we go from here?

So often we are caught up in the rush of our lives. Today we need to take a moment to look and to really see. Who is the one among us whom we do not know? The question almost forces the action we need to take: Get to know them!

Holy Spirit of God, descend upon me and fill my heart with love. Help me to witness to Jesus through my words and, above all, through my living.

1 John 3.7-10 • Psalm 98 • John 1.35-42

T hose who have been born of God do not sin, because God's seed abides in them; they cannot sin, because they have been born of God.   *1 John 3.9*

Seed that bears fruit in love

In his letters St. John measures our love for God by one standard: our sincere love for our neighbour. What a strong passage he gives us. We are born into God at baptism, when the seed of God's life is planted in us. It continues to grow, not bearing the fruit of sin, but blossoming into love for our neighbour.

We nourish our life as God's children through the sacraments. We open our hearts to the Holy Spirit of God, who teaches us all that Jesus spoke and did, so that we, in our turn, may do the works of Jesus, a promise given to us in the gospel. Our Christian life is a gift of grace founded deeply on Jesus' promise to be with us always.

Do I sometimes think all the responsibility is mine, and forget that I rest in the arms of God?

Where do we go from here?

Consider God's action in the life of Mother Elizabeth Anne Seton, who is honoured today. She left her wealthy life behind to care for those in need. What risk can we take today to show God's love to the world, trusting that we will never be abandoned?

Dear God, help me always to cling to your promise of life in trust and hope. The grace is yours; my gift is simply to continue to offer myself. Alleluia!

Isaiah 60.1-6 • Psalm 72 • Ephesians 3.2-3, 5-6 • Matthew 2.1-12

I n the time of King Herod, after Jesus was born in Bethlehem of Judea, wise men from the East came to Jerusalem, asking, "Where is the child who has been born king of the Jews? For we observed his star at its rising, and have come to pay him homage."

Matthew 2.1-2

All nations shall adore him

The adoration of Jesus by kings from different counties is called an "Epiphany," meaning a revelation of God to our world. The kings represented all the nations. They followed a star that they believed would lead them to a divine king, and so it did. To all who believe and trust him, Christ came to reveal God's presence with us. To follow him means to keep our eyes fixed on the star of faith, faith in his Word given to us in the gospels.

That first Christmas, only a few came before the Christ child to offer their gold, incense and myrrh, and to bow before him in love and praise. But Jesus brought the gift of God's love to all humanity. He gives us the gift to know him, and in knowing him, to know the Father. So lift up your heads and sing your Gloria, for God is among us.

Where do we go from here?

The tradition of chalking doors is a way to remind ourselves that at the turning of the year we will make hospitality a simple yet powerful means for showing God's love for the world. You can find instructions for this on the Internet.

O God, my joy will be to see the light of your face forever shining upon all peoples.

1 John 3.22–4.6 • Psalm 2 • Matthew 4.12-17, 23-25

J esus went throughout Galilee, teaching in their synagogues and proclaiming the good news of the kingdom and curing every disease and every sickness among the people. So his fame spread throughout all Syria, and they brought to him all the sick … and he cured them. *Matthew 4.23-24*

The kingdom of God has come

Our love for one another is the sign that the spirit of God is present among us. There are those who live in darkness and hate, and destroy the world by their thirst for power and war. They have not yet come to know Jesus and his message of love. There are those who are on the way—the seekers. The Holy Spirit guides us toward the light, toward the goodness we are seeking. All our good desires lead us to God, even when we cannot yet name our longing.

The good news is that God seeks us! Jesus brought the kingdom of God, seeking our love and our true repentance for our sins. Real repentance helps to restore the beauty of the divine image in us, showing us our true self and how much we need the help of God's grace.

Where do we go from here?

Today is Christmas Eve for those who follow the Julian calendar. It is another opportunity for us to celebrate the light of God coming into the world, so make sure that you send the traditional greeting to your Ukrainian friends: "*Khristos rodyvsya!*" (Christ is born!), which is answered by "*Slavite Yoho!*" (Let Us Glorify Him!).

O God, I acknowledge that I am a sinner. Fill me with your light, that I may see clearly the way to you and share with others the forgiveness you have given to me.

1 John 4.7-10 • Psalm 72 • Mark 6.34-44

As he went ashore, he saw a great crowd; and he had compassion for them, because they were like sheep without a shepherd; and he began to teach them many things. When it grew late, his disciples came to him and said, "This is a deserted place, and the hour is now very late; send them away so that they may go into the surrounding country and villages and buy something for themselves to eat." But he answered them, "You give them something to eat." *Mark 6.34-37*

Give them something to eat

The gospel shows Jesus' deep compassion and care for those who followed him: feeding the large crowd and healing all who came to him. What a patient love Jesus had for them. His focus was not just on teaching them—he cared also about how they would find food for their evening meal.

Our God is full of such infinite love and mercy toward all his creation. That love was revealed when God sent his Son to share our human life and to die for us that we might be saved. Could we ever match this love? Could we die for those who sin, or even for those we love?

Where do we go from here?

Today is the feast of Saint Brother André Bessette. What better model of love for the world could we hope for. Think of a way that you can open your life to the world in a new way. Ask how you could sacrifice some of your time or treasure for the sake of those in need.

**O God, help me to love and to forget myself
in the service of those with whom I live.**

1 John 4.11-18 • Psalm 72 • Mark 6.45-52

When they saw him walking on the sea, they thought it was a ghost and cried out, for they all saw him and were terrified. But immediately he spoke to them and said, "Take heart, it is I; do not be afraid."

Mark 6.49-50

Troubled seas

After spending a long day with crowds and the sick, Jesus went up the mountain to pray to his Father. How he must have loved the quiet and calm of the silent forest where he could rest without a shouting crowd pressing against him. As he prayed there, he knew his apostles were in trouble on the sea, so he left his solitude and went to them, walking on the surface of the water.

What selfless love he showed, leaving his quiet place of prayer and calling to them over the roaring sea, "Take heart, it is I; do not be afraid."

Am I able to walk across the sea of my own emotions, and forgive and give comfort where there is hurt or fear?

Where do we go from here?

In Canada, today we celebrate St. Raymond of Peñafort, who is a patron saint for lawyers, especially canon lawyers. This would be a good day to remember all those who serve the Church in administration of any kind. Send a message of appreciation to your chancery for the often thankless work they do that keeps the Church alive and functioning in your diocese.

**Lord, help me to love those around me
who are lonely or in pain.**

1 John 4.19–5.4 • Psalm 72 • Luke 4.14-22

"The Spirit of the Lord is upon me, because he has anointed me to bring good news to the poor. He has sent me to proclaim release to the captives and recovery of sight to the blind, to let the oppressed go free ...." Then he began to say to them, "Today this scripture has been fulfilled in your hearing."   *Luke 4.14-15, 18, 21*

Faith conquers the world

God loved us first before we loved him: we need to believe this. Love is a gift we have received from God; it unites, and does not divide. Hatred divides and is not from God. That is why if we hate and say we love, we lie. If we really love God, we will strive to love our brothers and sisters who are near us, and those who are far away.

When Jesus went home to Nazareth and spoke in the synagogue, he fulfilled what the Scriptures said of him. All were amazed at his teaching, for the Spirit of love was in him and they believed his word. Yet how quickly their praise turned to distrust and violence. Their praise and admiration did not penetrate to the heart.

Is my faith rooted in my inner spirit? Do I really believe in Jesus, and do I live my faith by doing practical deeds of love? Do I follow his commandments?

Where do we go from here?

The Bible needs to do more than sit on a shelf. Take it down today and read. Open it to several places; read and meditate on what you find there. Join with some friends to discuss one of the parables.

My Jesus, spread your love and your Word over the world like sunshine, giving light to all who are in darkness.

1 John 5.5-13 • Psalm 147 • Luke 5.12-16

O nce, when he was in one of the cities, there was a man covered with leprosy. When he saw Jesus, he bowed with his face to the ground and begged him, "Lord, if you choose, you can make me clean." Then Jesus stretched out his hand, touched him, and said, "I do choose. Be made clean." *Luke 5.12-13*

....

Eternal life in Jesus

To have faith in Jesus Christ is to have eternal life. In today's gospel Jesus cures the leper. The lepers lived in loneliness and separation from their fellow human beings. Jesus showed his true humanity by touching this poor man, something that no one would do for fear of contagion. The compassion of Jesus and his love for each individual brings us such hope. Divine Love was manifested especially on the cross when Jesus died for us. Oh, how wonderful to have such a God who shares eternal life with his creatures. Our hearts should explode with happiness to know we will be with our God forever. Jesus made this gift possible by his coming.

Where do we go from here?

Today we celebrate Pope Miltiades, one of three African popes, who served the Church at the time when the Roman Emperor Constantine converted to Christianity. Today is a good time to remember that we are part of a catholic—universal—church that has touched people from all over the world and in all walks of life. Pray today for the Pope and for all who lead the Church.

Let me rejoice always in the gift of your transforming grace and steadfast love that sustains me.

1 John 5.14-21 • Psalm 149 • John 3.22-30

J ohn answered, "No one can receive anything except what has been given from heaven. You yourselves are my witnesses that I said, 'I am not the Messiah, but I have been sent ahead of him.' He who has the bride is the bridegroom. The friend of the bridegroom, who stands and hears him, rejoices greatly at the bridegroom's voice. For this reason my joy has been fulfilled. He must increase, but I must decrease."   *John 3.27-30*

The blessings of obedience

When we read of the long journey of the people of God, we see that if they obeyed God's commandments, they were blessed and God accompanied them on the journey. Why is there so much unrest and violence among nations? Riots, war, a thirst for power at the expense of human lives: all these speak of the loss of dependence on God. John the Baptist knew who he was and did not deny Christ. John rejoiced that he was only a servant sent to announce the coming of the holy one of God. We also are here to serve our God and follow his commands. We are only stewards of his earth, called to love one another in humble service in Jesus' name.

Where do we go from here?

For many people, the winter blahs and blues are starting to take hold, maybe even in our own lives. After the holidays, when we were expected to visit others, today would be a good day to call a friend, to visit those who live alone, and to undertake it this time for no reason other than love.

**O God, bless us with leaders who love and obey
your laws and will lead the nations in truth and justice.**

Sunday | **JANUARY 12** | **Baptism of the Lord**

Isaiah 42.1-4, 6-7 • Psalm 29 • Acts 10.34-38 • Matthew 3.13-17

nd a voice from heaven said, "This is my Son, the Beloved, with whom I am well pleased." *Matthew 3.16-17*

This is the Beloved

The baptism of Jesus in the waters of the Jordan is a wonderful testimony of the Trinity's activity. The Father and the Holy Spirit confirm Jesus as the "chosen one." The Father speaks, identifying Jesus as the Son in whom God is pleased. The Holy Spirit overshadows Jesus. In his life and death, Jesus opens paradise, abolishes the stain of original sin and makes us heirs to the kingdom of God.

This is what baptism does for us. The readings for today are centred on this wonderful grace. Jesus made it possible for human beings to be with God and to know they are God's beloved. Everyone who is baptized receives the Trinity and is infused with the gifts and virtues necessary to gain eternal life. They receive the power to conquer sin and be transformed into the likeness of God. What a gift, and how thankful we should be.

Where do we go from here?

How can we say thanks to God? By helping God's people, of course! The people of Haiti still need our help, four years to the day from the earthquake that devastated so much of that impoverished land. Today is usually the feast of Marguerite Bourgeoys, and so, following her example, it would be a good day to help raise funds for those who are still in such need. The efforts of an individual encouraging friends and family can make a real difference in the lives of those who suffer.

**Father, mould us into the likeness of your Son,
that we may be worthy to see you face to face forever.**

18

1 Samuel 1.1-8 • Psalm 116 • Mark 1.14-20

A nd Jesus said to them, "Follow me and I will make you fish for people." And immediately they left their nets and followed him.

Mark 1.14-18

The kingdom of God is near

Deep in each human heart there is a longing for wholeness and eternal happiness. We lost these when sin entered creation. Jesus became a man to bring us back to our original purity and to open again that paradise closed by sin. He brought God's love back into our world, and gave his life that we might be with him in heaven.

Jesus calls anyone who is willing to leave all and follow him. The apostles received this call. Jesus gathered rough fishermen, and they responded, leaving their nets and boats to follow his summons. Jesus continues to call ordinary people, like you and me, to help spread the good news of God's kingdom to our thirsting world.

How can I help to spread the kingdom? Can I follow Jesus's way to truth and life?

Where do we go from here?

When it came to Jesus, Saint Hilary, whom we celebrate today, was a big believer in the truth. He worked tirelessly to spread the kingdom by eliminating anything that was hypocritical or just plain wrong. In our own lives, today would be a great day to look for those little lies we tell ourselves, the excuses we give for not living as we should. Lent is coming, so we should think about what we need to change.

**O God, help me to give my life as you did,
that all might know you, the true God.**

1 Samuel 1.9-20 • 1 Samuel 2 • Mark 1.21-28

J ust then there was in their synagogue a man with an unclean spirit, and he cried out, "What have you to do with us, Jesus of Nazareth? Have you come to destroy us? I know who you are, the Holy One of God." But Jesus rebuked him, saying, "Be silent, and come out of him!"
Mark 1.23-24

My heart exults in the Lord

Today in the book of Samuel we read how Hannah cried out for a child, for she was barren. She was judged wrongly, and her tears were rewarded by God. God is with us in our need and sees our inmost heart. Jesus was sent from the Father to make manifest God's tender love for each person. When Jesus went to the synagogue to teach, a man possessed by a demon confronted him. Jesus quieted him with authority and helped restore the man to health. He always respected each human person, cured them, lifted them up and restored their dignity as persons created by God. May we always follow this example, knowing each person as uniquely God's beloved, and helping them live their life as a unique human being destined for the kingdom of God.

Where do we go from here?

Intercessory prayer is an important element of our faith. It is okay to ask God for the things that will help us to live as faithful members of the body of Christ. Spend today listening to yourself and others, and make a list of those specific things that need prayer. Use that list over the next several weeks, and watch how God answers your requests.

Dear Jesus, help me to see you in each person, poor and rich, and treat each with loving dignity as a child of God.

1 Samuel 3.1-10, 19-20 • Psalm 40 • Mark 1.29-39

I n the morning, while it was still very dark, he got up and went out to a deserted place, and there he prayed. And Simon and his companions hunted for him. When they found him, they said to him, "Everyone is searching for you." He answered, "Let us go on to the neighbouring towns, so that I may proclaim the message there also; for that is what I came out to do." And he went throughout Galilee, proclaiming the message in their synagogues and casting out demons.
Mark 1.35-39

To do your will, Lord, is my delight

How can we know what the will of God is for us? Prayer before decisions and a sincere intention to do the right thing help us find answers and bring peace to difficult problems. Jesus always went into a quiet place and prayed to his Father before he went on his mission to bring help and peace to all who suffered any illness. If we keep our eyes fixed on Jesus, and follow his teaching, we can be sure we are doing the will of the Lord. It is when we abandon the way of truth and love, and seek material gain through deceit and power, that we lose sight of his will and lose our way.

Where do we go from here?

The desires of our heart tell us whether we are seeking God's will. If we desire to follow Jesus and want to do God's will, then we can be sure that the Holy Spirit will direct us into the path of truth. It is important to set aside time for prayer each day, perhaps early in the morning, and listen to what the Lord wishes to teach us.

O Divine Word, help me to speak the truth in my dealings with others. Keep my heart pleasing in your sight, for in your will are life and happiness.

Thursday | JANUARY 16

I Samuel 4.1-11 • Psalm 44 • Mark 1.40-45

A leper came to him begging him, and kneeling he said to him, "If you choose, you can make me clean." Moved with pity, Jesus stretched out his hand and touched him, and said to him, "I do choose. Be made clean!"   *Mark 1.40-41*

Show us your mercy, Lord

In the first reading, we see what a disgrace it was for Israel to lose the battle. They even lost the ark, the presence of God, because of the sins of Eli's sons. What hard lessons they had to learn after deviating from God's law, for sin carries its own consequences.

The mercy of God is infinite and there is always hope for each of us. Jesus did not ask the leper if he had sinned; he just cured him. Jesus did not change him back into a leper for not obeying him, but left the area for another town where he was needed. Jesus overlooked the man's disobedience for the sake of his gratitude, for he merely wanted to share his good fortune.

How can I overlook or pardon the actions of one who does not do what I think they should? Can I, like Jesus, see the good in every person?

Where do we go from here?

Jesus came into the world to manifest God's great desire to be merciful. As Christians, we in our turn must extend mercy to others. Is there someone in your life you find it very difficult to forgive? Pray that you may forgive that person. To be unforgiving only hurts us, makes our spirit small and closes our heart to love: God's love and our neighbour's.

**Help me, O Lord, to give mercy and love
to all who are different from me.**

1 Samuel 8.4-7, 10-22 • Psalm 89 • Mark 2.1-12

But the thing displeased Samuel when they said, "Give us a king to govern us."
1 Samuel 8.6

. . . .

The ways of kings

The Israelites wanted to have a king to rule over them so they could be like the neighbouring nations. They rejected God's leadership and chose a fallible human ruler. The people did not listen to Samuel and were slaves to the kings they chose. The Old Testament stories of kings who used their power to destroy others and to prosper at the expense of their own people are all too familiar to us today.

In the gospels, Jesus uses power to heal and to forgive sins. Oh, what a king we have in him who rules with justice and mercy. He alone can take away the spiritual wounds of sin. He is the only real king of our universe. The God of justice and love is the paradigm for all leaders.

Where do we go from here?

This text reminds us of the importance of praying for leaders and rulers, but we can also let it challenge us to reflect on what we allow to "rule" our lives. Am I listening to influences other than the voice of God, who wants to be all to me? What exercises a certain tyranny over me: what people think, an unhealthy relationship, or money? In your time of prayer, be silent and listen to hear God's voice and give him lordship in your life.

**Help all rulers of nations to follow you, Jesus,
for you rule with compassion and love.**

1 Samuel 9.1-4, 17-19; 10.1 • Psalm 21 • Mark 2.13-17

And as he sat at dinner in Levi's house, many tax collectors and sinners were also sitting with Jesus and his disciples—for there were many who followed him.   *Mark 2.15*

How God judges

God blessed Saul with every good gift of wisdom and judgment to rule. God chose him for a vocation that needed strength and courage as well as receptivity to the word of God. Saul forgot God. How different was the call of Levi the tax collector, who cheated on taxes and took more than was needed. Yet, he was called by Jesus to follow him, and he was faithful to him to the end of his life. What was different between Saul and Levi? Why did God reject Saul? Jesus always sees the intentions of our hearts. Saul was weakened by power. Levi knew the poverty of his heart and his need of healing, and he found strength, not in power but in Jesus' promise of life.

Only God knows the depth of hearts, so let him be the judge of others.

Where do we go from here?

God desires to fill us with so much love it overflows to our neighbour. Take time today to thank God for his love and ask him to increase your love. Notice those who come into your life in need of love, a kind word, a helping hand or a word of encouragement and give away the love you have received from God. God will give you more tomorrow.

**To condemn others is not for me but only for you,
O Lord, who reads all hearts.
Do not let me forget your mercy and forgiveness;
may I always extend that mercy to others.**

Isaiah 49.3, 5-6 • Psalm 40 • 1 Corinthians 1.1-3 • John 1.29-34

A nd now the Lord says,
who formed me in the womb to be his servant,
to bring Jacob back to him, and that Israel might be
gathered to him …
Isaiah 49.5

Being the face of God

This prophetic passage is taken from one of the four "servant songs" in Isaiah. The Church has always interpreted them in the light of Christ's mission: Jesus is the one who will bring the salvation of God to the ends of the earth. As disciples of Jesus, we are also formed as servants of salvation. How can we be a light of salvation, reflecting Jesus?

A story is told about Mother Teresa, who brought a dying man in from the street. He said to her, "I do not know your God, but I do know that he is loving and kind because of the kindness and compassion you have shown to me." Like Mother Teresa, I want to become a conduit of God's love and compassion to others. I will not convince anyone of my faith in Jesus by words if I am not like Jesus in practical deeds of loving kindness.

Where do we go from here?

God's light in me can reach to the ends of the earth—can touch the most forgotten places of the world through my prayers and intercessions for the needy of the world. Through prayer we are spiritually connected to all God's creation. I can also be a light in my immediate environment by my good deeds to those around me: by my patience, my willingness to help and my attentiveness of the needs of others. Make a difference today!

**Dear Jesus, teach me to give myself to those
around me in many small deeds of love.**

I Samuel 15.16-23 • Psalm 50 • Mark 2.18-22

"**N**o one puts new wine into old wineskins; otherwise, the wine will burst the skins, and the wine is lost, and so are the skins; but one puts new wine into fresh wineskins."

Mark 2.21-22

The law written on our hearts

Here Jesus teaches us that, with his coming, something new is happening. He does not do away with the old law, but in him, the law becomes new and vibrant, no longer a matter of rules written in a book. This new law has been written in our hearts through the gift of the Holy Spirit.

Jesus is the new wine, and as the Church, the people of God are the new wineskins. How can we translate his law of love written now in our hearts into concrete deeds of service to others?

How can we be loving members in our communities? How can God be central in the primary relationships in our lives?

Where do we go from here?

Do I want God to be first in my life? If I do, then how do I make God the primary reference for all I do in life? Carry these questions around in your heart, constantly coming back to them. Bring them to your times of prayer and offer them to God during the liturgy. Be sincere in your seeking and the answer will come. Take just one thing in your life that is not yet handed over to God and day by day seek to surrender it. We grow through a daily commitment to change one thing at a time.

Dear Jesus, send me forth to enter into loving relationships with my family first, and then the whole family of God.

Tuesday | **JANUARY 21**

Samuel 16.1-13 • Psalm 89 • Mark 2.23-28

> will sing of your steadfast love, O Lord, forever;
> with my mouth I will proclaim your faithfulness to all generations.
> *Psalm 89.1*

God's steadfast love

Today we celebrate the Feast of St. Agnes, who, at very young age, forfeited her life rather than deny her faith. Her bravery testified to God's steadfast love. She sang of God's love and proclaimed God's faithfulness to all generations. It's unlikely that any of us will ever have to give such a radical testimony to the faithfulness and steadfast love of the Lord.

Etty Hillesum, a young Jewish woman who died at Auschwitz, wrote in her journal: "I have strength enough, God, for suffering on a grand scale, but there are more than a thousand everyday cares that leap up on me without warning like so many fleas." This is the arena—the events of each ordinary day—where we need to witness to God's steadfast love in our lives, and trust that God will sustain us in faithfulness through his unending love, which remains forever firm and unchanging.

Where do we go from here?

Do I trust that God is sustaining me and will continue to sustain me through today's difficulties? We need only take on each day at a time and trust in God's sustaining love for that day. I can do nothing about tomorrow; it is in God's hands. If I can learn to live one day at a time with trust in God, then I will find lasting peace in times of joy and in times of trouble.

**Dear God, let me show I am a Christian
by my patience in all the small vexations of each day.**

1 Samuel 17.32-33, 37, 40-51 • Psalm 144 • Mark 3.1-6

They watched him to see whether he would cure him on the sabbath, so that they might accuse him…. He looked around at them with anger; he was grieved at their hardness of heart and said to the man, "Stretch out your hand." He stretched it out, and his hand was restored. *Mark 3.2-5*

An open heart

Jesus was angry at their hardness of heart. When he asked the Pharisees to explain the law about doing good on the sabbath, they were silent, and their silence was more eloquent than words. They had closed their hearts to anything but their own preconceived ideas of right and wrong, their notion of truth.

I would not want Jesus to look angrily at me because I wanted only to confirm my own self-righteousness. But I wonder, am I truly open to listen to God's word and to be changed by that word? Do I listen to others in order to really hear and enter into what they are saying, or do I listen in order to trap them with my preconceived ideas of righteousness and truth? Am I willing to give to others the mercy and forgiveness that God gives to me? All challenging questions! The way we listen to others is a fair barometer of how we are listening to God.

Where do we go from here?

The Pharisees were not open to the new possibilities that Jesus offered. Our preconceived ideas can keep us from growing. What to do? Be like a little child, eager to receive, open to all kinds of new things and new adventures.

**Jesus, your word is a real challenge to me today.
Let me ponder it and allow the Word to enter profoundly
into my heart. Give me the wisdom to live it daily.**

1 Samuel 18.6-9; 19.1-7 • Psalm 56 • Mark 3.7-12

A nd the women sang to one another as they made merry, "Saul has killed his thousands, and David his ten thousands." … So Saul eyed David from that day on. *1 Samuel 18.6-7, 9*

Lord, I will follow

The stories of the Old Testament so clearly show God's tender love in contrast to our sinfulness. In today's story from 1 Samuel, we see the seed of jealously and envy enter the heart of Saul. As the story continues, Saul allows that seed to grow and to erode the good soil of his heart, until finally he turns from the ways of God.

In David, we have another man who sins very seriously against the law of God and against his neighbour. But David is God's great struggler, accepting God's chastisement and repenting with great humility of heart again and again. God loves David with tender love, and continues to be with him and bless him. God seeks to bestow that same mercy and forgiveness on us every day. Our weakness only serves God as an opportunity to love us more—if we will.

Where do we go from here?

These two men from today's Old Testament stories show clearly how our choices shape our life. Jealousy narrows our hearts and our perspective. Saul cannot get beyond his struggle and need. David, who sins, acknowledges his sin and his need for God. A sure formula for growing in holiness is acknowledging our sinfulness and need and trusting utterly in God's loving mercy. God will never fail us.

Lord, let me be open to receive your grace
so that I may walk humbly in your ways.

1 Samuel 24.2-21 • Psalm 57 • Mark 3.13-19

He went up the mountain and called to him those whom he wanted, and they came to him.
Mark 3.13

The mountain of the Lord

Just one small phrase of Scripture pondered in the silence of our heart can be a source of infinite wisdom. Take the theme of "the mountain," which is a wonderful one to trace through Scripture: Moses' experience of the burning bush and receiving the Law, and the prophet Elijah's encounter with God in the gentle breeze all take place on a mountain. Isaiah uses mountain imagery to depict where the great Messianic banquet will take place, where God will heal our infirmities and wipe away every tear. Jesus frequently went up to the mountain to pray. In today's gospel, Jesus goes up the mountain to choose his intimate followers.

What does going up to the mountain mean for us? Our times set aside for silent prayer can be a call to go up the mountain in spirit to encounter God and to follow in his ways.

Where do we go from here?

Following a theme through the Scriptures is wonderful way to become more familiar with the Bible. At biblegateway.com you can type in a keyword and all the Scripture references will pop up. Why not try it? Share and discuss your study with others.

Lord, let me withdraw with you to the mountain of prayer, that you may teach me your ways and fill my spirit with the gentle, loving breath of your Holy Spirit.

Acts 9.1-22 • Psalm 117 • Mark 16.15-18

"Lord, I have heard from many about this man, how much evil he has done to your saints in Jerusalem; and here he has authority from the chief priests to bind all who invoke your name."
Acts 9.13-15

An instrument whom I have chosen

St. Paul was a strong personality: no fuzzy thinking or hesitation about him. He must have been a challenge to live with. So when the Holy Spirit sent Ananias to Paul, Ananias obeyed fearfully and reluctantly, offering a few choice words of advice to God about Paul's reputation.

I sometimes do the same thing, as if God needed me to point out possible consequences of God's request. When I catch myself, I picture God laughing, then saying to me, as he did to Ananias, "Just go! I can take care of the situation."

Both Ananias and Paul were called by God and listened to God's voice. It seems that God chooses some pretty unlikely characters to do God's work. After all, God chose me.

Where do we go from here?

I am one of the unlikely characters God has chosen to do his work. Will I go in the knowledge that God knows what he is doing? Whatever God asks, whether the task is great or small, it is the one best suited for me. The great saints were only men and women like you and me, and look what God accomplished in them. They said yes to being God's instruments and so can I.

Yes, Lord, here am I. Send me. And let me see with your eyes the unlikely other you have also commissioned to do your work.

31

Isaiah 9.1-4 • Psalm 27 • I Corinthians 1.10-13, 17-18 • Matthew 4.12-23

F rom that time Jesus began to proclaim, "Repent, for the kingdom of heaven has come near."   *Matthew 4.17-20*

Jesus, our light

Isaiah tells us, "The people who walked in darkness have seen a great light." He prophesies that God's people will be released from their burdens and set free from their oppressors. Jesus is the one Isaiah foretells. He delivers us from darkness and carries our burdens.

In today's gospel, we see Jesus walking along the Sea of Galilee, choosing his first followers. He begins his ministry by gathering those he will commission to continue his mission to proclaim repentance and forgiveness of sins—the deliverance from all that keeps us from the kingdom of heaven. Repentance is the key that opens the door to the kingdom. The Greek word for repentance is *metanoia,* which means a complete turning around, a real change.

The good news to begin this New Year is that our light has come! God is with us. Rejoice!

Where do we go from here?

What do you want to repent from? Is there something in your life you want to change and have been trying to change for years? Don't give up: let your desire to change be present to you, in your mind and in your heart. Take your desire to the Lord in prayer, along with all your failures: "Lord, I cannot do this alone, but you can do it in me." God always hears the prayer of the humble.

Lord, give me the gift of true repentance: touch me, heal me, open my eyes to see the nearness of your kingdom, and open my ears that I may hear your word and be healed.

2 Samuel 5.1-7, 10 • Psalm 89 • Mark 3.22-30

" I f a kingdom is divided against itself, that kingdom cannot stand. And if a house is divided against itself, that house will not be able to stand. And if Satan has risen up against himself and is divided, he cannot stand, but his end has come."   *Mark 3.24-26*

Kingdom living

Jesus teaches that division among people is a sign of the absence of the Holy Spirit, who is love. Jesus came to bring healing, peace and love. But we do not always open our hearts to receive these gifts. Division, prejudice, hate and jealousy are the results of our human choices, not God's will.

Our inner desires are manifest in our daily choices and actions. Do I refuse to forgive a hurt done to me? Do I cheat or hurt others to get ahead in my job? If the answer is "Yes," then my heart is not yet fully God's. Do I take time for prayer? Do I seek ways to help others? Am I kind and approachable? If the answer is "Yes," then the kingdom of God is near.

Where do we go from here?

Jesus never hesitates to challenge us. He knows that we can do what is necessary to bring the kingdom of God into our hearts. Are there divisions in my life: with my family or friends, in my workplace? I cannot change others, but I can change myself and make a difference. Think of just one way that you can be a person of peace and love in the midst of a situation of division. How we choose to live our life is not dependent on the choice of others. It is a challenge!

**Dear Jesus, may I walk in your ways
and do the deeds of loving compassion.**

2 Samuel 6.12-15, 17-19 • Psalm 24 • Mark 3.31-35

A crowd was sitting around him; and they said to him, "Your mother and your brothers and sisters are outside, asking for you." And he replied, "Who are my mother and my brothers?"

Mark 3.32-33

....

Being the family of God

Jesus' mother is his first and most perfect disciple. She is the one who said "yes" to all God asked of her, even to the sacrifice of her son. Mary is our model for being the one who does God's will. She pondered the word the angel spoke to her. She searched the depth of her heart to understand what God was asking. She wanted to say "yes," to be faithful.

Wanting to do God's will is the first step to finding God's will. We need to follow Mary's example, not to plunge unreflectively into things, but to wait and to listen to what the Holy Spirit is saying. God will speak in our hearts, if we give God the chance. If we say "yes" to God, then we, too, are Jesus' mother and brothers and sisters. We belong to him and to the family of God.

Where do we go from here?

Our desires hold the key to everything. What are your priorities? What we desire most is what will shape who we are and what we do. Do your desires need shifting? Do you need to change your priorities? Start today to look at how your inner desires are motivating your choices.

Lord, teach me the patience to wait and to listen.

2 Samuel 7.1-17 • Psalm 89 • Mark 4.1-20

And he said to them, "Do you not understand this parable? Then how will you understand all the parables? The sower sows the word. … And these are the ones sown on rocky ground: when they hear the word, they immediately receive it with joy. But they have no root, and endure only for a while; then, when trouble or persecution arises on account of the word, immediately they fall away."   *Mark 4.13-14, 16-17*

Staying power

The parable of the sower is rich in teaching. The image of the seed sown on rocky ground particularly resonates with me. It is so easy to get excited about new ideas, a new job, new friends. But will I have the staying power when I realize the cost of carrying through on my initial commitment?

Everything is an adventure when it is new, so exciting at first. God plants God's challenging and renewing Word in our hearts, but for it to firmly root and grow, we must be faithful in living that Word each day, whatever the cost. God will sustain us, but we need to persevere and endure.

Where do we go from here?

Can I set myself a task and stick to it? Endurance and perseverance are two qualities we need for spiritual growth. One of my tasks in the monastery is folding cards. It is a tedious job! I always want to jump up and walk around or do something more interesting, but set myself a time limit and persevere. Focusing on and doing this boring task prepares me for waiting on God's time and not running away from difficult spiritual challenges. Try it.

Lord, grant me the gift of faithful perseverance.

2 Samuel 7.18-19, 24-29 • Psalm 132 • Mark 4.21-25

" I will not enter my house or get into my bed;
I will not give sleep to my eyes or slumber to my eyelids,
until I find a place for the Lord,
a dwelling place for the Mighty One of Jacob."

Psalm 132.3-4

God's house

David wants to build a house for God's dwelling. He is full of zeal for the Lord's glory. But God tells David that he will not build a house for God; rather, God will build a house for David.

God has built a sanctuary in our hearts and dwells there. From our hearts come war and violence, or from our hearts come love and peace. Let us be filled with David's zeal to make God's inner dwelling our dwelling, where we learn to love God and do God's works in the world.

Where do we go from here?

Am I willing to stay up and give myself no rest until God is dwelling in my heart? Do I have an urgency about my life in God? There are so many other things that come at me and seem more important. Yet if all that I do comes from God and is in God, then all the problems and needs of life just fall into place. Test it out and see if it is not true. It takes practice.

**Lord, because my heart is your dwelling and mine,
let me be an instrument of peace and goodness.**

2 Samuel 11.1-4, 5-10, 13-17 • Psalm 51 • Mark 4.26-34

"The kingdom of God is as if someone would scatter seed on the ground, and would sleep and rise night and day, and the seed would sprout and grow …."

Mark 4.26-27

Growing in secret

Jesus tells us that the kingdom of God is already here. It is a seed planted in the hearts of men and women, a hidden treasure that grows in silence and darkness. The farmer scatters seeds and they grow unseen in the darkness of the earth.

I once knew a Sister who planted green beans, her first "farming" endeavour. She kept digging them up to see how they were doing. Not surprisingly, her first crop failed. God has planted his seed in our heart; the Holy Spirit prepares it and waters it. We need to be content with the darkness of our faith, and trust in God that the seed is growing. We continue to prepare the soil by our good deeds of love, but God brings them to fruition.

Where do we go from here?

There are times in our life when God seems to have disappeared and we wonder what we have done. If we look into our heart and find there the desire to love God and to do his will, then we have done nothing to displease God. God is taking us by the hand and leading us into a deep faith. When we consent to be patient and walk in the darkness of faith, we are trusting in God's unfailing love. Our trust brings us into a greater possession of God. God has promised never to fail us. Trust God.

**Lord, let my heart be the good soil
that will produce fruit for the kingdom.**

2 Samuel 12.1-7, 10-17 • Psalm 51 • Mark 4.35-41

A great windstorm arose, and the waves beat into the boat, so that the boat was being swamped. But he was in the stern, asleep on the cushion; and they woke him up and said to him, "Teacher, do you not care that we are perishing?"

Mark 4.37-38

Calm my stormy sea

Often life feels like a voyage on a stormy and turbulent sea, and safe havens are so far away they seem unreal. At these times, it is important to remember Jesus is always present with us. He may be sleeping peacefully on his cushion, apparently unaware of our peril, but he is attentive to hear us call out in our need. We have only to have faith in him, to reach out to him, to cry out, and he will hear us and calm the storms that threaten us.

Where do we go from here?

What fears do we carry in our heart? Why are we afraid? Our fears teach us so much about ourselves. Fear holds us in bondage and prevents us from going forward. We do not dare. Reflect honestly on what causes you fear. Often our fears are no more than illusions, such as what people will think. St. John in his first letter tells us that "perfect love casts out all fear." So try conquering your fears by loving and by praying for the grace you need.

Jesus, help me to overcome my fears and always have faith in your power to save me!

Malachi 3.1-4 • Psalm 24 • Hebrews 2.10-11, 13-18 • Luke 2.22-40

There was also a prophet, Anna the daughter of Phanuel, of the tribe of Asher. … At that moment she came, and began to praise God and to speak about the child to all who were looking for the redemption of Jerusalem. *Luke 2.36, 38*

The Spirit of God

Today's feast reminds us that the action of the Holy Spirit in our world did not begin at Pentecost! The Holy Spirit was working from the beginning of creation, moving over the waters of primal chaos to bring forth order and life, acting in the lives of prophets and kings. Now the Spirit leads Simeon into the temple on what must have been an ordinary day suddenly made extraordinary. Enlightened by the Spirit, Simeon takes the child Jesus into his arms and proclaims his canticle: "Master, now you are dismissing your servant in peace, according to your word."

Just as Simeon (and Anna, the other prophet in today's reading) recognized the Christ through the action of the Spirit, may we today see him in everyone we meet, enlightened by the same Spirit.

Where do we go from here?

Is your life at this moment like a stormy sea? Do you feel like the boat is about to capsize? Hang on, Jesus is still there and though he may seem to be asleep, he knows your distress. Jesus can and will still the storm at just the right time—until then, just ride the waves and trust the Lord. It is an extreme sport for the young and the old.

**Jesus, help me to recognize your presence
in the midst of the world today.**

2 Samuel 15.13-14, 30; 16.5-13 • Psalm 3 • Mark 5.1-20

"O Lord, how many are my foes!
But you, O Lord, are a shield around me,
my glory, and the one who lifts up my head."

Psalm 3.1, 3

The spiritual life

This psalm captures a truth about the spiritual life. Some problems loom over us like a dark cloud that lasts all day and returns in the morning. These problems taunt us, undermining our faith with their challenge: "There is no help for you in God." Yet, our Lord shields us, especially at times when fear seems all around, ready to extinguish hope like the night sky snuffs out daylight. In reality, God is our shield, our glory: "He answers me from his holy hill." Clouds do not last forever. The vapor dissipates with the sun that invariably shines. The spiritual life ushers in the consolation of God's abiding presence. God is with us at all times.

Where do we go from here?

Sit down with Psalm 3 and pray over it. The psalm contains a wide range of emotions. Study them. How do those emotions resonate in you? How does God answer the psalmist? How does the psalmist praise God? What does this psalm mean to you? How can it help you in your journey with God? Our foes and enemies are those things within us that prevent us from seeking God.

**O Lord, my shield and my glory, in dark times and
in times of consolation and light, I am yours.**

2 Samuel 18.9-10, 14, 24-26, 30—19.3 • Psalm 86 • Mark 5.21-43

He took the child's father and mother and those who were with him, and went in where the child was. He took her by the hand and said to her, "Talitha cum," which means, "Little girl, get up!" And immediately the girl got up and began to walk about ....
Mark 5.40-42

Incredulity

The word "incredulity" defines this gospel passage remarkably well, since incredulity wears many hats: amazement, disbelief, wonder, suspicion and astonishment. Sadness over the young girl draws forth the compassion of Jesus, who by now is known to the people. Yet he receives a derisive laugh from the bystanders when he suggests she is merely sleeping. The dead girl lies lifeless. Jesus, both merciful and wise, dismisses the crowd who taunt him, allowing the parents to remain. The parents will understand mercy. They enter into the command of Jesus, "Little girl, get up!" and they, too, come alive in new life. The girl receives her life's breath, and the parents receive credulity, belief.

Where do we go from here?

Jesus faces derision and disbelief when he does what his Father calls him to do. He came to heal our wounds and to restore us to life. Can I follow Jesus' example and do what God calls me to do in the face of misunderstanding and derision or in whatever circumstances I find myself? This is what it means to be a disciple.

Jesus, let me not be a bystander who derides, but rather like a parent, who hopes and prays with great trust.

2 Samuel 24.2, 9-17 • Psalm 32 • Mark 6.1-6

O n the sabbath he began to teach in the synagogue, and many who heard him were astounded. They said, "Where did this man get all this?"
Mark 6.2

Familiarity

Overfamiliarity can blind us to the wonder of encounter. I recall going into a museum to view the masterpieces on display. In my ignorance, I immediately scorned one piece whose duplicates I'd seen elsewhere many times. This marvellous work escaped my deep appreciation simply because of its familiarity. It took a guide to renew my interest and to help me rediscover its true value.

When Jesus returns to Nazareth, the people are not impressed. He is too familiar. "Is not this the carpenter, the son of Mary ...?" they ask each other. Their lack of faith in Jesus prevents them from being open to a "mighty work" performed in their midst.

If we want Jesus to come into our lives, to change us, to heal us of all our afflictions, we must begin with faith in his power to save. We are called to a strong faith in Jesus. It all starts with a word of faith, something as simple as "Jesus, I trust in you."

Where do we go from here?

The rosary is a very familiar prayer for us. We can begin just to rattle off the prayers without reflection. Try saying the rosary in a new way. Take time to reflect on the meaning of the mysteries connected with each decade. Savour each word of the "Hail Mary" as you put yourself in Mary's place and enter into the mystery with her.

**Lord, give me new eyes and a lively sense
of rediscovery to all that you are in my life.**

I Kings 2.1-4, 10-12 • I Chronicles 29 • Mark 6.7-13

He called the twelve and began to send them out two by two, and gave them authority over the unclean spirits. He ordered them to take nothing for their journey except a staff; no bread, no bag, no money in their belts ....
Mark 6.7-9

Gospel of peace

Sometimes I sit back and thank God I'm ordinary and not like the apostles who were asked to live like beggars. I can't imagine going off with one other person and casting out demons, carrying no food or money, lacking a decent pair of shoes and owning only one set of clothes.

But God gave the apostles a special mission; he wanted them to carry the virtue of courage and trust. These virtues would be their mainstay. Bread and provisions would come from the charity of those who were glad, even joyful, to hear the Good News.

I am not an apostle, but I pray for the heart of one so that I can be God's voice to those who have never heard the gospel message of peace and salvation.

Where do we go from here?

Do I possess more than I need? Stop a minute to count your real blessings: family, friends, enough to eat, a home, a job. Am I always trying to get more and perhaps neglecting the real blessings God has given me? It is something to think about. Discuss it with your family and see what you come up with together.

Lord, I need material things to live in the world and bring up my family, but I want to bring others your word and your peace as much as possible.

Sirach 47.2-11 • Psalm 18 • Mark 6.14-29

W hen his daughter Herodias came in and danced, she pleased Herod and his guests; and the king said to the girl, "Ask me for whatever you wish, and I will give it." … She went out and said to her mother, "What should I ask for?" She replied, "The head of John the baptizer." *Mark 6.22, 24*

Openness to grace

King Herod hears of Jesus and wonders about him. Could he be John the Baptist, raised from the dead? The sorry episode in which he executed John and put his head on public display haunts the king; in addition, he cannot forget the things John told him. John's message perplexed Herod, but also made him want to hear more.

Herod is like many in our world today. They hear the truth, and while they are intrigued by it, they cannot quite make the leap of conversion from a sinful lifestyle to embracing salvation. When Herod finally encounters Jesus, he is still puzzled. Like Herod, when we are not open every day to God's saving grace, it will fall on us without effect, and we will remain simply confused in the face of our one hope.

Where do we go from here?

How is your faith alive and active? How do you express your belief and commitment to Jesus in your daily life? What practices can you add to your life to open yourself more fully to God's grace? We don't want just to be intrigued by the gospel truth but to live it in all truth. If our life is not producing the fruits of the Holy Spirit—joy, peace, love and more—then something is missing.

Jesus, help me to be open to every grace you wish to give me today, and to bring the good news to others!

1 Kings 3.4-13 • Psalm 119 • Mark 6.30-34

H e said to them, "Come away to a deserted place all by your-selves and rest a while." For many were coming and going, and they had no leisure even to eat. And they went away in the boat to a deserted place by themselves.   *Mark 6.31-34*

....

Come away

Jesus' response to the disciples recounting the success of their first mission is interesting: "Come away by yourselves to a lonely place, and rest a while." When we are involved in church ministries—especially when the work is going well—our first tendency is to keep at it, to strive for more success. But Jesus had a different perspective. Every life needs a balance between apostolic activity and contemplative rest. We need to step outside the busy stream of activity and take time to thank God, who is the real source of our success! Contemplation gives us the energy we need to minister. Jesus gives us the example of both prayer and ministry.

Where do we go from here?

Are there times of silence and contemplative rest in your life? Silence is essential for our well-being, both physically and spiritually. Designate a period of time, about 15 minutes: still yourself and your thoughts and just "be" in God's presence. Take a walk in the country or a park and just look around you at the colours, the shapes, the birds. Hear the sound of the trees in the wind or the movement of water. Listen to the absence of noise. Walk softly, for God is here.

**Jesus, help me to take time for contemplation
and rest in my busy life.**

Isaiah 58.6-10 • Psalm 112 • 1 Corinthians 2.1-5 • Matthew 5.13-16

When I came to you, brothers and sisters, I did not come proclaiming the mystery of God to you in lofty words or wisdom. ... My speech and my proclamation were not with plausible words of wisdom, but with a demonstration of the Spirit and of power, so that your faith might rest not on human wisdom but on the power of God. *1 Corinthians 2.1-5*

The power of God

When I was young, I really enjoyed bowling with neighbourhood friends. Though our conversations weren't serious, occasionally one of us spoke a small word of wisdom that comes to mind many years later. These could not have been "lofty words"; after all, we were only teenagers. But for all our limited years, I believe that a certain "power of God" entered in.

Bowling with my friends was like the spiritual life in another way. It took a certain amount of muscle to bring down those pins. Yet the more relaxed and flexible we were when throwing the ball, the better the chance we had of achieving our goal.

Where do we go from here?

Relaxed and flexible—very nice words, but is it possible to practise being relaxed and flexible? Getting things done immediately seems to be the motto of our society. Stop and take some time to do something silly, to enjoy having fun with your family. Make a habit of setting aside some useless, non-productive time. It is wonderful!

**Lord, give me a supple and flexible spirit.
You have the words of everlasting life.**

I Kings 8.1-7, 9-13 • Psalm 132 • Mark 6.53-56

A nd wherever he went, into villages or cities or farms, they laid the sick in the marketplaces, and begged him that they might touch even the fringe of his cloak; and all who touched it were healed.

Mark 6. 56

....

Healing

The people in today's gospel demonstrate faith in Jesus' power to heal. Even touching the fringe of his garment is enough—no words are necessary. And yet, this kind of faith is only the beginning. For every time God responds to our prayers with a "Yes," there are times when he seems to say "No." We want healing and other interventions from God, but God knows best what we need and when we need it.

Faith often begins with light; it tends to end in darkness. God is there in the dark, waiting to grasp our trembling hands.

Where do we go from here?

What do we do when God seems to say no to our prayers? Looking back on my life, there were times when all the answers seemed to be no, the struggles were great and I really did not think I would make it through. But I did. The struggles lifted and God's light shone in my heart. The movement of light and darkness finally taught me to trust and to know that God is there always. It also taught me to be able to share that hope with others.

**Lord, teach me to pray, to be in tune
with your saving will.**

I Kings 8.22-23, 27-30 • Psalm 84 • Mark 7.1-13

So the Pharisees and the scribes asked him, "Why do your disciples not live according to the tradition of the elders, but eat with defiled hands?" He said to them, "Isaiah prophesied rightly about you hypocrites …."
Mark 7.5-6

True devotion

The Pharisees and scribes question Jesus. They don't seek understanding or greater insight. Their purpose is self-justification. These men demand that others perfectly obey the tradition, but they do not practise true obedience. They give only lip service, without giving God the gift of their life. Jesus calls them hypocrites.

A hypocrite is one who has perfected the art of duplicity, one who puts all his or her energy into looking good rather than being good. What a waste of energy. If we find ourselves spending all our effort in noticing and criticizing the failings of others—the ways in which they are not measuring up to our standard—are we behaving like the Pharisees and scribes? Better to question our responses to God and others. I am the only one I have any hope of improving.

Where do we go from here?

Today is the Feast of our Lady of Lourdes. St. Bernadette had a simple, trusting faith in Mary and in the promises of her Son. The pilgrims to Lourdes continue to witness to the power of a simple faith and to prayer. It is good to be simple and uncomplicated in our loving relationship to God. Pray today for the gift of truly being a child of our Father in heaven.

Lord, give me a heart of love that finds your goodness everywhere—especially in my neighbour.

1 Kings 10.1-10 • Psalm 37 • Mark 7.14-23

Whidden the queen of Sheba heard of the fame of Solomon (fame due to the name of the Lord), she came to test him with hard questions … "Blessed be the Lord your God, who has delighted in you and set you on the throne of Israel! Because the Lord loved Israel forever, he has made you king to execute justice and righteousness." *1 Kings 10.1, 9*

....

Acknowledging God's grace

The Queen of Sheba, a pagan queen, recognized that Solomon's great wisdom and success were God's gifts to him. But Solomon forgot. He turned from following the Lord and did not keep the covenant.

All that we are comes from God. Along life's journey, we sometimes claim ownership over our life and deeds, forgetting that God created us, sustains us and graces us at every moment. Step by step, the way of holiness is to relinquish the feeble control of our life and return it to God in love. With St. Paul, we can say "I can do all things in God who sustains and perfects me." Then, and only then, are we enabled to do truly great things.

Where do we go from here?

God has gifted each of us with gifts, both of nature and grace. Humility is truth. We can acknowledge the gifts we have while at the same time knowing they are gifts given to us for the sake of others. Our life and talents should be put at the service of our brothers and sisters. How is God calling you to serve today?

**Lord, lead me in your ways that I may give glory
to you and serve you wholeheartedly.**

I Kings 11.4-13 • Psalm 106 • Mark 7.24-30

Now the woman was a Gentile, of Syrophoenician origin. She begged him to cast the demon out of her daughter. … Then he said to her, "For saying that, you may go—the demon has left your daughter." So she went home, found the child lying on the bed, and the demon gone.

Mark 7.26, 29-30

In Jesus' name

Jesus begins his ministry by teaching and preaching to his own people first. In several instances in this gospel, he is diverted from this mission by the great faith he finds among the Gentiles. This is the context for the story of Jesus' encounter with the Syrophoenician woman, who dares to counter Jesus' rebuke. She focuses not on herself, but on the child she loves. Jesus is amazed at her faith, and, it seems, is deeply touched by her selfless love and concern that risks her own dignity.

Can we, in Jesus' name, love the other even in the face of rebuke and rejection, allowing ourselves to become small and poor? A tall order! Our example is Jesus, who did not cling to his own great dignity in the face of ridicule and death itself. His was indeed the victory.

Where do we go from here?

Can I love my brother and sister in the face of their ingratitude and rejection? Can I let go of my hurt and forgive another's thoughtlessness? Jesus did this for us on the cross. We can follow his example only through grace. Pray for the grace to love without return. It is possible. If there were more love in our world, hate would be conquered.

Dear Lord, give me a humble, steadfast heart.

I Kings I I.29-32; I2.I9 • Psalm 81 • Mark 7.31-37

I n distress you called, and I rescued you;
I answered you in the secret place of thunder;
I tested you at the waters of Meribah ....
I am the Lord your God,
who brought you up out of the land of Egypt.   *Psalm 81.7,10*

God with us, even in our breath

Our breathing can be a reminder of the fact that we exist only because God is with us. Ancient monks prayed the Jesus Prayer to the rhythm of their breathing. This is a very simple prayer, but a profound reminder of how we find ourselves before God. Stop for a moment and become aware of the rhythm of your breath. Breathe in, saying, "Lord Jesus Christ, son of David, be merciful"; exhale, saying, "to me a sinner."

God sustains every breath we take. Every breath is a gift of God. Let us live our life for the Lord, trusting in God's infinite love for us and for others. Giving heed to the psalmist's words, let us open every moment of our life to be in-spired by the Holy Spirit.

Where do we go from here?

God gave me life and sustains me at every moment. I belong to God. The rhythm of my breathing puts me in tune with the rhythm of God's presence in my life. I breathe in and receive this new moment of life from God; I breathe out and return the gift of my life to God. Being aware of our breathing can make our life a constant ebb and flow of receiving and giving. Try it and share this practice with others.

**Dear God, may my whole life praise and
thank you for your love and kindness to me.**

I Kings 12.26-32; 13.33-34 • Psalm 106 • Mark 8.1-10

I n those days when there was again a great crowd without anything to eat, he called his disciples and said to them, "I have compassion for the crowd, because they have been with me now for three days and have nothing to eat. *Mark 8.1-4*

A liturgical event

If we look first at the account of Jesus' feeding the multitude in Mark 6.30-44, we find an important key to unlock the meaning of today's gospel. It is not by coincidence that Jesus had the crowds "sit down in groups on the green grass. So they sat down in groups, of hundreds and of fifties" (Mark 6.39-40). Why does Mark include the seemingly meaningless statistics of *how* the crowd sat down? This is not a description of a haphazard social gathering. What we are looking at is a *liturgical* event. The miracle of division of bread and fish foreshadows the Body and Blood that will soon be poured out for the whole world.

In Mark 8, we see the interior of the heart that is presented to us in Mark 6: unending depths of love and compassion poured out with *thanksgiving*—which is translated "Eucharist." Jesus will not let anyone go away hungry.

Where do we go from here?

The gospels often show Jesus feeling deep compassion for the needs of others. A compassionate person is one who notices the other person as special and worthy of love. Today, seek to imitate Jesus' compassion. Notice the people around you; let them stand out as individuals. See their needs and try to help.

**Lord, help me to realize more and more
deeply your love for us in the Eucharist.**

Sunday | FEBRUARY 16

Sirach 15.15-20 • Psalm 119 • 1 Corinthians 2.6-10 • Matthew 5.17-37

"So when you are offering your gift at the altar, if you remember that your brother or sister has something against you, leave your gift there before the altar and go; first be reconciled to your brother or sister, and then come and offer your gift."

Matthew 5.23-24

A clarion call

This gospel passage occurs right in the heart of the Sermon on the Mount, that clarion call for all Christians to follow Jesus. God wants his whole family to live in right relationships with each other. As St. John tells us, "... those who do not love a brother or sister whom they have seen, cannot love God whom have not seen" (1 John 4.20).

If we have strained relationships with a brother or sister, we must clear them up before our hearts can be at peace to worship God. Forgiveness, reconciliation and, by extension, supporting one another are central to being children of God. This does not come easily. But God's grace is greater than any hurts we may have suffered. We ask for his help.

Where do we go from here?

Our Christian faith is very practical in its expression. We are called to love. One of the difficult aspects of love is forgiveness. I have known people who have gone for years without being able to forgive another: thoughts of revenge and carrying grudges sour our life. Love opens our heart and expands us. In loving, we become free. Is there a relationship in your life that needs healing? Ask God to give you a new heart to love this person.

Loving God, expand my heart so that I may truly forgive all my brothers and sisters.

53

James 1.1-11 • Psalm 119 • Mark 8.11-13

I f any of you is lacking in wisdom, ask God, who gives to all generously and ungrudgingly, and it will be given you. But ask in faith,
never doubting, for the one who doubts is like a wave of the sea,
driven and tossed by the wind; for the doubter, being double-minded
and unstable in every way, must not expect to receive anything from
the Lord. *James 1.5-8*

The wisdom from above

Difficult and confusing times often are the push we need to turn to
God for help and guidance. We need these nudges. Often we approach God with our own demands, and tell God the answer we
want. Yet, true wisdom calls us to deep and trusting faith in the response that will be best for us. Of course, we use our intelligence and
experience to discern the right way to handle a situation. We are not
made to be helplessly passive. But can we stand before God with the
simplicity and trust of a child, knowing that all we need and desire
will be given to us abundantly, even when our prayers do not seem
to be answered?

Where do we go from here?

James teaches us that trials are not optional—yet God has pledged
that he will not abandon us. We will not be tempted beyond our
strength. God has promised that his grace in our life is sufficient.
Trials stretch us and, through grace, help us to reach new heights.
God is with us always!

**Give me a trusting and grateful heart
in all the circumstances of my life.**

James 1.12-18 • Psalm 94 • Mark 8.14-21

N o one, when tempted, should say, "I am being tempted by God"; for God cannot be tempted by evil and he himself tempts no one. But one is tempted by one's own desire….

James 1.13-14

The power of desire

The heart of St. Catherine of Siena's teaching is that we must have *the right kind of desire*. We must let those desires be ruled by the Spirit working in our hearts through our reason.

Remember the parable of the rich man's barns. He lived only for his material gain, and envisioned building huge barns to show off the greatness of his grain-farming endeavour. Yet, his life was required of him that night. Those possessions for which he lived—whose are they now?

Perhaps the Lord's words sum up for us the perspective we should have: "See, I am coming soon, my reward is with me, to repay according to everyone's work. I am the Alpha and the Omega, the first and the last, the beginning and the end" (Revelation 22.12-13).

Where do we go from here?

Our actions are motivated by what we believe is good for us. What kind of good things are shaping your life? Are you being motivated by real goods or by fleeting realities that appear to be good? God and the things of God are the ultimate source of goodness. How do all things I am accumulating and seeking in my life measure up to the standard of God's goodness?

Lord, fill my heart with desire for you; let it overflow in me and wash away all the sins that hinder my union with you.

James 1.19-27 • Psalm 15 • Mark 8.22-26

Y ou must understand this, my beloved: let everyone be quick to listen, slow to speak, slow to anger; for your anger does not produce God's righteousness. Therefore rid yourselves of all sordidness and rank growth of wickedness, and welcome with meekness the implanted word that has the power to save your souls. But be doers of the word, and not merely hearers who deceive themselves. *James 1.19-22*

Quick to listen

Listen to and act on the word of God! Authentic hearing of the word of God involves the use of our heart, mind and soul, not just our ears. God speaks to us in every moment and every event in our lives, expressing and communicating God's great desire for a deeper union in love, joy and peace with us.

Yet it is not enough to listen; we must act on what we have heard, understood and experienced with the message of God. There is no merit in simply listening to God's teachings without acting on them. We must allow the word of God to take effect in our lives by reaching out to those in need.

Where do we go from here?

The letter of James is so straightforward. It is useless simply to listen to the word of God without putting it into practice. Every day, or on Sunday, we hear the word of God in the liturgy. Do we put it into practice? Every time we come away from the liturgy, we need to bring a word or phrase of Scripture to ponder and live during the week.

**Lord, grant me the grace to have a listening
and understanding heart.**

James 2.1-9 • Psalm 34 • Mark 8.27-33

J esus … asked his disciples, "Who do people say that I am?" And they answered him, "John the Baptist; and others, Elijah; and still others, one of the prophets." He asked them, "But who do you say that I am?" Peter answered him, "You are the Messiah."

Mark 8.27-29

. . . .

Who do you say Jesus is?

If someone were to ask you, "Who do you say that Jesus is?" how would you answer? Or if Jesus were to ask you, "Who do you say that I am?" how would you answer him? If I carefully consider how to answer this personal question, my answer will change my life.

In acknowledging Jesus as the Messiah, I also enter into the call to discipleship. Am I ready to change the direction of my life and my heart? Am I prepared to follow Jesus and his teachings, to dedicate my life in his service, to carry my cross and offer him all that I have—with all my heart, mind and soul? These are just some of the many challenges in following Jesus that will surely turn my life upside down—and make it fulfilling.

Where do we go from here?

Who do you say Jesus is? Who is he for you? Who is he in your life? Take time to ponder these questions. Look at your relationship with Jesus. How vital is it in your daily life? You are called to be a disciple, which means a real commitment to Jesus and to the gospel teaching. Let Jesus be alive in your life and share the good news with others.

Jesus, teach me to love as you love.

James 2.14-24, 26 • Psalm 112 • Mark 8.34–9.1

" I f any want to become my followers, let them deny themselves and take up their cross and follow me. For those who want to save their life will lose it, and those who lose their life for my sake, and for the sake of the gospel, will save it. *Mark 8.34-35*

Finding life

Jesus has strong words for us in today's gospel—though they seem to contradict his other teachings. Did he not also say, "I have come that they may have life and have it to the full"?

We get our clue to his meaning from the phrase "for my sake, and for the sake of the gospel." We need to see with Jesus' eyes in order to choose true life and to have the courage to die to what is not really life at all: the greed, possessiveness and selfishness so prevalent today, and the denial of our own creatureliness that makes us indifferent to God as our source of life and salvation. Let us stand tall in our convictions, no matter what the cost, knowing that, in making Jesus' word and example our own, we are choosing true life.

Where do we go from here?

Choose life; choose to freely follow Jesus in word and action. Jesus asks us to be his disciples even when that means misunderstanding and ridicule. Read the gospel of Mark. What is Jesus asking of you through the gospel? Take a sentence to carry with you through the day and allow yourself to be transformed.

Jesus, as I go through my day, help me to see with your eyes all you bring into my life. Only when my choices come from your perspective can I be truly and fully alive and life-giving to those around me.

1 Peter 5.1-4 • Psalm 23 • Matthew 16.13-19

The Lord is my shepherd, I shall not want.
He makes me lie down in green pastures;
he leads me beside still waters; he restores my soul. ...
Surely goodness and mercy shall follow me all the days of my life,
and I shall dwell in the house of the Lord my whole life long.

Psalm 23.1, 2, 6

The Lord is my shepherd

The psalmist affirms what the prophet Isaiah speaks about concerning Jesus: "He will feed his flock like a shepherd; he will gather the lambs in his arms, and carry them in his bosom" (Isaiah 40.11). Jesus himself said, "I am the good shepherd. The good shepherd lays down his life for the sheep" (John 10.11). These words are powerful indeed. They refresh our weary souls; they free us from fears and anxieties.

The Lord wants us to know this truth and invites us to believe in our hearts that we are always being led into his green pastures. He is the good shepherd who continually seeks us out, to fill us with his love, peace and joy. As followers of Jesus, we, too, are called to shepherd his other lost sheep, bringing them back to the communion of his flock.

Where do we go from here?

God has promised to lead me in the right path. Each day brings so many choices. If we listen to the guidance of the Holy Spirit we will choose to follow the right path. We should stop frequently during the day to reflect on our motivations and the effects that certain ways of acting will have in our life.

**Lord Jesus, strengthen my trust and confidence
that you are always near.**

Sunday | FEBRUARY 23

Leviticus 19.1-2, 17-18 • Psalm 103 • I Corinthians 3.16-23
Matthew 5.38-48

The Lord spoke to Moses, saying: Speak to all the congregation of the people of Israel and say to them: You shall be holy, for I the Lord your God am holy. ... I am the Lord. You shall keep my statutes. *Leviticus 19.1-2, 18-19*

Be holy; God is holy

Be holy as your heavenly Father is holy! Be a saint! Be perfect! Be human! This is our calling, our vocation, because everyone is created in the image and likeness of God. Vatican II clearly emphasized this universal call to holiness for all people from every walk of life, not only for the priests and religious. What does it mean? It simply means that each one is mandated to live one's vocation to the best of their ability, in whatever state that might be: a nun, a store clerk, a doctor, a mother. We must try to be what God created us to be—holy—and with God's grace we will succeed through the help and guidance of the Church. If this amazing reality were accepted and lived by everyone, there would be peace, joy and love in the whole world.

Where do we go from here?

The gospel calls us to holiness. What does it mean to be holy? It means we are living the gospel and are true disciples of Jesus, that we are loving and caring for people. I think it also means we have a good sense of humour. The saints were intense people, but they knew how to laugh and not take themselves or life too seriously. We take Jesus seriously and our call to follow him along the narrow path in joy and freedom.

**Lord, open my mind and heart to accept
my vocation to be holy, to be a saint.**

James 3.13-18 • Psalm 19 • Mark 9.14-29

Who is wise and understanding among you? Show by your good life that your works are done with gentleness born of wisdom. … the wisdom from above is first pure, then peaceable, gentle, willing to yield, full of mercy and good fruits, without a trace of partiality or hypocrisy. And a harvest of righteousness is sown in peace for those who make peace.   *James 3.13, 17-18*

The intentions of the heart

Why do we feel jealous? We are jealous because somebody has something we do not have and we envy her for what she has. If we do not acknowledge or admit this feeling in ourselves, we end up acting it out in other ways, causing all kinds of trouble. It destroys friendships, leads to friction in the community or family, and creates a "monster" deep in our hearts. If we confront this feeling, we realize two things: we are insecure and we are not being rational. That is why it is important to start our day in prayer. We ask God for the gift of wisdom and understanding to face each day and situation in a loving way, to be a good example to those around us, to reflect the image of God that is in us all.

Where do we go from here?

Is there jealousy or selfish ambition in my heart? Jealously kills our relationships. Ask God for the grace to expand your heart in love. God loves each of us in a unique way. We are called to love others in that same way. There is room to love everyone and no need to selfishly grasp another's love. Unselfish love loves the other into freedom, into being all she or he can be.

Father, let the light of your truth guide us to your kingdom through a world filled with lights contrary to your own.

James 4.1-10 • Psalm 55 • Mark 9.30-37

Submit yourselves therefore to God. Resist the devil, and he will flee from you. Draw near to God, and he will draw near to you. Cleanse your hands, you sinners, and purify your hearts, you double-minded. Lament and mourn and weep. Let your laughter be turned into mourning and your joy into dejection. Humble yourselves before the Lord, and he will exalt you.   *James 4.7-10*

Listening to the Spirit of God

James speaks with bold directness in his letter, but it comes from his great desire for our holiness. Our right relationship with God and all creation is the only stance from which we will experience true peace, joy and love. A simple but challenging program is placed before us. How do we submit to God? By resisting the devil and drawing near to God. But to do this we need to recognize the influence of the evil one that can be so subtle. That's where the gift of the Holy Spirit comes to our aid. Fidelity to even very short moments of prayer and listening to the good spirit deep inside bring clarity and courage for living in peace, joy and love as grateful children of God.

Where do we go from here?

The word "submission" is not a popular one in our "I will do it my way" culture. Submitting ourselves to God is not slavery but freedom. Do you consider yourself a reflective person? Do you take time to listen to the inner voice of the Holy Spirit by taking time for silent prayer before God? Do you take time to deepen your faith by reading? Read a book about the faith, about prayer, about God. It is important to nourish our faith.

**Send your Spirit upon me today, that every choice
I make may be a loving submission to your will.**

James 4.13-17 • Psalm 49 • Mark 9.38-40

W hat is your life? For you are a mist that appears for a little while and then vanishes. Instead you ought to say, "If the Lord wishes, we will live and do this or that." As it is, you boast in your arrogance; all such boasting is evil. Anyone, then, who knows the right thing to do and fails to do it, commits sin.

James 4.14-17

Seeking the Lord

The true followers of Jesus are convinced of their reliance on God's loving plan of salvation. Jesus himself lived his earthly life always seeking and doing the will of the Father. God provides us each day with the graces needed to fulfill God's divine plan. The truth is that, by God's will, we live, and by his strength we are able to do our duties according to the state of life to which we have been called. Sometimes we put God aside and we fill our days with our own plans, which are often hurtful to us and to others. Today, the Lord invites us to a deeper and loving surrender to God's loving will.

Where do we go from here?

It is true that we have no idea what tomorrow will bring. So many of the events of life are beyond our control and we become anxious and frustrated. We do need to plan ahead, but then give our plans and our whole life into God's keeping. Trusting in God's provident care brings peace. The secret is to use all our gifts to live our life well and to provide for our family, while with deep faith giving everything to God with total love and trust. Start today with the little things.

Jesus, help me follow and seek to walk in your ways.

James 5.1-6 • Psalm 49 • Mark 9.41-50

" or truly I tell you, whoever gives you a cup of water to drink because you bear the name of Christ will by no means lose the reward. ... Salt is good; but if salt has lost its saltiness, how can you season it? Have salt in yourselves, and be at peace with one another."

Mark 9.41, 50

The little ones

Woe to anyone who causes the little ones to sin. To love God means to love everybody and to seek their good, especially the poor and helpless. In this passage, the "little ones" refers not only to children but to adults who are weak in any way. It includes the intellectually weak, the mentally challenged, the emotionally fragile, the casualties of society, the poor. They are most dear to the heart of Jesus. Whoever leads these "little ones" away from the right path by bad example, neglect, or even by simply ignoring them is not hearing the gospel and putting it into practice. Every one deserves to be loved and to love.

Where do we go from here?

Jesus is using hyperbole here to emphasis the serious and devastating nature of sin. Sin deprives us of more than a hand or foot; sin deprives us of our life in God. Sin involves our relationship to our neighbour. God is love, and if we belong to God we, too, must love. Take time today to help someone in need and to pray for those society pushes aside. They are God's precious children.

Lord, fill our hearts with compassion and understanding for the needs of the "little ones."

James 5.9-12 • Psalm 103 • Mark 10.1-12

Beloved, do not grumble against one another, so that you may not be judged. ... You have heard of the endurance of Job, and you have seen the purpose of the Lord, how the Lord is compassionate and merciful.   *James 5.9, 11*

....

The game of grumbling

Do you recall how the Israelites grumbled against Moses and complained to God in the wilderness? If we're honest with ourselves, we are like them. We complain. People grumble against one another, blaming others for the sad situation they're in. We see this attitude with our political leaders, in parishes, in communities, workplaces and families. St. Benedict warns his brothers not to grumble, so it is also a reminder for us all. To grumble is very often to judge others. Grumbling is pride that tells us we deserve better. And when we are grumbling, we often fail to see the many things God has given us.

Next week we will begin the Lenten season. Perhaps we can join each other in fasting from grumbling or complaining, and show grateful hearts to God and those around us.

Where do we go from here?

Grumbling does not change anything, only serves to make us unhappy and grumpy. When you begin to grumble and complain, change your complaint into a prayer of thanksgiving to the Lord for all your blessings. Name a few of your blessings; doing so will lighten your heart and make your day brighter. Counting our blessings is a good way to begin the day.

Giver of good gifts, teach us to cherish your gifts and the blessings that surround us. Help us to put away pride and grumbling in our lives.

James 5.13-20 • Psalm 141 • Mark 10.13-16

"Let the children come to me; do not stop them; for it is to such as these that the kingdom of God belongs." *Mark 10.14*

Be as little children

The main difference between adults and children is that adults do not trust as spontaneously as little children do. To feel secure, all a child needs is a loving look and a gentle touch from someone who cares. They will believe someone they trust.

Perhaps a good example of this is the story of St. Peter on the stormy sea, when he tried to walk on the water to meet Jesus. As soon as his trust wavered, he began to sink. What a difference it made for Peter when he was changed from a timid disciple to the bold leader of Pentecost, proclaiming in a thunderous voice that the kingdom of God is at hand.

Where do we go from here?

How do we receive the kingdom of God like a little child? Ask yourself a few questions. Do you still feel a sense of wonder at the beauty of a tree or the sunrise? Can you stop and watch an ant carrying a piece of food and be amazed at its industry and perseverance? Can you find joy in the smile of another person? Life is exciting for children: so many things to discover, to do, to be. Children have the sense that they are still in the making. But that is true of all of us, until the end of our life. Spend a day looking at the world in a new way—with the eyes of a child.

**Lord, help me to see you in the weak of this earth
and to glorify you by helping the poor.**

Isaiah 49.14-15 • Psalm 62 • 1 Corinthians 4.1-5 • Matthew 6.24-34

"Do not worry about your life, what you will eat or what you will drink, or about your body, what you will wear. … But strive first for the kingdom of God and his righteousness, and all these things will be given to you as well." *Matthew 6.25, 33*

Why worry?

Jesus' instructions to not worry about food or clothing or life seem rather harsh. Of course we worry about these things! After all, others depend on us—our spouse, our children, other relatives. But Jesus doesn't expect us to stop worrying completely. Rather, he wants us to put our concerns in proper order: to seek first the kingdom of God and then everything else will fall into place. How do we do this? We can't neglect our daily responsibilities, but we need to bring something of God into our lives by prayer, deeds of charity, generous self-giving to our family members and others who have a legitimate claim on us. In other words, we make the search for the kingdom the motive for everything we do.

Where do we go from here?

If we seek the kingdom of God first, everything else comes into focus. If we get in touch with our heart, with the God who dwells within us, we will find the kingdom of God here and now. Learning to live life from our centre puts our whole life in order. We so often allow all of life's changing circumstances to toss us this way and that. We can change all that by allowing ourselves to be formed by the God-life within.

Lord, dare I believe that by seeking your kingdom before all else, I will surpass even Solomon in all his splendour? Yes, because then I will shine with your splendour!

1 Peter 1.3-9 • Psalm 111 • Mark 10.17-27

As he was setting out on a journey, a man ran up and knelt before him, and asked him, "Good Teacher, what must I do to inherit eternal life?" Jesus said to him … "You lack one thing; go, sell what you own, and give the money to the poor, and you will have treasure in heaven; then come, follow me." When he heard this, he was shocked and went away grieving, for he had many possessions.

Mark 10.17, 21-22

Eternal life

What is this eternal life to which we are heirs? In John's gospel, Jesus tells us that eternal life is to know the one true God and Jesus Christ whom God has sent. This knowledge is the magnanimous gift that is ours through the outpouring of the Spirit in baptism. And the way that we may be sure we know God is to keep God's commandments (see 1 John 2.3). For the one who keeps God's commandments, truly the love of God is perfected in that person. What commandments? You know: love God and love your neighbour! So what are you doing today to inherit eternal life?

Where do we go from here?

Eternal life is a participation in the life of the Trinity: when we live in God, we possess eternal life. We already carry that life in our heart's core. Our body will die, but our spirit is eternal and will never die. Reflect on the eternal life you already possess. An English Dominican wrote: "Life is eternal and love is immortal, and death is only a horizon, and a horizon is nothing but the limit of our sight." Did you know you carried eternal life within you?

**Lord, by your anointing, I am an heir of eternal life;
help me to remain true to that anointing.**

1 Peter 1.10-16 • Psalm 98 • Mark 10.28-31

Therefore prepare your minds for action; discipline yourselves; set all your hope on the grace that Jesus Christ will bring you when he is revealed. Like obedient children, do not be conformed to the desires that you formerly had in ignorance. Instead, as he who called you is holy, be holy yourselves in all your conduct; for it is written, "You shall be holy, for I am holy."

1 Peter 1:13-16

The call to holiness

God created us in his image and likeness; therefore he calls us to be holy because God is holy. Sin has marred the beauty of our image and likeness to God. Jesus' coming among us and the gift of baptism has restored that likeness. We have to reclaim our inheritance as God-image and polish our mirror likeness to God. As St. Peter teaches us, we must prepare our minds and hearts to enter into the discipline inspired by the gift of the Holy Spirit, and rely entirely on the grace of Jesus Christ.

Where do we go from here?

Do you believe you are called to be a saint? God says you are! Holiness means to live our life in God. The Holy Spirit dwelling in your hearts will show you what holiness means for you. Learn to listen. The Church gives us so many means to attain holiness: the liturgy, the word of God, the sacraments, especially the daily Eucharist. The word of God forms us in God's life and the Eucharist nourishes us with the very life of God.

Lord, help me to deepen my life in the Spirit.

Joel 2.12-18 • Psalm 51 • 2 Corinthians 5.20–6.2 • Matthew 6.1-6, 16-18

Yet even now, says the Lord, return to me with all your heart, with fasting, with weeping, and with mourning; rend your hearts and not your clothing. *Joel 2.12-13*

God's fast

Wow! God is really serious about our repentance! This is a pep talk worthy of a major sporting event. "Come on, team, get out there and do your job!" Clearly God thinks we can do it, and God already has in mind to take pity on God's people.

Forty days is a long time, and even before we begin, we feel the weariness and discouragement that makes itself felt ever more intensely as Lent progresses. When that happens, we need to remember the words of Isaiah, which Paul quotes in his letter to the Corinthians: "In an acceptable time I have listened to you, and on a day of salvation I have helped you" (2 Corinthians 6.2). God doesn't want our penance to make us miserable but to bring us into God's joy.

Where do we go from here?

Today we begin another Lent. Lent is really not meant to be a gloomy time. Lent is our preparation for the great Christian feast of Easter. All the readings at each Mass develop a theme. The beginning weeks of Lent focus on our obligation of love to our neighbour and show us its essential unity with our love for God. The latter weeks of Lent focus on Jesus and his total gift of himself in love. Follow the readings and study them to receive a new perspective on Lent.

**Lord, I claim the joy you have promised,
which no one can take from me.**

Deuteronomy 30.15-20 • Psalm 1 • Luke 9.22-25

Happy are those who do not follow the advice of the wicked …
or take the path that sinners tread, or sit in the seat of scoffers;
but their delight is in the law of the Lord,
and on his law they meditate day and night. *Psalm 1.1-2*

God's work

Already it is the second day of Lent and I am wondering why I have
not noticeably changed in spite of yesterday's fast and firm resolutions. Thoughts like these gravely tempt me to want immediate results from *my* actions. This ignores two important points. First, God
accomplishes whatever good is in us; as St. Paul tells the Corinthians:
"It is God who gives the growth" (1 Corinthians 3.6). And second,
this takes time. As the psalm says, we are like trees that yield their
fruit in due season. Even fast-growing trees need years to reach maturity, for that is the way of nature—measured and orderly. Early fruit is
bitter and late fruit insipid.

Where do we go from here?

Take time to reflect on Psalm 1. We are like mighty trees that
take time to grow and mature. God is eternal and is not unduly
impressed by the passage of time. Every so often, I have reminded
God that here, time is long, and could he perhaps not speed things
up a bit. Yet waiting is good for us. We need time to allow ourselves to grow, deepen and mature. God gives us that time. Let us
do the same for our neighbour. Only in eternity will we see the
finished product.

Lord, give me the patience to do your will
and receive what you have promised.

Isaiah 58.1-9 • Psalm 51 • Matthew 9.14-15

"The wedding-guests cannot mourn as long as the bridegroom is with them, can they? The days will come when the bridegroom is taken away from them, and then they will fast."
Matthew 9.15

The fast pleasing to the Lord

The prophet Isaiah lays down some very clear and exacting conditions for efficacious fasting, all of which can be reduced to the three great Lenten penances: prayer, genuine fasting and almsgiving. And these three can be reduced to one simple and all-encompassing practice: the gift of self, to God and to others. From this perspective, we can clearly see that giving up ourselves is the same as giving ourselves to others. We give ourselves to God through our self-giving to others; as Jesus told us, what we do to even the least of the members of his family, we do to him. Or again, whoever loses himself for Jesus' sake will gain his life. It is not important that we do big things, but it is important that we do something and with the right intention.

Where do we go from here?

Prayer, genuine fasting and almsgiving are Lent's holy triad. Prayer is not just a vocal exercise or a litany of requests of God. Prayer is a relationship with God—this is what the season of Lent is directing us to. Fasting and almsgiving go together. If we fast from food, then we give the money we save to the poor. If our fasting is the gift of ourselves to God, then the fruit of that gift is generous self-giving to others. Giving our time and talents in the service of others is a far greater gift than giving money.

**Lord, may my Lenten penances help me to realize
how empty my life is when you are not there.**

72

Isaiah 58.9-14 • Psalm 86 • Luke 5.27-32

"Those who are well have no need of a physician, but those who are sick; I have come to call not the righteous but sinners to repentance."
Luke 5.31

The divine physician

Concern about their physical health is the primary concern of many North Americans, who spend an incredible amount of time and money getting and remaining healthy and fit, physically as well as mentally. Jesus found Levi busy pursuing his own welfare and enjoying the company of others who were like-minded. But like a truly good physician, Jesus could see past Levi's exterior, and recognized his deeper need. He invited Levi to come with him and find abundant life.

This abundant life is what we really seek when we chase after the well-being of the body, though we seldom realize it. Jesus calls each of us to follow him, too, and to find the abundant life he promises. The wonderful thing about Jesus the Physician is that, unlike most doctors today, he continues to make house calls. Listen! Is that your doorbell ringing?

Where do we go from here?

Our external grooming, absorption with fashion and looking good puts the emphasis on the wrong thing. Our heart needs to be beautiful, radiating God's life. Have you ever met a person who is not beautiful by worldly standards but whose smile and joy exude the inner beauty of a heart that belongs to God? We want to clothe ourselves with the beauty of Christ and the inner glow of the life of the Spirit. This is beauty that does not fade.

Jesus, how often have I missed your house call?
Open my ears to hear your voice calling me.

Genesis 2.7-9, 16-18, 25; 3.1-7 • Psalm 51 • Romans 5.12-19
Matthew 4.1-11

Jesus said to him, "Away with you, Satan! for it is written, 'Worship the Lord your God, and serve only him.'"   *Matthew 4.10*

Temptation

Today's readings refer to two of Satan's most cunning temptations: that of Eve and Adam, and that of Jesus. We know how both these encounters ended, and we are fortunate to have today's second reading to contrast them and put them in context. From Eve and Adam we have inherited a mortal nature all too ready and able to sin; from Christ we inherit a supernatural life capable of resisting sin. Satan tempted Jesus yet another time in the garden of Gethsemane, so we should not be surprised that temptation comes our way again. The letter to the Hebrews warns us that resistance might mean shedding blood, but the victory is ours in Christ Jesus our Lord! During Lent, as we test our resources, building them up where they are found wanting, let us keep our eyes fixed on Jesus, enduring our crosses for the sake of the same joy that came to him.

Where do we go from here?

Jesus experienced everything we experience, except sin. He freely chose to become like us, to sanctify our life and to give us courage in the face of temptation and sin. Being tempted and sinning are two different things. Let us keep our eyes fixed on Jesus and pray in times of temptation to be strengthened by the Holy Spirit so that we might not sin.

Lord, it is good to know that you have passed this way before us; give us the courage to follow you to the end.

Leviticus 19.1-2, 11-18 • Psalm 19 • Matthew 25.31-46

The Lord spoke to Moses, saying: Speak to all the congregation of the people of Israel and say to them: You shall be holy, for I the Lord your God am holy.   *Leviticus 19.1-2, 11-12, 17-18*

Jesus, touch me

The Jews in Jesus' time held the opinion that if you touched something holy, then you shared in the holiness of what was touched. Jesus tells us that the needy are his surrogates in the world. To attend to them is to attend to him, and therefore, if they represent the One who is holy, then they, too, share in his holiness. So if the poor and the needy are holy, we have only to reach out and touch them to be made holy ourselves!

In the first letter of St. John, we are told that "those who do not love a brother or sister whom they have seen, cannot love God whom they have not seen" (1 John 4.20). We know we love God when we keep God's commandments, and God's commandment is this: Love one another.

Where do we go from here?

Here we have it again: true holiness is linked to practical deeds of love. Touching the poor, the outcast, the homeless and the sinner is to touch Jesus. A woman once came to the door of the monastery begging and I went and prepared several bags of food for her. When I gave her the bags, she gave me a big, long hug. I think she was testing me to see how far my giving went. She smelled so it was not a very pleasant experience, but I did not draw away. I believe Jesus touched me that day.

Lord, teach me your perfect law of love.

Isaiah 55.10-11 • Psalm 34 • Matthew 6.7-15

Wh3n the righteous cry for help, the Lord hears, and rescues them from all their troubles. The Lord is near to the brokenhearted ....

Psalm 34.17-18

May God be praised

The prophet Isaiah tells us that God's word will accomplish what it says. What an incredible promise this is and how powerful are God's words. The psalmist tells us to magnify and exalt God together, because he has answered him. We can rejoice like the woman who found her lost coins. The poor, the lame, the deaf, the leper, even the dead are saved from their distress by the power of Jesus' word. This same word, like a two-edged sword, cuts to the core of our being to bring healing and comfort. When we are brokenhearted, we can claim the promise of the psalm: God is near. And, more amazing still, we can take Jesus' own words on our lips and expect the same incredible results: "Our Father ...."

Where do we go from here?

The psalms are the very heart of the Old Testament. They are the cry for help, the joy and the praise of Israel. The psalms have also become Christian prayer. Meditate on Psalm 34, along with today's gospel. What do you learn from these two readings? The psalm tells us that God is near to the broken-hearted. Do you believe that in time of difficulty and sorrow? Believe it is true!

**Lord, help me to trust in the power of your words
and know your comfort in every difficulty.**

Jonah 3.1-10 • Psalm 51 • Luke 11.29-32

"This generation is an evil generation; it asks for a sign, but no sign will be given to it except the sign of Jonah. … The people of Nineveh will rise up at the judgement with this generation and condemn it, because they repented at the proclamation of Jonah, and see, something greater than Jonah is here!" *Luke 11.29, 32*

Conversion

Jonah must have been a very effective preacher. The people of Nineveh had forty days to prepare for God's judgment, but after just one day of preaching, they believed Jonah's message; they proclaimed a fast and repented in sackcloth. Not only did they repent, but they also became a sign to the people of Jesus' generation. Jonah preached and the whole city was converted, man and beast alike. When Jesus preaches, who is converted? During the forty days of Lent, we continually hear the plea: Repent, be converted, and believe the gospel! Well, have I done so? A full week of Lent has passed already, and the preaching of someone greater than Jonah calls to me. Jesus says, "Return to me with your whole heart, for I am gracious and merciful." He wants to give us a new heart and a new spirit, if we will only offer him a humble and contrite heart.

Where do we go from here?

Today, take one thing that is holding you back from loving God or your neighbour and begin letting go of this behaviour. It won't happen overnight, but it won't happen at all if you do not begin. Ask God for a new heart and a new Spirit. Conversion and turning our life around begins in this moment with one act of renunciation.

There are many messages clamoring for my attention, but only one will cleanse my heart and renew my spirit.

Esther 14.1, 3-5, 12-14 • Psalm 138 • Matthew 7.7-12

n the day I called, you answered me,
you increased my strength of soul.   *Psalm 138.3*

Cry to the Lord in your need

Two necessary qualities for effective prayer are perseverance and confidence. Without confidence, our perseverance is like shifting sand; without perseverance our confidence bears no fruit. Queen Esther prayed with confidence and perseverance; in mortal anguish she lay prostrate from morning until evening. Recalling God's faithful help to Israel, she pleaded with God: "Now help me, who am alone and have no one but you, my God." Her confidence rested firmly on God's reputation as a faithful and caring God.

Jesus paints a vivid picture of both confidence and perseverance in prayer, reminding us that no father will fail to provide his children with what they need. Then he adds an unexpected twist: the gift of the Holy Spirit (see also Luke 11.9-13). Yes, the Spirit is available if we ask. The Spirit comes to us from the Cross (see John 19.30).

Where do we go from here?

When things are difficult, do we really believe God will be faithful to his promise? In times of darkness, don't forget the times of light. God's light will come again. We can trust it. For us, light and darkness are two opposing qualities, but for God there is no difference—God is with us in both. God's light is so brilliant that for us it becomes darkness. Never lose faith in God's promises. God is with you, sustaining you until the darkness again becomes light.

Lord, you know all my longings; my groans are not hidden from you. I trust your loving care to provide for all my needs.

Ezekiel 18.21-28 • Psalm 130 • Matthew 5.20-26

"So when you are offering your gift at the altar, if you remember that your brother or sister has something against you, leave your gift there before the altar and go; first be reconciled to your brother or sister, and then come and offer your gift. Come to terms quickly with your accuser while you are on the way to court with him, or your accuser may hand you over to the judge, and the judge to the guard, and you will be thrown into prison.   *Matthew 5.23-25*

Be reconciled

Of all the things that Jesus commands us in the gospels, this must be the most difficult. To be reconciled, we must be in actual contact with the estranged brother or sister. When we are told to forgive, we can accomplish this in the privacy of our own heart, in our own home, our own room. This is true when we are told to pray for those who persecute us or speak evil of us. For true and sincere reconciliation, some form of personal contact is usually necessary, provided this contact is safe and will not cause us harm. When we stand eye-to-eye with one whom we have cut off, or been cut off from, it is hard to hide one's insincerity!

Where do we go from here?

To say I am sorry to someone who has hurt me is very hard. To be the first one to do so is even harder. It does not matter whose fault it was—God asks me to say I am sorry for our disagreement. Even if my apology is not accepted, God is pleased with my effort. Apologize and then let go. Jesus never promised it would be easy; he did promise he would be with us.

Mary, reconciler of sinners, pray for me.

Deuteronomy 26.16-19 • Psalm 119 • Matthew 5.43-48

"For if you love those who love you, what reward do you have? Do not even the tax-collectors do the same? And if you greet only your brothers and sisters, what more are you doing than others? Do not even the Gentiles do the same? Be perfect, therefore, as your heavenly Father is perfect."   *Matthew 5.46-48*

Be perfect

This command to be perfect can certainly seem a bit overwhelming. In spite of the fact that most of us think we are pretty good folks, few of us would be ready to claim perfection. For one thing, we do not really understand the perfection Jesus is talking about. Jesus says that pagans love their own, and greet their brothers and sisters. This is not the perfection he recommends. He tells us that his Father pours out blessings of rain and sun on everyone, bad and good, just and unjust. If we are to be perfect like that, we must pour out our love, freely and without discrimination, on folks who don't belong to our religion or church or family—maybe even folks we don't like—as well as the people we love. It is not easy, but then nothing perfect ever is.

Where do we go from here?

The gospel is certainly demanding! Our love and giving is not tit for tat. We do not love another person because they are good or love us. We love them freely, without counting the cost, as Jesus has loved us. Jesus loved us when we were yet sinners. What do you do if you give yourself to another and that person neither thanks you nor is grateful? It is something to think about. Jesus loves us anyway, without fail.

Lord, you expect a lot of me; show me how to live out your commandments each moment of each day.

Genesis 12.1-4 • Psalm 33 • 2 Timothy 1.8-10 • Matthew 17.1-9

Jesus took with him Peter and James and his brother John and led them up a high mountain, by themselves. And he was transfigured before them, and his face shone like the sun, and his clothes became dazzling white. … As they were coming down the mountain, Jesus ordered them, "Tell no one about the vision until after the Son of Man has been raised from the dead." *Matthew 17.1, 2, 9*

On the mountain

In today's gospel, we see Jesus taking Peter, James and John up the mountain with him. On the mountain, Jesus allows his glory to shine forth for a moment. He is strengthening these beloved disciples for what is to come on the mount of Calvary. Moses and Elijah appear, representing the law and the prophets. As Jesus is about to fulfill his mission in his death, he draws all time into that epic moment.

We have entered the second week of Lent, and the Church sends us comfort for the Lenten journey. In all the circumstances of life, in our moments of hardship and grief, God is with us. We are never alone. Everything is in God's hands. The glory on Jesus' face is the glory he has won for us. We, too, will one day shine like the sun.

Where do we go from here?

Today remember some of your "Tabor" experiences. Bring them out especially at those times when the going is tough. This is what Jesus did for his disciples. He knew that he would die soon and wanted to give them a moment of light. Our memory is gift. Use it as a storage space for all the good moments in your life. They will bring you hope in times of grief and hardship. God is near.

**I thank you, Jesus, for the light and comfort
of the Holy Spirit to guide me.**

Monday | **MARCH 17**

Daniel 9.3, 4-10 • Psalm 79 • Luke 6.36-38

"**B**e merciful, just as your Father is merciful. Do not judge; and you will not be judged; do not condemn, and you will not be condemned. Forgive, and you will be forgiven; give, and it will be given to you. A good measure, pressed down, shaken together, running over, will be put into your lap; for the measure you give will be the measure you get back."   *Luke 6.36-38*

Be merciful

What a challenge the gospel gives us: be merciful to others as our heavenly Father is to us. What does that mean? It means to forgive even as we have been forgiven, not to judge or condemn others, and to give generously. God is our model. How many times has God forgiven me and loved me back to new life? God's love is given without measure; not because I deserve it, but only because God is Love. God intends that we pour out abundantly on others the good measure we have received.

Where do we go from here?

Read this short passage carefully. Stay with it awhile prayerfully in the presence of God. There is a rhythm to the text: be merciful—you have received mercy; do not judge—you have not been judged; do not condemn and you will not be condemned; forgive and you will be forgiven. It is the rhythm of the divine life. If we are generous with others, as God has been generous with us, our treasure in heaven is overflowing.

Dear Father in heaven, let me take time today to reflect on your loving presence in my life, and with gratitude, to spend your gifts on others.

Isaiah 1.10, 16-20, 27-28, 31 • Psalm 50 • Matthew 23.1-12

Then Jesus said to the crowds and to his disciples, "The scribes and the Pharisees sit on Moses' seat; therefore, do whatever they teach you and follow it; but do not do as they do, for they do not practise what they teach."
Matthew 23.2-3

To live the truth

Today's gospel gives a succinct definition of a hypocrite: someone who says one thing and does another. How often have you heard the saying "practise what you preach"? The closer we come to God, the more our life becomes unified and simple. We become an integral whole, where who we are and what we do is one. Our action flows from our heart. We preach by our life, not merely through lip service to the gospel. Love of God is one with love of neighbour.

The question is, do we want to *look* good, or really *be* good? The more we practise deeds of love, the more love grows within us. The practice of virtue, of godliness, becomes second nature to us. In the end, the virtue we practise becomes the person we are. Herein lies happiness and freedom.

Where do we go from here?

Who we are and what we do as we grow in the Spirit will become more integrated. If we fill our minds and hearts with good thoughts and desires, then our actions will proceed from our hearts and will reflect the goodness that is there. We want to learn to live our life from the inside out. Then it is the God-life within that teaches us what to do with the changing circumstances of time and place. Living this way brings peace and harmony.

Lord, teach me to love and be generous to others.

2 Samuel 7.4-5, 12-14, 16 • Psalm 89 • Romans 4.13, 16-18, 22
Matthew 1.16, 18-21, 24 or Luke 2.41-51

For the promise that he would inherit the world did not come to Abraham or to his descendants through the law but through the righteousness of faith.

Romans 4.13

Righteousness

Pondering just one word or a phrase from a Scripture passage can bring abundant insight. The word that struck me in today's reading from St. Paul's letter to the Romans is "righteousness." In the Old Testament, this word is frequently used to describe God. For us, to be righteous is to be like God, to be acceptable in the sight of God, to be what we are supposed to be. St. Joseph is the paradigm of the righteous person. He sincerely searched to understand and perform God's will. This gentle, silent man of God served Jesus and Mary, entering into the divine plan of salvation with a generous and total commitment. God calls each of us to be righteous, men and women of God.

Where do we go from here?

Righteousness describes God. When I am righteous I am like God. St. Joseph was a righteous man. His heart and his actions reflected God. To be righteous is to be as one should be: upright and dealing justly with others. Pray to St. Joseph for the gift of a righteous spirit, reflecting the goodness of God. Do you know someone who has these qualities? St. Joseph is a wonderful friend and intercessor in our needs.

St. Joseph, intercede for us that we might follow Jesus and do the Father's will.

Jeremiah 17.5-10 • Psalm 1 • Luke 16.19-31

"There was a rich man who was dressed in purple and fine linen and who feasted sumptuously ... at his gate lay a poor man named Lazarus, covered with sores, who longed to satisfy his hunger with what fell from the rich man's table ...." *Luke 16.19-20*

Sharing with others

How we live here on earth forms us for eternal life. The great theme of all of Scripture is the relationship of our love for God to our love for our neighbour. How we love and serve those around us is the scale that measures our love for God.

Today's gospel recounts the poignant story of Lazarus and the rich man. The problem is not being rich; rather, it is having and not sharing. The rich man is blinded by his lifestyle, and he cannot see the needs of others. He asks Abraham to send someone from the dead to his brothers before it is too late. Abraham points out that if they have not believed the Scripture, neither will they believe if someone rises from the dead.

Jesus has risen from the dead, and reconnected us to God. Do we believe? Is our belief reflected in service to others?

Where do we go from here?

By his death and resurrection, Jesus has defeated evil. So why does it seem like things are getting worse? God is only waiting until as many people as possible can be saved to come in glory. We simply have to choose day by day to make God's victory our own and live as children of the light. The example of a good person is a powerful testimony to God's victory over death and evil. Let us believe in the resurrection and share the good news with others.

Dear God, I do believe. Help my unbelief.

Genesis 37.3-4, 12-13, 17-28 • Psalm 105 • Matthew 21.33-43, 45-46

S ing to him, sing praises to him;
tell of all his wonderful works.
Glory in his name;
let the hearts of those who seek the Lord rejoice.   *Psalm 105.2-3*

Sing a new song

The psalms are the mainstay of our communal monastic prayer. We pray them every day throughout the day, and this daily recitation engraves their wisdom in our minds and on our hearts. These verses of Psalm 105 give us a program for life. We are created to sing God's praises, to tell forth in our very persons God's wonderful works. Seeking the Lord brings joy to the heart. We seek the Lord to find our strength in God. Without God, nothing is possible; with God, everything is possible. Holding the continual remembrance of God in our hearts gives us life. Remembering all God's deeds in history and in our lives gives us courage and hope. The Eucharist is the celebration and remembrance of God's wonderful works above all others.

Where do we go from here?

St. Augustine says to sing a new song: "A song is a thing of joy … it is a thing of love. Anyone, therefore, who has learned to love the new life, has learned to sing a new song." We sing a new song when heart and deeds flow from one source, from God who gives us life. We read of God's great work in Scripture. We experience God's wonderful work in our lives. Each day, take time to remember all that God has done in your life—the blessings of his love. Become a new song of praise and thanksgiving to God.

Jesus, I give thanks for your presence in the Eucharist and for daily celebrating this great gift.

Micah 7.14-15, 18-20 • Psalm 103 • Luke 15.1-3, 11-32

"So he set off and went to his father. But while he was still far off, his father saw him and was filled with compassion; he ran and put his arms around him and kissed him."

Luke 15.18-24

....

The merciful father

This parable is about the mercy of God. God loves us even while we are sinners, and God runs to us to welcome us back with compassion even before we can recite all our excuses. The main characters in the parable are the father, the son who sins, and the elder son. In any parable there are many levels of meaning. In this parable, the behaviour of each of the characters teaches us so much: the son who sins and repents, the father who forgives and welcomes, and the elder son who cannot rejoice in the happy event. How do I see myself? Am I a person of mercy and compassion, or am I a repentant sinner, trusting in God's mercy? Or am I the elder son, filled with jealousy at another's good fortune? Probably I have been all three.

Where do we go from here?

This is a wonderful parable about God's loving mercy and forgiveness. The son in the parable does not even get a chance to say he is sorry, before the Father runs to him and holds him in a great embrace of love and forgiveness. Jesus is trying to tell the people that this is the way God, his Father, loves us. Meditate on this parable, ponder your relationship to God and let Jesus' words heal you.

Lord, give me a loving spirit of mercy toward others, a patient spirit with myself and a trusting spirit with God.

Exodus 17.3-7 • Psalm 95 • Romans 5.1-2, 5-8 • John 4.5-42

"Everyone who drinks of this water will be thirsty again, but those who drink of the water that I will give them will never be thirsty."
John 4.13-14

Give me a drink

The Sundays of Lent are full of powerful gospels. In today's short passage, we find many meaningful tidbits. For example, Jesus rests at a place that is connected to Jacob and Joseph, Old Testament figures who carried God's promise. Jesus is the fulfillment of the promises given to these ancestors in faith. His dialogue with a Samaritan woman, an outcast in the eyes of the Jews, also has great meaning. Jesus reaches out in love to everyone. And then there is the simple detail that Jesus, God and man, is tired and thirsty. He understands our fragility and need.

What else touches you in this short passage? Take a little time to read the whole passage or listen attentively at Mass to the reading, and let one short passage resonate with you.

Where do we go from here?

What teaching in this parable has touched you in a new way? Every year as we read this passage again, it should be a new word for us. God's word is always new and we are always different when we hear it. Jesus excludes no one from his love or teaching. He reaches out to the rich and to the poor. Jesus is also willing to be needy. He is thirsty and asks this woman for a drink of water. Jesus continues to ask you to feed him in the hungry, to clothe him and comfort him in the needy. In his turn he will give you living water.

Lord, let me make time to ponder the Scripture and listen to your transforming Word.

2 Kings 5.1-15 • Psalm 42 • Luke 4.24-30

A s a deer longs for flowing streams,
   so my soul longs for you, O God.
   My tears have been my food day and night,
while people say to me continually, "Where is your God?"
Hope in God; for I shall again praise him, my help and my God.
Psalm 42.1, 3, 5

Longing for God

St. Augustine says that our souls are restless until they rest in God. Deep in our hearts we always seek God, in whom we live and have our being. In the beginning, God created us for himself, and we carry within ourselves the desire to return to God. If we do not quench our spiritual thirst with God, we will run after lesser goods. The psalmist longs for God, needs God and reaches out to God. Life would not be complete without God's presence. When we pray the psalm, all these sentiments become our own, offered for all in need. God always hears our longing and comes near.

Where do we go from here?

Offer to God an empty, thirsting heart that he can fill with his love. This can become a prayer to God. Sit in a quiet prayer space in your home or in the presence of the Blessed Sacrament. In the silence, offer God your emptiness and pray that he may expand that emptiness until it becomes an immense receptacle to receive his love.

**Lord, increase my desire for you
and let me seek your presence.**

Isaiah 7.10-14; 8.10 • Psalm 40 • Hebrews 10.4-10 • Luke 1.26-38

I n the sixth month the angel Gabriel was sent by God to a town in Galilee called Nazareth, to a virgin engaged to a man whose name was Joseph, of the house of David. The virgin's name was Mary. And he came to her and said, "Greetings, favoured one! The Lord is with you." *Luke 1.26-28*

Fear not

God is always telling Israel and those whom God chooses for a special mission, "Do not be afraid." The angel's first greeting to Mary, too, is "Do not be afraid." We can be afraid of so many things, and fear tends to paralyze us, unless it is the fear that is connected to zeal for the Lord. Mary's fear is the fear of a humble heart in the face of a mission far beyond her ability to fulfill it. When the angel assures her of God's will and power to do this, Mary says yes.

Perhaps today God will call me to a task far beyond my ability. Let me say yes, and see what happens.

Where do we go from here?

God says to each of us: "Fear not; I am with you." Today, God wants me to say "yes" to his plans. He wants to use my "yes" to bring the good news of his love to someone. We can witness to God's love not just by words but in a kind deed. Our good deeds of love to another speak much louder than anything we can say. Look around for the one whom God is sending to you. Like Mary, say "yes": I am your servant. Send me.

Lord, give me the trust that if you call me to a task, you will give me what is needed.

Deuteronomy 4.1, 5-9 • Psalm 147 • Matthew 5.17-19

"**D**o not think that I have come to abolish the law or the prophets; I have come not to abolish but to fulfill. For truly I tell you, until heaven and earth pass away, not one letter, not one stroke of a letter, will pass from the law until all is accomplished."
Matthew 5.17-18

Seek first the kingdom

Jesus has brought the law to its fulfillment. We do not despise the law but live from the heart, and in that, the law is fulfilled. Jesus always seems very concerned that his disciples are real. He wants their service to be for God and not for the sake of appearances or for self-importance. Each person is beloved of God, unique and special, but we receive our strength and truth from God who is the source of our life. Jesus lived his life on earth always in communion with his Father, and he wants us to do the same. Let us seek no reward but loving union with God.

Where do we go from here?

St. Augustine said, "Love and do whatever you want"—a statement that can easily be misunderstood. What he meant was that love goes beyond the law. We will be keeping the law and doing so much more. Law gives a structure to society. Good structures do not limit our freedom but allow everyone an equal freedom to live in peace.

Let me seek you in all that I do
and desire only my reward.

Jeremiah 7.23-28 • Psalm 95 • Luke 11.14-23

"When a strong man, fully armed, guards his castle, his property is safe. But when one stronger than he attacks him and overpowers him, he takes away his armour in which he trusted and divides his plunder. Whoever is not with me is against me, and whoever does not gather with me scatters."

Luke 11.21-23

Playing games

These people are really playing games with Jesus. They do not want to admit that the power of God is in him, so they cry "devil." The others are asking for special signs from heaven, and they totally miss the signs he has already given. They really do not want him to do or be anything special, because then they will have to respond to him in a different way. Even more challenging, they will have to change.

What do I want Jesus to be? What do I want Jesus to be for me? Do I want him to be less than he is in my life, so that I can be in control?

Where do we go from here?

It is so easy to play games, to be unreal. We need to reflect on how much of our life we want to turn over to Jesus. To follow Jesus means a real commitment of my life. There can be no game playing. We all like to be in control of our life and of others' lives as well. Jesus says to each of us, "Come follow me." Will you?

Dear Lord, may you increase and I decrease.

Hosea 14.1-9 • Psalm 81 • Mark 12.28-34

I will heal their disloyalty; I will love them freely,
for my anger has turned from them.
I will be like the dew to Israel;
he shall blossom like the lily,
he shall strike root like the forests of Lebanon.

Hosea 14.4-5

....

God waits upon us

Faith is a gift of God. Our life is a gift of God. God helps us in our weakness and heals all our wounds if we say yes. How often I take myself too seriously, acting as if everything depends on me: "I can do it by myself." The truth is that it is grace that makes us whole and opens our hearts to receive from God all that is needful. The prophet Hosea writes of God's love, of God's seeking out Israel. You can almost hear God's plaintive cry: "Return to me!" God waits upon us to come, so that God may heal our faithlessness and love us freely. In God's shadow, we will grow and flourish.

Where do we go from here?

"Return to me with all you heart." God speaks through the prophet Hosea of his tender love. What do you need to do to return to the Lord? God is waiting and desires your coming. Ask the Holy Spirit to guide you in the ways of God.

**I can do all things in the strength provided by God.
Let this be my great confidence and hope, Lord.**

Hosea 5.15–6.6 • Psalm 51 • Luke 18.9-14

" Come, let us return to the Lord;
for it is he who has torn, and he will heal us …
Let us know, let us press on to know the Lord;
his appearing is as sure as the dawn…."

Hosea 6.1, 3

He comes like the gentle rain

Lent is the special time given to us by the Church for repentance and returning to the Lord. These themes run through the readings given during this season, always coupled with the theme of God's love and healing mercy. The Scripture is never "iffy" about God being near and accessible to us; this is God's promise and God is faithful. God is never the source of the ills of life, but God uses them to bring us back to his love. Isaiah gives us the beautiful imagery of nature to assure us. God's coming is as sure as the dawn and will be like the gentle spring rains that water the earth and bring forth new life.

Let us lift our faces to the heavens and image God descending to water the barrenness of our spirits with the gentle rain of his grace.

Where do we go from here?

The liturgy continues to repeat the Lenten message: "return to the Lord." Yes, come, let us return to the Lord. God is not hard to find. He is so near to each of us; his Holy Spirit abides in our heart. Here I am, Lord, to do your will. The words of Mary at the Annunciation, "Be it done unto me according to your Word," should echo and re-echo in our life with God.

**Dear God, let me constantly rejoice
in your gentle and tender love for me.**

1 Samuel 16.1, 6-7, 10-13 • Psalm 23 • Ephesians 5.8-14 • John 9.1-41

For once you were darkness, but now in the Lord you are light. Live as children of light—for the fruit of the light is found in all that is good and right and true. Try to find out what is pleasing to the Lord. Take no part in the unfruitful works of darkness, but instead expose them. For it is shameful even to mention what such people do secretly; but everything exposed by the light becomes visible, for everything that becomes visible is light.

Ephesians 5.8-14

Live in the light

St. Paul calls us to live as children of light. When we live in the light of the Holy Spirit we understand what is good, right and true. St. Paul exhorts us to find out what is pleasing to the Lord. How do we do that? We rely on the Holy Spirit. God does not want it to be difficult to know his will. An open, seeking heart that listens to the voice of the Spirit of God will find, day by day, what is the Lord's will. We need only to be still, so that we can hear the gentle, inner whisper of the Holy Spirit directing us in the way to God.

Where do we go from here?

Our Lenten journey is almost over for another year. St. Paul tells us now that we have had this preparation time: "Try to find out what is pleasing to the Lord." This is our daily task. What would you have me do today, Lord? Jesus sent the Holy Spirit to continue to teach us and to understand all the words of Jesus. Pray every day for the guidance of the Holy Spirit.

Lord, quiet my heart, that I may hear your voice.

Isaiah 65.17-21 • Psalm 30 • John 4.43-54

I will rejoice in Jerusalem, and delight in my people;
no more shall the sound of weeping be heard in it,
or the cry of distress. ...
They shall build houses and inhabit them;
they shall plant vineyards and eat their fruit.   *Isaiah 65.19, 21*

Rejoice! God is near

Do we think of Lent as a sombre and gloomy time? The readings during Lent do speak of repentance and fasting, but they also speak of joy, new life and re-creation. Since Christ's resurrection, his disciples can never be a gloomy people. The prophet Isaiah offers some of the most comforting passages in the Old Testament. Today's reading tells us God is going to create newness, and we shall rejoice and be glad. God will wipe away all tears and take away from us all distress. What a wonderful message! God does this even now when we trust ourselves to the Holy Spirit and walk in God's ways.

Where do we go from here?

God is creating a renewed earth. We will be reborn in Jesus from his wounded side and become children of the day at his resurrection. We have only a few more weeks to walk intensely with Jesus, who has set his face toward Jerusalem and the complete gift of himself for our sake. Let us walk very closely with Jesus during his journey. Let the word of God penetrate our minds and hearts and bring us to know the Lord and to commit ourselves to God in a deeper way.

God, let me receive this newness even now.
Give me a heart of praise!

Ezekiel 47.1-9, 12 • Psalm 46 • John 5.1-16

There water was flowing from below the threshold of the temple toward the east .... On the banks, on both sides of the river, there will grow all kinds of trees for food.   *Ezekiel 47.1, 12*

The temple

The temple is the heart of Jesus, which was pierced by the sword and from which flow living waters. It is as if God's "water broke," bringing to birth the Church that flows abundantly with waters of baptism. The temple is also the heart of Jesus, ever overflowing with love and compassion, and desiring to be present to us in our places of abandonment, isolation, paralysis or despair. Even when we have lost hope, can no longer pray and do not expect anything, Jesus comes to us, sees us, loves us and asks, "Do you want to be healed?" His heart flows with such an overabundance of love that he yearns to bring us life in all fullness, to nourish us, to quench our thirst, to heal us, so that we, in turn, may bear fruits of love and compassion.

Where do we go from here?

Pray with the image of water: picture a fast-moving creek flowing over a rocky bed, cleansing and making the rocks smooth. The rocks, with time, become round and perfectly smooth, with no rough edges. In silent stillness, see yourself standing under a waterfall that is a symbol of God's grace and mercy: you are cleansed and all the rough places are slowly washed away.

Lord Jesus, let me "be still," like a tree planted close to the river of life flowing from the sanctuary of your most Sacred Heart, so that my life may not be barren but bear life-giving fruit and leaves that bring healing to others.

Isaiah 49.8-15 • Psalm 145 • John 5.16-30

Therefore the Jews started persecuting Jesus, because he was doing such things on the sabbath. But Jesus answered them, "My Father is still working, and I also am working." For this reason the Jews were seeking all the more to kill him, because he was not only breaking the sabbath, but was also calling God his own Father, thereby making himself equal to God.   *John 5.16-17*

Communion with God

After healing the paralytic, Jesus yearns to heal the Pharisees, who are frightened and desperately defending the only way they know to love God: to fulfill obediently the law. Jesus heals on the sabbath to be like God, who gifted them with the law and who, as the psalmist sings, "is gracious and merciful, slow to anger and abounding in steadfast love … good to all, and his compassion is over all that he has made." To these Pharisees, Jesus opens the possibility of going deeper into communion with God, of entering into a filial relationship with God and a transformational oneness with God. Not only would they fulfill the law, but they would have the freedom to do the works of God their Father, "who will have compassion on his suffering ones" (Isaiah 49:13).

Where do we go from here?

It such a sad thing to see someone who could be helped refusing that help. How grieved Jesus must have been when his love was rejected, his power to heal and give life left unused because of stubbornness of heart. God wants to do wonderful, unbelievable things within us and through us. Give God permission.

O, that I too may be gracious and merciful, because you, my beloved, are my Abba, Father.

Exodus 32.7-14 • Psalm 106 • John 5.18, 31-47

"**H**ow can you believe when you accept glory that comes from one another and do not seek the glory that comes from the one who alone who is God?"
John 5.44

To search

We search and strive after life in so many ways, but in doing so, we bypass Jesus, who yearns to give us life in all its fullness. In the same way, we try to love God on our own, rather than receiving love as a gift from Jesus, allowing God's love to flow in and through us. Life and love are gifts that are freely and abundantly given to those who are receptive to Jesus. Where does our reluctance to believe and to receive come from? Jesus gives us a clue. It has something to do with seeking glory in the wrong places.

Jesus is totally oriented toward the glory of God his Father. It is the Father who is his source and his finality. He relies neither on himself nor upon the opinions of others. Empty of these, he is total receptivity. All he is and does flows from this filial relationship.

Where do we go from here?

Is there some area in my life that I am not bringing to Jesus? Make that question a prayer to God and be willing to let go when the answer comes. Kneel or sit in silence with that question, turning your gaze inward and wait. God will speak in your receptive heart.

Father, grant me the grace to resist filling my emptiness, relying upon myself and seeking the admiration of others. Grant that I may abide in your love and continually receive my life and my love as sheer gifts from you.

Wisdom 2.1, 12-22 • Psalm 34 • John 7.1-2, 10, 25-30

N ow some of the people of Jerusalem were saying, "Is not this the man whom they are trying to kill?" *John 7. 25*

The threat of difference

Astonishment has turned into murmuring; gossip has turned into malicious taunting; discomfort, into hatred. Unconscious fear has led these authorities to discredit, hunt, exclude and destroy the one who is so other. Jesus is outside of their frame of reference and they are unable to subdue him.

Meek and humble of heart, Jesus persists in welcoming, calling, loving and healing the "wrong" sort of people at the "wrong" times and in the "wrong" places. He lovingly crosses social and religious boundaries to include others with the ease and inner freedom of one who has been sent by One with true authority. No wonder the "authorities" were terrified; by killing Jesus, they exorcized their fear.

Like Jesus, let us choose the way of inclusion and love.

Where do we go from here?

What is our frame of reference for acceptance? If we did not know who Jesus was, would he perhaps be outside it? Our judgment of beauty and truth is often too narrow, defined in a very superficial way. Try to see the heart of another beyond the superficial façade they use to protect themselves from rejection and hurt. Dare to throw away the mask you sometimes hide behind.

Jesus, when I am tempted to murmur, gossip, accuse or exclude, may I recognize my fear of discomfort, my fear of fear, and my fear of the other. Give me the grace to continue to act justly and walk humbly with you in your way of love.

Jeremiah 11.18-20 • Psalm 7 • John 7.40-53

When they heard these words, some in the crowd said, "This is really the prophet." Others said, "This is the Messiah." But some asked, "Surely the Messiah does not come from Galilee, does he?" ... So there was a division in the crowd because of him. *John 7.40-41, 43*

Do not judge

Jesus' words had offended them again. Some of the people came to a rash conclusion. If they had taken time, asked a few questions or gathered information, they would have discovered that, although Jesus came from Galilee, he was indeed born in Bethlehem. In their need for closure on the question, they slammed shut the door of their minds, and dismissed both the question and Jesus. Even if they had known where he came from, they likely would have looked for another question to justify their fear and their reckless judgment. Jesus had just stood in their midst and cried out to them, "Let anyone who is thirsty come to me." His cry of love was met with their intractable judgment, disguised as discernment, which came from their lamentable self-sufficiency. They simply were not thirsty.

Where do we go from here?

The text from John really emphasizes the importance of listening and the futility of worrying about what others think. The listening of the crowd is so superficial. The division was already present in their closed hearts. What did they truly want? What do you honestly want of Jesus?

Beloved Lord Jesus, I thirst. Forgive me for the times when my rash judgments and self-sufficiency have turned me away from the living water you offer.

Ezekiel 37.12-14 • Psalm 130 • Romans 8.8-11 • John 11.1-45

When Mary came where Jesus was and saw him, she knelt at his feet and said to him, "Lord, if you had been here, my brother would not have died." When Jesus saw her weeping, and the Jews who came with her also weeping, he was greatly disturbed in spirit and deeply moved. ... Jesus began to weep.
John 11.32-33, 35

God weeps

Here, we witness Jesus' deep and personal love for individuals. When he sees Mary's pain, Jesus is moved. He is touched to the core of his being by the horror and sorrow experienced by those who are left behind when a loved one dies. Jesus breaks down and cries. Is Jesus, in this moment, suddenly also painfully aware of the great void and immense sorrow that his mother, his disciples and his friends will experience when he is laid in his tomb? How agonizing for him to know that he will be the occasion of such suffering. When faced with the suffering and death of loved ones, we can be tempted to feel betrayed by God and blame him: "Lord, if you had been here...". This passage tells us that our God weeps with us and shares our sorrow.

Where do we go from here?

Jesus weeps; his heart is torn at the grief of his friends. God has given Jesus tears to shed for his creatures. What an awesome thought. Our God is not a distant and unmoved deity, but a personal God of love and mercy who has become one with his creatures, so that we may be one with God.

Lord Jesus, how you loved Lazarus and his sisters. How you love all those I love! May I ever know and trust that love, especially in times of suffering and great loss.

Daniel 13.1-9, 15-17, 19-30, 33-64 • Psalm 23 • John 8.1-11

"Teacher, this woman was caught in the very act of committing adultery. Now in the law Moses commanded us to stone such women. Now what do you say?" *John 8.4-5*

Compassion for sinners

"Let anyone among you who is without sin be the first to throw a stone at her." Jesus' response to the scribes and Pharisees is a masterpiece of psychology, and shows clearly Jesus' respect and compassion for every person. He condemned neither the woman who was caught in the act of committing adultery nor the scribes and Pharisees; yet he did not condone the sin. By his gentle and compassionate attitude, he confronted the sin while being compassionate toward the sinner. We can imagine the embarrassment of the scribes and Pharisees as they became aware of their own sins. Yet Jesus did not stare at them. Instead, he bent down until they had quietly departed. We can also imagine the woman's fear as she stood there alone, and then her relief as she heard Jesus say, "Neither do I condemn you. Go your way, and from now on do not sin again."

Where do we go from here?

The Pharisees deliberately make the woman stand before them in her shame. Jesus, however, never shames the sinner, but calls them to new life. Have you ever met someone who is eager to tell all about the latest scandal? He or she is like the Pharisees, self-righteous and gloating over another's misfortune. Search for ways to build up the good name of another. Do not participate in gossip.

Lord Jesus, so live in me that I may always see others through your eyes of compassion and love. May I be slow to condemn and quick to excuse the apparent faults of others.

Numbers 21.4-9 • Psalm 102 • John 8.21-30

"When you have lifted up the Son of Man, then you will realize that I am he, and that I do nothing on my own, but I speak these things as the Father instructed me." ... As he was saying these things, many believed in him.   *John 8.28, 30*

Healing presence

The lifting up of the Son of Man refers to Jesus' being lifted up on the cross—his "hour of glory," according to St. John. Just as Moses lifted up the serpent in the desert, and all who had been bitten were healed by looking on the bronze serpent, so those who look on Jesus raised on the cross, having faith in him and in the One who sent him, will be healed.

Throughout Chapter 8 of John, Jesus dialogues with the Jews in order to evoke a response of faith in him as the One who is sent from above. But they continue in their blindness, because they think they know where he came from. Jesus knows where he comes from and where he is going; he knows that the Father is always with him, because he always "does what is pleasing to him."

Where do we go from here?

"I know him and I know where he comes from." Words like these cut us off from everything but our preconceived notions. What we are so sure we know we usually do not know at all. Why would seeing Jesus on the Cross help us to realize who he was? Those standing by did cry out that truly this was the Son of God. The heart recognizes the presence of goodness and love.

Live, Jesus, live! So live in me that all I do is done in you, and all I think and all I say are your thoughts and words this day.

Daniel 3.13-20, 24, 49-50, 91-95 • Daniel 3 • John 8.31-42

Then Jesus said to the Jews who had believed in him, "If you continue in my word, you are truly my disciples; and you will know the truth, and the truth will make you free." They answered him, "We are descendants of Abraham and have never been slaves to anyone. What do you mean by saying, 'You will be made free'?"

John 8.31-33

True freedom

God's word is always a creative Word, alive and active. When we welcome the Word as Mary did, we are transformed and become true disciples of Jesus. St. Augustine said, "Of what use is it for the Word to take flesh and be born in Bethlehem if he is not born in my heart?" When we welcome the Word, he gives us power to become sons and daughters in the Son. This is the truth we learn from pondering the Word: that we are children of the one Father, brothers and sisters of Jesus. This truth sets us free from sin and selfishness, and opens us to a new vision of reality. If the Son makes us free, we are free indeed. Free to worship our Father through Jesus, and free to love our brothers and sisters, even to the point of laying down our life for them.

Where do we go from here?

The word of God will truly make us free if we welcome it into our hearts. Jesus promises the freedom of the word to the Pharisees, who think they are already free. They are not willing to receive the gift of a new freedom; Jesus can do nothing for them. Let our response to the Lord be "Yes, Jesus, make me free!"

Jesus, through pondering your word, may you be born in my heart, and renew all your mystery in me.

Genesis 17.3-9 • Psalm 105 • John 8.51-59

S eek the Lord and his strength; seek his presence continually. Remember the wonderful works he has done …
Psalm 105.4, 5

Seek God's presence

In this beautiful psalm, we are invited to tirelessly seek the face of the Lord. The psalmist recounts the great deeds the Lord has accomplished for God's people, beginning with the covenant with Abraham, God's care of the Patriarchs, God's providence in the life of Joseph, and God's wonders shown through the lives of Moses and Aaron. God proves God's faithfulness in leading the people of Israel with joy to the Promised Land.

Jesus is our true "Moses," who frees his people from the power of darkness, and leads them through the desert of this life to their true home in heaven—feeding them with his own flesh and blood and guiding them by the power of his Spirit. Without God we wander hopelessly, but with him, all our wandering leads to the kingdom.

Where do we go from here?

We do not have to rely on our own strength to get through each day. God will be our strength and courage, our light and hope for each day. Carry in your heart each day a word of thanksgiving, remembering the grace of God in your life. Remember God's wonderful works in the past and pray that God may walk with you today, tomorrow and always.

**Lord, may the radiance of your glory light up my heart
and guide me through the shadows of this world
as I journey toward my true homeland of everlasting life.**

Jeremiah 20.7, 10-13 • Psalm 18 • John 10.31-42

O Lord, you have enticed me, and I was enticed;
you have overpowered me, and you have prevailed. ...
But the Lord is with me like a dread warrior ....

Jeremiah 20.7, 11

The cost of discipleship

In chapter 20, the prophet Jeremiah complains that God has seduced him and taken him by force. He describes what it cost him to be chosen by God, recounting his inner struggles and suffering, his loneliness and hopelessness bordering on despair, to the point of cursing the day of his birth (20.14-18; 15.10). His anger, complaints and disappointments are like those in the heart of a lover.

God's call did not make Jeremiah a superman; he was no ready-made saint. His natural defects of character and background, his fragility and vulnerability demonstrate God's power at work in human weakness. He allowed himself to become the clay in the Divine Potter's hand, and he continued to be faithful to his mission in spite of so much opposition and ridicule, knowing the Lord was with him.

Where do we go from here?

We are called to be like Jesus. The way is not always easy—Jesus did not promise his disciples would not suffer. We will suffer, as he did, the world's rejection and hardship. Sanctification is not something we achieve by hard work or human perfection; it is a gift we enter into—God's gift. Our work is listening to God's inner word and humbly assenting to the Spirit's healing work, honestly aware of what is hindering us in following the Spirit's promptings.

Here I am, Lord, to do your will. Help me to be faithful, no matter what the cost.

Ezekiel 37.21-28 • Jeremiah 31 • John 11.45-57

My dwelling place shall be with them; and I will be their God, and they shall be my people.   *Ezekiel 37.27*

God's sanctuary

Ezekiel spoke these words of hope and encouragement when the Israelites were far from their homeland, exiled as a result of their sins and infidelity to the Sinai Covenant. Yet God never gave up on them. While exile in Babylon was a punishment for their sins, it was simultaneously a purification, preparing them for a more intimate and permanent union with their God, when "he would set his sanctuary among them forevermore."

This promise is fulfilled in Jesus, the new Temple and dwelling place of God. Jesus promises to come with the Father and the Holy Spirit to dwell in the hearts of his disciples. This promise will find its ultimate fulfillment in the New Jerusalem, where "the home of God is among mortals. He will dwell with them as their God; they will be his peoples, and God himself will be with them" (Revelation 21.3).

Where do we go from here?

God is always faithful to his promises. Ask God to be God in your life. Bring God into your workplace by your patience and good humour, your helpfulness and kindness. Our actions speak louder than words. One day someone will ask you why you are so upbeat and that will be the opening to share your faith.

**To those who love you, Lord, you promise to come
with your Son and make your home within them.
Come with your purifying grace, and make of my heart
a place where you can dwell.**

Matthew 21.1-11 • Isaiah 50.4-7 • Psalm 22 • Philippians 2.6-11 • Matthew 26.14–27.66

The crowds that went ahead of him and that followed were shouting, "Hosanna to the Son of David! Blessed is the one who comes in the name of the Lord! Hosanna in the highest heaven!"

Matthew 21.9

Palm Sunday

Palm Sunday is the gateway to Holy Week, the prelude to the great feast of Easter. In his letter to the Philippians, St. Paul tells us to have the same mind as Christ, who emptied himself for our sakes. As we enter into this holiest of all weeks and move toward the great celebration of Easter, let us pray to put on the mind of Christ Jesus, to love and serve in his name, and to follow Jesus in our daily life. If we share in his cross, we shall also share in the glory of his resurrection. Jesus is our sure hope and our joy!

Where do we go from here?

Enter with great faith into Holy Week. Participate, as much as possible, in all the Holy Week liturgies. The liturgy is structured so that we can profoundly walk with Jesus through his Passion and rise with him on Easter morning. The Scripture readings are the richest of the entire liturgical year. Allow yourself this transforming experience of God's presence.

**Jesus, I follow you and seek to love as you love.
Help me to grow in your love.**

Isaiah 42.1-7 • Psalm 27 • John 12.1-11

Six days before the Passover Jesus came to Bethany, the home of Lazarus, whom he had raised from the dead. ... Mary took a pound of costly perfume made of pure nard, anointed Jesus' feet, and wiped them with her hair. The house was filled with the fragrance of the perfume.   *John 12.1, 3*

Pure love

Mary's act of pure, extravagant love filled the whole house with perfume. Jesus praised her and understood her anointing as a preparation for his burial, for he was about to pour out his life on the cross in pure, self-giving love to the Father on behalf of humankind. Somehow they understood each other, heart to heart; both of them were extravagant in their love.

When motivated by pure, disinterested love, our actions, no matter how insignificant they may appear on the surface, have far-reaching effects, filling the house of the Church and our world with the perfume of holiness, beauty and truth.

Where do we go from here?

The house is filled with the perfume of Mary's gift to Jesus. She doesn't care what the others will think of her, whether they will sneer or condemn her for her life. She sees only Jesus and knows with her whole being that she will receive love and forgiveness. Pray for such a gift of love, see only Jesus and seek to please him.

O Lord, help me to seek you with all my heart. Free me from the snares of selfishness, and grant me the grace to live each day as a witness of your friendship and truth.

Isaiah 49.1-6 • Psalm 71 • John 13.21-33, 36-38

S imon Peter said to him, "Lord, where are you going?" Jesus answered, "Where I am going, you cannot follow me now; but you will follow afterward." Peter said to him, "Lord, why can I not follow you now? I will lay down my life for you." Jesus answered, "Will you lay down your life for me?" *John 13.36-38*

Humility

Peter focuses on himself and on what he wants to do for the Lord. Jesus knows that Peter is not yet ready, but assures him that he will follow later. First Peter needs to experience his own weakness; three times he denies that he ever knew Jesus. He needs to grow in humility and in the awareness of his own helplessness.

We can experience trials that test our faith and love so much that we may even doubt the existence of a God who is Love. The Lord does not allow these things to happen in order to crush us, but rather to purify our hearts so that we can love more deeply and come to realize that, of ourselves, we are powerless. In God who strengthens us with his Spirit, we can do great things—works that will truly glorify God's name.

Where do we go from here?

St. Paul says that when he was powerless, then he was strong. We do not easily let go of control over our life. Yet spiritual growth comes when we know that we are weak but God is strong and sustains us in love. Do not be afraid of weakness. It is precisely then that God's grace lifts you up.

Jesus, help me to cling to you in all the circumstances of my life, whether painful or joyful, knowing that all things, even my sins, work together for good if I love you.

Isaiah 50.4-9 • Psalm 69 • Matthew 26.14-26

Then one of the twelve, who was called Judas Iscariot, went to the chief priests and said, "What will you give me if I betray him to you?" They paid him thirty pieces of silver. And from that moment he began to look for an opportunity to betray him.

Matthew 26.14-16

True and false friendship

At the very moment when Jesus is about to lay down his life for love of the human race, and is about to hand over his body and blood as food and drink, one of his trusted disciples asks the chief priests: "How much will you give me if I betray him to you?" Judas seems to be completely blinded by his selfishness. He can think only of himself and what he will get by betraying a friend. Can we sometimes identify with Judas? Are we so wrapped up in our own ego that we become insensitive to the needs of those whose lives we touch, even our friends and those who love us, that we let them down for a paltry advantage to ourselves?

Where do we go from here?

Friendship is about how much I love, not first about how much I am loved. A true friend is one who loves as Jesus loved, generously and unselfishly. What can you do for others today? How can you love unselfishly and give yourself away in love? Ask the Holy Spirit to fill you with love to share.

Jesus, through the power of your Passion, heal the wounds of selfishness in my heart, and grant me the grace to be a loyal and faithful friend to all those who touch my life.

Exodus 12.1-8, 11-14 • Psalm 116 • 1 Corinthians 11.23-26 •
John 13.1-15

J esus] got up from the table, took off his outer robe, and tied a
towel around himself. Then he poured water into a basin and
began to wash his disciples' feet ....   *John 13.4-5*

Jesus the servant

There are few incidents in the gospel that so reveal the character of
Jesus and the depth of his love as this passage in St. John. In the
other gospels, Jesus speaks the words of institution at the Last Supper
("This is my Body … This is my Blood. Do this in memory of me"),
but in John, Jesus washes the disciples' feet. This gesture replaces the
words of institution. It specifies what the Eucharist is in fact meant to
do: to lead us into the humble service of others.

Jesus took the form of servant when he washed his disciples' feet.
He asks us also, "Do you know what I have done?" If we accept Jesus
and his way of life, we are his disciples. He has set us an example of
love: the greater we are, the more humbly we should behave.

Where do we go from here?

Humility and love are connected. Jesus served humbly because he
loved. Loving as Jesus loves gives us new eyes to see the needs of
others, to see the dignity and beauty in every other person. Love
gives me the capacity and the desire to serve others. Peter did
not want Jesus to wash his feet. Love also helps us to let others
serve us, for that too is a manifestation of humble love. Read and
meditate on this passage from John.

**Loving Lord Jesus, you showed by example what
I should do: be generous in loving and serving you and all
my brothers and sisters, especially the sick and the poor.**

113

Isaiah 52.13–53.12 • Psalm 31 • Hebrews 4.14-16; 5.7-9 • John 18.1–19.42

[Jesus] said ... "I am thirsty." ... one of the soldiers pierced his side with a spear, and at once blood and water came out.
John 19.28, 34

Merciful love

Today as we reflect on the merciful love of our Saviour, we are filled with hope and courage. St. Catherine of Siena reminds us that it was not the nails that held Jesus on the cross, but the love in his heart—his thirst to complete the task the Father had entrusted to him.

He thirsts for our love in return. No matter what sin we have committed, no matter how far we have strayed from him, let us rely completely on his infinite mercy. The greatest gift we offer Jesus for his love is to open our hearts to receive the fruits of his Passion: to allow him to flood our hearts with his love and compassion. May Jesus enable us to radiate his love to everyone we meet.

Where do we go from here?

St. John was the Apostle of love. There is the tradition that at the end of his life, his only message was: love, love, love. There seems no getting away from the fact that following Jesus is to love—not just those who are easy to love or those who love us, but everyone, even our enemies. A discipleship of love calls us to days filled with good deeds and prayer. Pray especially for those men and women who sow seeds of hate in our world.

Jesus, be merciful to me, a sinner. Help me to believe in your infinite love for me and for all people, and help me to be compassionate to others.

Gen 1.1–2.2 • Ps 104 *or* 33 • Gen 22.1-18 • Ps 16 • Exod 14.15-31;15.20, 1 •
Exod 15 • Isa 54.5-14 • Ps 30 • Isa 55.1-11 • Isa 12 • Bar 3.9-15, 32–4.4 • Ps 19 •
Ezek 36.16-17, 18-28 • Ps 42 *or* 51 *or* Isa 12 • Rom 6.3-11 • Ps 118 • Matt 28.1-10

A wind from God swept over the face of the waters.
Genesis 1.2

God's Spirit hovers

The first lines of the Book of Genesis give us a wonderful insight into
the pattern of God's activity in our created world. In the beginning,
God's Spirit hovered over the "formless void." He spoke his Word,
and creation came to be. At the Annunciation, God's Spirit overshad-
owed Mary, and the Word took flesh in the void of her virgin womb.
On the evening of the first Easter Sunday, the Risen Jesus filled the
void of the frightened and heart-broken disciples, and breathed on
them, saying, "Receive the Holy Spirit" (John 20.22). It is the same
Spirit who hovers over the waters of baptism, making us children
of God. The Spirit continues to hover over the chaos of our lives—
whether it be sin, illness or whatever wounds we carry—waiting to
transform the chaos into something beautiful for God.

Where do we go from here?

The night of nights and the Feast of Feasts: the great Easter Vigil.
This night is the peak of the liturgical year, the night of our spiritual
rebirth. Tonight the Church sets before us the whole mystery of
our salvation. Listen attentively to the readings and to the whole
liturgy. It is the story of God's mercy and our salvation. Prepare for
Easter by meditating on these. Easter blessings!

O Risen Saviour, breathe your Spirit afresh on me!
Penetrate and possess my whole being so completely
that my life may radiate your light and love to others.

Acts 10.34, 37-43 • Psalm 118 • Colossians 3.1-4 or 1 Corinthians 5.6-8
• John 20.1-18 or Matthew 28.1-10 or Luke 24.13-35

T he angel said to the women, "Do not be afraid; I know that you are looking for Jesus who was crucified. He is not here …. Then go quickly and tell his disciples, 'He has been raised from the dead, and indeed he is going ahead of you to Galilee; there you will see him.'"
Matthew 28.5-7

The presence of the Risen Jesus

Do we, like the two Marys, seek Jesus in places where we ourselves have laid him safely to rest, thinking that we'll always find him there? Have we put his statue in a shrine we can visit to ask for our needs or to light a candle? The Good News is that Jesus is risen and can no longer be tied down by earthly limitations. He is always taking the lead, going ahead to "Galilee" where we shall "see him." Galilee for the disciples meant their workplaces, their homes, the places where they battled the storms. Today, Jesus assures us that he will be there, waiting, in every situation in which we may find ourselves.

Where do we go from here?

"Do not be afraid" is a message God uses repeatedly throughout the Bible. God knows how weak we are, and how timid in the face of life's challenges. Jesus knows how hard life is because he lived it and then conquered forever all evil and adversity. Allow Jesus to walk with you and see if his victory is not true. Then share the good news with others.

**Risen Lord Jesus, open my eyes to recognize
your presence in all the circumstances of my life
and in every person I encounter.**

Acts 2.14, 22-33 • Psalm 16 • Matthew 28.8-15

S o they left the tomb quickly with fear and great joy, and ran to tell his disciples. Suddenly Jesus met them and said, "Greetings!" And they came to him, took hold of his feet, and worshipped him. Then Jesus said to them, "Do not be afraid; go and tell my brothers to go to Galilee; there they will see me."

Matthew 28.8-10

Paschal joy

In this word picture that is so full of action, the women run quickly to tell the disciples the amazing news. We can experience their joy and awe as they discover from the angel that their beloved Lord and Master is alive! They speed to tell their companions, but the Master has taken the initiative, as always, and comes to greet them himself. Their excitement is palpable as they fall at his feet and clasp them. Yet he sends them on their way to spread the Good News.

Joy is the echo of God's life in us. When this echo resounds within us, we are led to the prayer of praise and thanksgiving at all times.

Where do we go from here?

The women ran with fear and great joy to tell the disciples that Jesus was alive. What was this fear? Their joy was great and yet it was so hard to believe it was true—the fear was that it could not be real. Jesus' last words as he ascended were "Do not be afraid! Be bold; tell the good news to everyone. They will not all believe but still continue to spread this unbelievable good news." Jesus tells each of us the same thing.

**Jesus, may I joyfully recognize you
in those whom I meet today.**

Acts 2.36-41 • Psalm 33 • John 20.11-18

S he turned round and saw Jesus standing there, but she did not know that it was Jesus. Jesus said to her, "Woman, why are you weeping? Whom are you looking for?"

John 20.14-15

Seek and you will find

We find Mary Magdalene weeping near the tomb, overcome with grief. She had seen her beloved Lord Jesus crucified on Calvary. Now, restless with love and longing, she seeks solace near him, only to find that even his dead body has disappeared. She is inconsolable. What she does not realize is that she is seeking among the dead for one who lives. He is actually very near to her. Jesus finds comfort in the knowledge of her love and the anguish of her loss. He speaks a simple word of great love and longing: "Mary!"

Mary comes seeking, but Jesus does the revealing. It is always that way. If we seek him in our times of anguish and distress, he will find us.

Where do we go from here?

Jesus calls each of us by name. He knows us better than we can ever know ourselves. Jesus knows our sins, our desires, our tears and our joys. He buried them all deep in his heart on Calvary and rose with them into new life at his resurrection. Trust everything to Jesus and walk in the light of his love.

"Come, then, Lord Jesus ... Come to me, seek me, find me, take me in your arms, carry me." (St. Ambrose)

Acts 3.1-10 • Psalm 105 • Luke 24.13-35

Peter looked intently at him … and said, "Look at us."
Acts 3.4

Love's gaze

We see how the cripple looked expectantly to the apostles, and what a gift they gave him. "I have no silver or gold, but what I have I give you; in the name of Jesus Christ of Nazareth, stand up and walk" (Acts 3.6). Let us, too, look expectantly today to Jesus our Lord and healer, because for God to gaze on us works wonders. His look cleanses us, makes us beautiful, enriches and enlightens us.

Jesus looks with love upon us, and his mercy sets us free. Can we dare to open our hearts to this look of love, and be taken in by his penetrating eyes, full of compassion, love and humour when he sees our childish waywardness?

Where do we go from here?

Peter gave to the cripple what he had received from Jesus: healing and forgiving love. He gazed on the man with the eyes of God, and the works of God flowed through him. We have been given the same power to do the works of God in the world. Have the faith and courage to give to others what you have received.

Father, grant me the grace to be transformed by your look of healing love and to see others with the eyes of Jesus.

Acts 3.11-26 • Psalm 8 • Luke 24.35-48

While they were talking about [what had happened on the road to Emmaus], Jesus himself stood among them and said to them, "Peace be with you." They were startled and terrified, and thought they were seeing a ghost. He said to them, "Why are you frightened and why do doubts arise in your hearts? Look at my hands and my feet; see that it is I myself." *Luke 24.36-39*

Jesus with us

The disciples were scared and confused after Jesus' arrest and death. When he appeared in the room with them, they were terrified, and thought they were seeing a ghost. Jesus was quick to reassure them and make it clear that he was not a disembodied spirit but was there in the flesh. By asking the disciples to look at his hands and feet, he was proving to them without doubt, by the marks of the nails, that he was real. The risen Lord is the same person they knew before.

We all have painful and frightening experiences in our lives from time to time. We know if we turn to Jesus and rest with him, we will experience his peace. He will assure us by his presence that he is with us, to encourage us and to help us be witnesses of his resurrection.

Where do we go from here?

Don't panic when the situation seems impossible. There is a way through it. Stop and listen. Jesus says to us in every difficult situation and insurmountable problem, "Peace be with you!" It is true. Ask Jesus, "What shall I do? Help me!" If you listen and trust, the way through will be there for you.

May nothing disturb my peace or draw me forth from you, O Lord, but may I penetrate more deeply every moment into the depths of your mystery.

Acts 4.1-12 • Psalm 118 • John 21.1-14

W hen Simon Peter heard that it was the Lord, he put on his clothes, for he was naked, and jumped into the sea. *John 21.7*

Peter's naked heart

Peter's nakedness is an amazing, thought-provoking detail in today's gospel. Peter's heart must have been anguished with guilt from boasting that he would never deny Jesus. It's interesting that he pulled on clothes before he jumped into the sea. What exactly was he covering?

Though Jesus lovingly welcomed Peter and the disciples to breakfast, the charcoal fire must have pricked Peter's conscience, since his denial of Jesus happened while he was waiting around a charcoal fire during Jesus' trial. After breakfast, Jesus gave Peter the opportunity to reaffirm his love, asking him three times if Peter loved him. At the third questioning, Peter's anguished heart cried out, "Lord, you know everything; you *know* that I love you." His naked confession of love for the Lord turns his guilty denial of Jesus inside out.

Where do we go from here?

Peter did not mind being naked before the other men in the boat, but he put on his clothes to meet Jesus. We sometimes clothe ourselves with the appearance of goodness rather than taking upon ourselves the arduous task of holiness. In God's presence, it is a futile gesture. God sees our nakedness and need. None of the details are an accident. Jesus did want Peter to remember his guilt, but only so that he could heal it.

**Lord, I too feel naked and guilt-ridden when I sin.
Clothe me in your loving compassion and forgiveness.
Truly, I love you, Lord.**

Acts 4.13-21 • Psalm 118 • Mark 16.9-15

O give thanks to the Lord, for he is good;
his steadfast love endures forever!
Psalm 118.1

Gratitude

Gratitude is a little virtue with all the power of an acorn on its way to becoming a mighty oak. A gracious word of thanks and appreciation can move mountains! The high point of thanksgiving is found in the Liturgy of the Eucharist. We pray in the Preface, "Father in heaven, it is right that we should give you thanks and glory." We are grateful to our Eternal Father for the wonderful gift of the Eucharist, where we meet God.

There is still another way of giving thanks. In times of stress and pain, hurt or disappointment, we can turn to our Father and whisper through our tears, "Thank you. You know what is best for me." Nothing touches the heart of Jesus so much as entrusting everything—our desert times and our joy—to him.

Where do we go from here?

Fill this day with little acts of giving. Intentionally look for ways to help, to be kind, to upbuild and cherish your neighbour. It is a good practice to remember and to thank God for the difficult moments. The power of God's grace and the comfort of the Holy Spirit sustain us in life's hardship. We are never alone—this is a great gift we should never cease thanking God for.

Father, I thank you for all your gifts.

Acts 2.42-47 • Psalm 118 • 1 Peter 1.3-9 • John 20.19-31

"**R**eceive the Holy Spirit."
John 20.22

Breath of Jesus

These words bring us back to Genesis, where God breathed into man's nostrils the breath of life, and the man became a living being (Genesis 2.7). Remember that breath-taking moment when Jesus said, "It is finished," then bowed his head and gave up his spirit. Today, the Risen Jesus breathes his own Spirit into the chaos of our lives. As we listen to God's word being announced, let us turn to our Father and ask him to breathe the Spirit into our hearts, and so renew the face of the earth.

> Your fragrant breathing stills me
> Your grace, your glory fills me
> so tenderly your love becomes my own.
> (John of the Cross)

Where do we go from here?

To be a person of silence in our noisy and fast-moving world is a real challenge. Taking time to reflect on life, on our goals and being silent in the presence of God with our hopes and dreams is necessary for human wholeness. God created us with a mind to think and a spirit to receive. Our humanity needs to slow down from time to time just to "be," not to do or be useful. Only then can you truly appreciate the goodness that is in you, which exists not because of your actions but because you are you. Every person is of infinite value.

**Risen Jesus, breathe your new life into my heart
and give me stillness of soul and mind in you.**

Acts 4.23-31 • Psalm 2 • John 3.1-8

When they had prayed, the place in which they were gathered together was shaken; and they were all filled with the Holy Spirit and spoke the word of God with boldness.   *Acts 4.31*

Confidence in prayer

The place where we gather doesn't often shake when we pray, as it did for Jesus' disciples. But we are certainly always filled with the Holy Spirit when we lift our minds and hearts to our eternal, ever-mindful Father.

Today we can draw renewed confidence from the disciples of Jesus. Remember in these days of Easter that Christ has truly risen; he lives and has conquered all the power of the evil one forever. Remember that whatever we pray in faith and hope and love, Jesus can take and use to move mountains, though we may not feel it. He waits to hear us, receive us and take us with all our longings into himself to fill us with his love.

Where do we go from here?

The boldness with which the Apostles proclaimed the good news was a consequence of their receiving the Holy Spirit. It is the same for us. We have received the Spirit at baptism and have been strengthened in all the gifts of the Spirit at Confirmation. We have all we need to live our Christian life in boldness and to share the good news without fear or restraint.

Eternal and loving Father, I come to you as your beloved child in Jesus' name. Help me, Lord, to pray to you and to believe that you hear me.

Acts 4.32-37 • Psalm 93 • John 3.7-15

"**A**nd just as Moses lifted up the serpent in the wilderness, so must the Son of Man be lifted up, that whoever believes in him may have eternal life."
John 3.14-15

Courage to believe

Do I have the honesty to look at Jesus on the cross, and acknowledge that, despite my love for him, I have also failed him through my sin, and that is why he is there? Do I have the courage to confess my guilt and ask for mercy?

Nicodemus was a teacher, and should have understood what Jesus told him about being born of the Spirit. I call myself a Christian, someone seeking to listen to the Lord so that I may know who I am and how I am to be. But do I presume to know myself apart from Jesus? Do I understand how free I can be when I give all of myself to God, even that which is sinful in me? Am I resentful of what the Lord asks of me?

I can trust that Jesus knows better, because he loves me more than I love myself— infinitely more.

Where do we go from here?

Take time to reflect on the seven-fold gifts of the Holy Spirit: wisdom, understanding, counsel, knowledge, fortitude, piety and fear of the Lord. These gifts are ours to be used, to transform us into God. We are equipped to live a courageous life of faith each day.

Lord Jesus, help me to believe in your power to save me; help me so to trust in your love, that I may never be afraid to seek your mercy, but rejoice in you with all the breath you give me.

Acts 5.17-26 • Psalm 34 • John 3.16-21

"Indeed, God did not send the Son into the world to condemn the world, but in order that the world might be saved through him. Those who believe in him are not condemned; but those who do not believe are condemned already, because they have not believed in the name of the only Son of God."   *John 3.17-18*

Be thou my vision

There is a lot of despair in the world today. But believing in God means seeing the world and the people in it as God sees it and us. Do I look around and see beauty, light and wonder, or am I so disenchanted by news of violence and hate that I begin to lose hope?

In an age where daily reports of destruction no longer shock us, these words of Scripture invite us to enter into a spiritual combat against hopelessness: to be creatures of hope and love. For it is indeed a beautiful world in which the Lord delights; we have the capacity to be beautiful by believing in him. "God saw everything that he had made, and indeed, it was very good" (Genesis 1.31).

Where do we go from here?

Why are we so quick to condemn others and ourselves when God, who knows us so well, does not condemn us, but sent his Son Jesus to save us? It is important to have a good self-image in order to love truly. When we can understand the beauty and goodness in our deepest heart, then we can find that same beauty in others.

Lord, my God, I ask you for the grace to see the world as you see it. Grant that, in your name, I may be a light of hope to those who live in darkness, that they may come to seek and find you, who are the light of the world.

Acts 5.27-33 • Psalm 34 • John 3.31-36

The Father loves the Son and has placed all things in his hands.   *John 3.35*

The Father delights in me

When I sit in prayer before the Lord and look at my hands, I see that they are empty. There is nothing I can give God that has not first been given to me. Even the love I have for God is God's gift to me: my desire to sit with God is God's gift.

What an unfailing wonder it is that God delights in my response to his gift. God, who created me to love God and to know that God loves me, delights in me. God's desire for me is so great, that he sent his Son to speak that desire to my heart. God gave the Spirit without measure to his Son, that I might receive a share in it. God loves the Son so much that God placed in his hands … me.

Where do we go from here?

Set aside 15 or 20 minutes for silent prayer. Hold your cupped hands before you or set out an empty bowl to represent your spiritual life. Get in touch with your emptiness. What might arise first are things that are bothering you or you wish were different, or your sins. All things that are filling you—let them go. In your mind, see them falling away. Now are you empty? Be totally naked before God, allowing him to look into the deepest recesses of your being. Look with him. What do you see? Are you afraid? You are not yet empty. Your hands are cupped and the bowl is rounded to receive. God will pour your life back into you, renewed.

Heavenly Father, grant me to understand more deeply the wonder of your infinite love. Remind me, when I forget, that there is nothing to fear, for you are with me.

Acts 5.34-42 • Psalm 27 • John 6.1-15

W hen they were satisfied, he told his disciples, "Gather up the fragments left over, so that nothing may be lost."
John 6.12

Precious crumbs!

It seems odd that the Lord should be concerned about scraps of food, "leftovers." Are the twelve baskets full to teach us about the abundance of his kindness? With the Lord, we will always have more than we could ask for or imagine.

This gospel "tidbit" suggests that you and I are not beneath his notice or concern. We are infinitely precious to him. Furthermore, Jesus instructed his disciples to save the leftovers. By listening and believing, we are disciples. No one is outside the reach of the Lord's mercy and love.

Where do we go from here?

Reflect on this short text. What do the fragments suggest to you? What is Jesus saying? What does this text teach you about Jesus? About yourself? Jesus had the disciples gather up the fragments only when everyone was satisfied. We can get enough of bodily food but we can never be fully satisfied with the food Jesus gives. The more we receive, the more we want—full satisfaction comes with eternal life.

Lord, I thank you for your gift of faith: for the gift of knowing that I am known and loved by you at every moment.

1 Corinthians 15.1-8 • Psalm 19 • John 14.6-14

Jesus said to [Thomas], "I am the way, and the truth, and the life. No one comes to the Father except through me."
John 14.6

Learning to live

These words are so familiar, it would be easy to hear them without listening to what Jesus is inviting us to know and desire. He came to save us from ourselves, to teach us how to get up when we fall. He shows us where to turn when we are in need of help and mercy. He came to show us how to be human.

I want to be true to myself, the person God created me to be. I want to know how to live well the life I have been given. Jesus is the answer to all my desire.

Where do we go from here?

Does your life seem chaotic? Do you like to have a good plan in place that covers every situation? God has given us one in Jesus and the sending of the Holy Spirit. We have an infallible way: we can know what is true and we have been given abundant life. The gospels give us the full game plan. Read the gospel of John: study it, pray it and search to understand what Jesus is asking of you through this gospel.

**Lord Jesus, grant me the grace to listen with my heart.
Be with me in all I say and do, in rest and in activity.**

Acts 2.14, 22-28 • Psalm 16 • 1 Peter 1.17-21 • Luke 24.13-35

Jesus himself came near and went with them ....
Luke 24.15

You will never walk alone

In the story of the journey to Emmaus, we encounter two despondent disciples, all hope gone, aimlessly wandering the roads. They move as far from the source of their pain as their weary legs will carry them. We, too, encounter the One who walks with them. Gently present to their pain, the One who meets them in their wandering brings the word of God to bear on their situation, leading them gradually to faith, which allows them to recognize him in the breaking of bread.

This gospel passage takes us on a journey from the darkness of unbelief and incomprehension of God's ways to the light of faith and to joy in the Risen Lord, a joy to be shared with all people.

Where do we go from here?

I think of the beautiful words of the song "You will never walk alone." The song exhorts, "Walk on, walk on with hope in your heart and you'll never walk alone." The Scripture is full of God's promise that he is with us always. It is one thing to know it and another to believe it by the way we live our life. Take God's promise and live it in joy and hope. Knowing in your deepest heart that God is faithful is a living faith. Pray for such faith.

**Lord, you joined your disciples on the way to Emmaus.
Accompany me on my journey through life.
May your word light up my way.**

Acts 6.8-15 • Psalm 119 • John 6.22-29

"Very truly, I tell you, you are looking for me, not because you saw signs, but because you ate your fill of the loaves."
John 6.26

....

Look beyond the bread you eat

In these times of economic hardship, we can readily sympathize with those who flocked to Jesus because he provided food in abundance. What they didn't realize was that Jesus was offering them so much more. Jesus asked the crowd to look beyond the signs and wonders to himself as the Revelation of God, who provided not only for their material well-being, but for the kind of food that "endures for eternal life," if they only had faith in him.

Where do we go from here?

What is the "much more" that Jesus wants to offer to you? Do you know what your deepest spiritual needs are? Look into your heart and see how you are needy in the things of God. Do you live your life from your faith in Jesus? Ask God to increase your faith until it becomes the principle from which you live your life. Our faith needs to go much deeper than words.

**Lord, you are drawing me through earthly realities
to an awareness of your Presence. Give me eyes to see
the Giver behind your gifts, and to entrust myself
wholeheartedly to you in faith.**

Acts 7.51–8.1 • Psalm 31 • John 6.30-35

"What sign are you going to give us then, so that we may see it and believe you?"
John 6.30

Only have faith

Like us, the Jews in this gospel story have preconceived ideas of what the Messiah should be like. They refuse to believe in Jesus unless he meets their expectations. They demand that Jesus prove himself to their liking. Jesus, on the other hand, asks us to surrender to him in faith first, and then we will experience that he is the true bread from heaven, prefigured in the manna. He will give us, not a sign or a gift, but his very self.

Where do we go from here?

Do I need signs and wonders to believe that the Holy Spirit is within me? Am I able to discern God's presence in the everyday events of my life? The Church, the sacraments, the Eucharist and the Scriptures are the spiritual mainstays of our life. We find healing through the sacrament of reconciliation and the deepening of our life in God through the Eucharist, and we can discern God's will for us in meditation of the Scriptures. These are the signs of God's presence for us.

Father, by Mary's consent and the power of the Holy Spirit, your Word came to dwell among us. Open my heart to receive Jesus in the same spirit of faith as Mary did.

Wednesday | MAY 7

Acts 8.1-8 • Psalm 66 • John 6.35-40

"**A**nyone who comes to me I will never drive away …."
John 6.37

A faithful promise

What consoling and life-giving words! If we simply come in faith, we need have no fear of rejection. The Father has created us in love and entrusted us to the care of the Son, who offered his life to ensure that we will always find a welcome in God's heart. His arms outstretched on the cross are a constant reminder of his willingness to embrace sinners. For us and for all people, Jesus endured the cross, and looking upon us, he speaks these gracious words: "Father, forgive them; for they do not know what they are doing" (Luke 23:34). Nothing can separate us from the love of God made visible in Jesus.

Where do we go from here?

There is nothing we can do that will separate us from God. God will never reject us and we have to imitate God by never rejecting him. When you sin, repent and receive the healing of the sacrament. To prepare for the sacrament of reconciliation, go beyond the list of sins you have committed as you examine your conscience. Why are you falling into these sins? What are the deeper roots of your sin? In the sacrament, ask for the grace to understand what needs to be healed in your deepest spirit. Over the years, I have found the sacrament can be the source of very deep healing.

Father, there are days when I feel weighed down by my sin and find it difficult to trust in your love. At these times, let your word light up my way.

Acts 8.26-40 • Psalm 66 • John 6.44-51

" The bread that I will give for the life of the world is my flesh."
John 6.51

To be your bread, Lord, to be a sign of your love

Jesus, the Word Incarnate, is the true bread from heaven, the food of eternal life for which we all hunger, whether we realize it or not. His death on the cross opens heaven to us and makes possible the gift of faith. Having received this faith, we in turn are called to be bread for the life of the world. Our union with Jesus sends us out to tend to the hidden hunger in the human heart, to offer nourishment. We are entrusted with God's word for others. "And this is eternal life, that they may know you, the only true God and Jesus Christ whom you have sent" (John 17.3). Let us lose no opportunity to encourage others to recognize Jesus as the One who satisfies all their desires.

Where do we go from here?

In union with Jesus we, too, are called to be bread for others. Like Jesus did, we are to turn over our life to our brothers and sisters in service and in prayer. Those who are impossible to reach by our words, God can reach through our prayers. You can unite your prayers with those of others and they rise before the throne of God with powerful effect. How can you be bread today for a brother or sister?

What else have I in heaven but you? Apart from you I want nothing on earth. To be near God is my happiness. (Psalm 72)

Acts 9.1-20 • Psalm 117 • John 6.52-59

"Those who eat my flesh and drink my blood have eternal life…."
John 6.54

Are you hungry?

This passage treats the Eucharist directly. Jesus tells us unambiguously that his flesh is real food. What Jesus says is that to partake of his flesh is to share in his life here and now. The one who eats his flesh has eternal life.

We eat ordinary bread to feed the body. It must be consumed if it is to become part of us, and to keep us alive. Just so, for us to have eternal life we must eat eternal bread. We must take Jesus' life, the living bread, into our selves. His flesh, given for the life of the world, becomes ours. We become one flesh with him through participation. "It is no longer I who live, but it is Christ who lives in me" (Galatians 2.20).

Where do we go from here?

Meditate on the words of Galatians 2.20. Can you say, "It is no longer I who live," but Jesus? That is our lifetime project to allow Jesus to live in us. What can you do today to make that more of a reality in your life? We grow step by step into holiness. We do need to take the steps, first walking and then running in the way of holiness. It is for everyone.

Lord Jesus, you nourish me with your body and blood that I may become your body. In the strength of this food, may I live always by your life, and rise in glory on the last day.

Acts 9.31-42 • Psalm 116 • John 6.53, 60-69

"This teaching is difficult; who can accept it?"
John 6.60

....

You've got to be kidding!

We can sympathize with the crowd's reaction to Jesus' declaration that they must eat his flesh. Without faith, it is impossible to accept such an outrageous statement. But Jesus is adamant. In spite of their incredulity, he will do nothing to make his words more acceptable. They must either trust him or move on.

St. Thomas Aquinas, in one of his hymns, gives expression to our reason for taking Jesus at his word. "What God's son has told me, take for truth I do. Truth himself speaks truly or there is nothing true." And so we say with the apostles, "Lord, to whom can we go? You have the words of eternal life" (John 6.68). We choose to stay, because Jesus gives the ultimate meaning to our lives.

Where do we go from here?

There have been times in my contemplative vocation when I stayed and others left. But the truth is I wanted to leave, too. During one such time, Jesus' words to the disciples came to mind: "Do you also wish to go away?" My answer was the same as Peter's: "I have come to believe in you." When we come to believe in Jesus and our call to follow him, we cannot leave, even if we would like to. We then are choosing from the inner core of our heart and not the chaos of the present situation.

What return can I make to the Lord for his goodness unto me? I will take the cup of salvation and will call upon his name. (Psalm 15)

Sunday | **MAY 11**

Acts 2.14, 36-41 • Psalm 23 • 1 Peter 2.20-25 • John 10.1-10

" I came that they may have life, and have it abundantly."
John 10.10

Eternal life

Eternal life is a constantly recurring theme in the New Testament. We all seek eternal life. Deep down in the human heart is a craving for fullness of life, a vague longing for something more. We possess eternal life from the moment of our baptism. "Whoever believes has eternal life" (John 6.47). This life we have received is a sharing in the life of the Holy Trinity, Father, Son and Holy Spirit. The Spirit cries out within us, "Abba!" letting us know that we are beloved children of the Father. This is not just a dream, but is even now a foretaste of our life in heaven.

We now possess what the whole world is seeking. All Christians have the germ, the seed of eternal life, and we become more aware of this great gift as we grow in our awareness of God through prayer.

Where do we go from here?

The Holy Spirit prays within, with sighs beyond words. The Holy Spirit understands what we need and will guide us along the way Jesus has chosen for us. That is why Jesus sent his Spirit to us— to teach us gradually. We cannot receive everything at once. The Holy Spirit enlightens us as we are able to understand and receive. The Holy Spirit is the love and mercy of God.

Father, I ask that the eyes of my heart may be opened and that I may know the hope to which you call me: life in heaven for all eternity.

Acts 11.1-18 • Psalm 42 • John 10.11-18

" I know my own and mine know me...."
John 10.14

....

Jesus knows me

What does Jesus mean when he says, "I know my own and my own know me"? Perhaps we can get a glimpse when we read Psalm 139. Indeed, the whole psalm is an eloquent expression of the many ways Jesus knows me through and through:

> O Lord, you have searched me and known me;
> You know when I sit down and when I rise up;
> you discern my thoughts from far away ....
> you knit me together in my mother's womb.

Until we fully comprehend that Jesus thirsts for us, we will never begin to know who he wants to be for us, and—wonder of wonders!—who he wants us to be for him.

Where do we go from here?

Meditate on Psalm 139 in the light of this short passage from John's gospel. In what ways do you feel God has searched your heart? Think about God forming you in your mother's womb. Are there some things you wish God didn't see? Work on them one by one. We are always in a hurry to get things done, to be perfect now. It simply does not work that way. God is eternal and walks with us for the long haul. Isn't that great? Start moving: baby steps are all right. Just keep going, relying on the Lord.

**Loving Father, grant me the grace to know and believe
that you are "madly in love" with me.**

Acts 11.19-26 • Psalm 87 • John 10.22-30

"The Father and I are one."

John 10.30

Communion

It is good to realize that when we come to Jesus in the Eucharist, we have immediate access to the Father. The power within us to lift up our hearts to the Father and say "Abba" comes from the Holy Spirit, who comes to us from Jesus. So in a special way, when we kneel before the Blessed Sacrament, we have direct access to the Father; the heart of our life is to share in the movement of the Son to the Father.

The whole essence of the spiritual life is to become aware that God is present as Abba (Papa). The response to God's presence as Abba is perfect trust and abandonment. Through Eucharistic Adoration, we begin to share in the Heart of Christ toward the Father and toward the world.

Where do we go from here?

Many parishes now have exposition of the Blessed Sacrament. Praying before the Blessed Sacrament is a grace-filled experience. It can be an opportunity for silent listening, learning from the indwelling Spirit. Consider taking some time in eucharistic adoration to deepen your relationship with God.

**Father, gather me into the current of love
that bears your Son toward you.**

Acts 1.15-17, 20-26 • Psalm 113 • John 15.9-17

"Y ou did not choose me but I chose you. And I appointed you
to go and bear fruit, fruit that will last …."
John 15.16

....

Love one another

Today we keep the feast of the apostle St. Matthias, the one chosen to
take the place of Judas, who betrayed Jesus. In stark contrast to that
rejection, overflowing love from the lips of Jesus is found in today's
gospel. "As the Father has loved me, so I have loved you; abide in my
love …. You did not choose me but I chose you."

Each of us is chosen and loved from all eternity. The one thing the
Lord asks of us, begs us, is to return his love by loving our neighbour.
"Love one another as I have loved you. No one has greater love than
this, to lay down one's life for one's friends." That is the condition for
abiding in him, and, conversely, only by abiding in him can we love
one another.

Where do we go from here?

You are God's chosen one. You are God's beloved chosen. In the
gift of the Holy Spirit, you have been equipped to live a life of
service in the Church. Reflect on the mystery of your particular
invitation to live the God-life and to share that life with others.
What are the gifts God has given you? Are you using them well?
How can you use them better for God's glory and the good of
your brothers and sisters?

**Father, may Christ dwell in my heart through faith;
may love be the root of my life.**

Acts 13.13-25 • Psalm 89 • John 13.16-20

will sing of your steadfast love, O Lord, forever.
Psalm 89.1

Good news

To be, for weeks, the glad disciple of a single thought
has left me dazed yet happy as a thrush.
It is the thought that He, giver of the gifts we bring,
He who needs nothing, has need of us,
and that if you or I should cease to be
He would die of sadness. (Paul Murray, O.P.)

Now what can beat good news like that? Indeed, it is true that we are put on this earth for a little space so that we may learn to bear the beams of love (see William Blake). We never cease to be amazed that the Infinite God should seek the love of weak creatures like us! "As the Father has loved me, so I have loved you; abide in my love" (John 15.9).

Where do we go from here?

To abide is a permanent condition. Our call to discipleship means to abide in love, not just loving now and then, in this situation but not another. We follow Jesus by "becoming" love, by being a person of love. It is the way Jesus followed. It is the way we follow through the guidance of the Holy Spirit, who is love. In our time-bound world, we learn to abide in love by loving.

**My God, fill me with your love that I may taste
in my inmost heart how sweet it is to love
and to be enfolded in your love.**

Acts 13.26-33 • Psalm 2 • John 14.1-6

" I go to prepare a place for you ...."
John 14.2

All the way to heaven is heaven, because Jesus is the way

In face of his imminent death, Jesus, instead of focusing on himself, has time for others: time to see their needs, their anxiety, and their pain. And he desires to reassure his friends. The time ahead will be very difficult for them, but their separation will not be final. Jesus has closed the gap between God and us. He is the bridge, the way to the Father. If we remain in him, he will take us to our destination. There will be a time of reunion for all who trust in God, all those for whom Jesus is the way, the truth and the life.

Where do we go from here?

Jesus, the Son of God, came forth from the Father, was born in time, lived among us, took upon himself our sins, all the hardships of life, even death, and has now returned to the Father. He is now the bridge, the way by which we can pass through life on our way to the Father. Like Jesus, we are meant to pass through life doing the works of God and showing the way to others.

**Jesus, you had utter confidence in the Father.
Give me that same trust in you, that I may follow
in your way with a serene heart, knowing that in
all my journeying, you are drawing me closer to the Father.**

Acts 13.44-52 • Psalm 98 • John 14.7-14

"**W**hoever has seen me has seen the Father."
John 14.9

The living image

Jesus' whole purpose in life was to reveal the Father. Now, as he prepares to leave this world, he discovers that even those closest to him have missed the point. "Look, show us the Father, and we will be satisfied," Philip demands. So Jesus makes one last attempt to break through to them. He puts it as simply and clearly as possible: "Whoever has seen me has seen the Father." It is Jesus—merciful, compassionate, forgiving, tender, friend of sinners and outcasts—who shows us the face of God. In him we see our God made visible.

What if someone were to ask you, "Show me Jesus and I will be satisfied"? Could you respond, "To have seen me is to have seen Jesus"? Would they still be interested in knowing Jesus?

Where do we go from here?

Can you be so bold as to say to someone, "To see me is to see Jesus"? When we see Jesus in another person, then we have also seen the Father. How does Jesus look in me? When people see in me patience, kindness, love, willingness to heal others and to bind up their wounds, they see Jesus. And when they see in me someone who abides in love and is always ready to be there for another, then they see Jesus. Live your life by the gospel teaching and Jesus will shine forth from you.

**Lord Jesus, may my life so reflect your love
that I may draw others to you.**

Acts 6.1-7 • Psalm 33 • 1 Peter 2.4-9 • John 14.1-12

C ome to him, a living stone, though rejected by mortals yet chosen and precious in God's sight, and like living stones, let yourselves be built into a spiritual house ....

1 Peter 2.4-5

God's holy people

St. Peter's great love of his Master is portrayed in simple yet profound words in his first letter written in Rome. Only by drawing close to Jesus, he tells us, can we be built into a spiritual temple, "offering spiritual sacrifices which please God through Jesus Christ." By our baptism we are incorporated into Jesus. In, with and through him we are introduced into the family of the Blessed Trinity, Father, Son and Holy Spirit, and thereby become members of God's chosen people. As Christians who are aware of this great dignity that is sheer gift and grace, we cannot but proclaim God's wonders. This is what evangelization is all about. We are truly a "chosen race, a royal priesthood, a holy nation, God's own people" called to proclaim God's mighty deeds.

Where do we go from here?

Through baptism, we exercise a royal priesthood and can offer spiritual sacrifices acceptable to God. At the Eucharist, we are empowered through our royal priesthood to offer Jesus in union with the ministerial priest. When we gather together for liturgy, Jesus is with us in a unique and powerful way: in the Eucharist, in the word of God, in the ministerial priest, and in the assembly. Jesus comes to us to transform us and we offer Jesus back to the Father to transform the world.

Lord, give me a spirit of prayer and praise this day.

Acts 14.5-18 • Psalm 115 • John 14.21-26

"They who have my commandments and keep them are those who love me; and those who love me will be loved by my Father, and I will love them and reveal myself to them." … the Advocate, the Holy Spirit, whom the Father will send in my name, will teach you everything, and remind you of all that I have said to you."
John 14.21, 26

Indwelling love

Jesus asks his disciples to keep his commandments. Their obedience is made possible through their love for him. The keeping of Jesus' commandments with love opens up the life of the disciples to the love of the Father and the full revelation of the Son. They will receive the Father's love by keeping the word given by the Father in union with Jesus. The Father and the Son are to come to the disciples and make their home in them, making them temples of the word to preach to all peoples. Jesus promises the Advocate, the Holy Spirit, to teach them and strengthen the word they have received.

Where do we go from here?

Jesus told his disciples, and we are among those disciples, that there was much more they needed to learn. He knew he was leaving them with a lot to digest, and in his love and mercy he knew they and we could not receive it all at once. Jesus does not leave us without help; he promises to send the Holy Spirit who will teach us everything and remind us of Jesus' teaching as we live day by day and seek to follow Jesus. What more could we ask?

Jesus, help me to keep your word and obey it through love that you may dwell in me. May your light fill each day I live, that I may bring your love to others.

Acts 14.19-28 • Psalm 145 • John 14.27-31

"Peace I leave with you; my peace I give to you. I do not give to you as the world gives. Do not let your hearts be troubled, and do not let them be afraid."

John 14.27

The gift of peace

The peace that Jesus is leaving to his disciples is a promised peace, a peace not of this world. It is a peace that will help the disciples not to be troubled and afraid. Jesus even asks them to rejoice that he is going to the Father. Jesus must have briefly experienced the joy of being united with his heavenly Father before the oncoming darkness of the agony, torture and crucifixion. How Jesus longed that the ruler of this world would not overcome his disciples.

All is fulfilled in the loving obedience of Jesus to the Father. The power of this world is overcome by the peace of eternity, the eternal rule of God and the peace within each of us.

Where do we go from here?

The peace Jesus gives is a peace that resides in our deepest heart. This peace is there when we are assailed by the often chaotic circumstances of life. God's peace keeps us stable in a world of flux. Pray for this peace and ask the Holy Spirit to teach you how to enter into the peace of your heart's core and make your home there. It is from within that we can face all life's difficulty while we are sustained in God's peace.

**Jesus, create in me your peace, that I may embrace
in prayer those who suffer from loss of faith
and peace of mind.**

Acts 15.1-6 • Psalm 122 • John 15.1-8

" I am the vine, you are the branches."
John 15.5

Luscious grapes

I am a branch of Jesus the vine. Only by remaining firmly attached to
the vine can I be life-giving or remain alive. Cut off, or even partially
cut off, the sap of the vine ceases to flow through me and I begin
to die. Because of my separation, the vine cannot be seen in its full
beauty. Each branch is called to bear fruit, fruit that tempts people to
taste its sweetness and to give praise to the Vine and the Vinedresser.
How sad if even one person were to go away and seek elsewhere because my branch produced sour grapes or none at all.

Where do we go from here?

Jesus calls us to bear good fruit that will nourish others. Like the
branch on the vine, we receive our nourishment and life from the
source. United with Jesus, we will have whatever we need to grow
to spiritual maturity. Regular prayer keeps us in union with Jesus. If
we are earnest about our life in God, there are ways to slip times
of prayer into even the busiest days.

**Lord Jesus, I want to bear plentiful fruit for your honour
and glory. Open my eyes to the ways I inhibit the flow
of your life through me.**

Acts 15.7-21 • Psalm 96 • John 15.9-11

"**A**s the Father has loved me, so I have loved you …."
John 15.9

A recipe for joy

Imagine if someone were to come up to you and say, "I can tell you something that will fill you with overflowing joy." Wouldn't you at least listen? Yes? Then here it is. In today's gospel, Jesus tells us something utterly mind-boggling. If you take the time to rest in his Word, by the end of your prayer time, you will be bubbling over with joy, a joy so full that you will be bursting to tell others how to come by it. Try it! Jesus loves you with the very same love with which his Father loves him. Stop a while and bask in that love.

Where do we go from here?

Sit in church before the Blessed Sacrament. Sit with your hands in your lap, palms up, ready to receive. Certain postures are conducive to silencing us and bringing us into the prayer of the heart. Think of a special moment in your life when you felt at peace, so loved. Let that memory surround you. Then receive that love as God's love and let it grow until it is all around you. Stay silent, not asking anything, just being in the presence of God's immense love for you.

Jesus, draw me into your embrace, that I might experience something of the height and depth of God's love for me.

Acts 15.22-31 • Psalm 57 • John 15.12-17

" I have called you friends ...."
John 15.15

....

What makes a friend?

Think about your best friend. What makes this relationship special? What about your friendship with Jesus? How do these compare? In today's gospel, Jesus calls us his friends, "because I have made known to you everything I have heard from my Father." He shares with us what is most precious to him, the wisdom his Father has imparted to him, all that has gone into making him who he is—the image of his Father. He longs for us to listen to him, and to share with us the secret of his life with his Father. Time with Jesus in quiet prayer will deepen our friendship with him and change us. As we rest in Jesus, his love will begin to flow through us and we will be able to fulfill his command to love one another.

Where do we go from here?

In the beginning of a new friendship, getting to know one another is so important. As friendship develops, trust and understanding are built up, words become less necessary, and it is enough just to be with a friend in a communion of love and understanding. Friendship with God follows a similar pattern. We come to know God through studying our faith, praying the Scriptures, taking time for prayer. Gradually, our friendship with God becomes an intimate communion in love—we abide in God.

Jesus, may your word take flesh in my life, your truth shine forth in my actions, and your love burn brightly within me.

Acts 16.1-10 • Psalm 100 • John 15.18-21

" f they persecuted me, they will persecute you ...."
John 15.20

Unrequited love

God loved the world so much that he sent his only Son, and yet we hear in today's reading that the world hated Jesus and will hate those who are privileged to be his disciples. The words of Jesus, which we try to incarnate in our lives, may provoke hostility. Jesus says people act in this way because "they know nothing of him who sent me." But let us not lose heart. Jesus has won the victory and his grace is with us always. May we continue to proclaim the Good News in spite of adversity, but most of all, may we show his love to all by our forgiveness and compassion.

Where do we go from here?

Love and forgiveness are essential qualities for followers of Jesus. Forgiveness is the hallmark of Christianity. Think of the example of John Paul II, who forgave his attempted murderer. Empty your mind and heart of past injuries and resentments. Instead, allow God to fill the empty space of your heart with thoughts of forgiveness and love. You are the one who will benefit most from being a forgiving and loving person.

**Jesus, in these times, too, people are hostile toward you.
As I try to be true to you in the face of opposition,
may my words always be firmly grounded in your teaching,
and may my actions reflect your forgiving love.**

Acts 8.5-8, 14-17 • Psalm 66 • 1 Peter 3.15-18 • John 14.15-21

Blessed be God,
because he has not rejected my prayer
or removed his steadfast love from me.

Psalm 66.20

God's steadfast love for us

As frail, insecure, wounded creatures, we are in constant need of the reassurance of God's love for us and his attentiveness to our requests in prayer. In the Old and New Testaments, God gives us this assurance of his love, as we can see from the following example: "I have loved you with an everlasting love; therefore I have continued my faithfulness to you" (Jeremiah 31.3). We can be secure in the knowledge of God's love for us and trust that our prayers are heard and answered. "Very truly, I tell you, if you ask anything of the Father in my name, he will give it to you. Ask and you will receive" (John 16.23, 24). With such assurances we are encouraged and enabled to continue our earthly journey as pilgrims.

Where do we go from here?

Reflect on John 14.15-21. Pray over the text. Jesus promises us that if we follow his commands, he will send us the Holy Spirit to be with us forever. If we follow Jesus, we will be loved by the Father and Jesus will reveal himself to us. In following Jesus and through the power of the Holy Spirit, we are brought into life in God—eternity begun in this life and received in all its fullness in the next. Make regular reading of the Bible part of your life.

**Lord, grant me a spirit of praise and thanksgiving,
and may the words of the psalms find a home
in my heart and on my lips.**

Acts 16.11-15 • Psalm 149 • John 15.26–16.4

T he Lord opened her heart to listen eagerly to what was said by Paul.
Acts 16.14

A listening heart

The Lord always takes the initiative in our lives. In the case of Lydia, the Lord opened her heart to listen eagerly. It's interesting that the text does not say that her ears were opened, as one might expect. Paul and Barnabas preached to Lydia the word of God that led her to faith and baptism. As a direct consequence of this, she put herself at the service of the Church, insisting that Paul and Barnabas stay with her and her family, as she offered them generous hospitality.

Our heart is our deepest centre, where the Blessed Trinity dwells, where we are one with God. "To speak to the heart is to satisfy the heart, which is dissatisfied with anything less than God," says St. John of the Cross (Stanza 35, "The Spiritual Canticle").

Where do we go from here?

We can hear God only when our hearts are open and we are eagerly waiting to hear God's voice. We listen with our heart when we learn to live from our inner heart core. Take time for silent prayer. Close your eyes and look deep into your centre. Imagine looking into a deep well—the living water of God's life is at the bottom.

**Open my heart, Lord, to eagerly receive, live,
be converted and be transformed by the word
that you will speak to me today.**

Acts 16.22-34 • Psalm 138 • John 16.5-11

Then he brought them outside and said, "Sirs, what must I do to be saved?" They answered, "Believe on the Lord Jesus, and you will be saved, you and your household."

Acts 16.30-31

The gift of faith

Faith is one of the most precious of God's gifts to us at baptism. As Jesus says in John 6.29, "This is the work of God, that you believe in him whom he has sent." In his commentary on this line, Hans Urs Von Balthasar says, "God's work is that man believes rather than achieves." Belief in Jesus Christ, then, is the way to arrive definitively at salvation.

Where do we go from here?

We are a society of achievers. Our life in God is not something we can achieve; rather, it is a gift we receive. By working hard, we cannot become holy. God gifts us with the grace we need to become holy—all is God's gift. Our work is to say yes, to keep our heart open to receive. God does not force grace upon us, but stands at the door and knocks.

Dear Lord, with the father who pleaded with Jesus to heal his son, I pray, "I believe; help my unbelief!"

Acts 17.15, 22–18.1 • Psalm 148 • John 16.12-15

"Though indeed he is not far from each one of us. For 'In him we live and move and have our being …'."
Acts 17.27-28

The soul's centre is God

Saint John of the Cross says that the soul's centre is God ("Living Flame of Love," Stanza 1; 12). He teaches us that love is the inclination, strength and power for the soul in making its way to God, for love unites it with God. The more love we have, the more deeply we enter into God, and centre ourselves in God. In the words of Saint Augustine, "God is higher than my highest and more inward that my innermost self." God is not far from any of us; in God we truly live and move and have our being.

Where do we go from here?

God created us, we come forth from God and God continues to sustain us in existence at every moment. God knows you and cannot forget you for a moment or you would cease to exist. Whether we realize it or not, we live and move and have our being in God. Stop to thank God for the gift of daily breath, for your body, your accomplishments. All that you are is God's gift.

Lord, teach me to allow the Blessed Trinity to penetrate and possess my whole being so completely that my life may radiate God's light and love to others.

Acts 18.1-8 • Psalm 98 • John 16.16-20

" Very truly, I tell you, you will weep and mourn, but the world will rejoice; you will have pain, but your pain will turn into joy."
John 16.20

....

They shall be comforted

From our own experiences, we know that life has its share of sorrows and joys. Job says, "The Lord gave, and the Lord has taken away; blessed be the name of the Lord. … Shall we receive the good at the hand of God, and not receive the bad?" (Job 1.21; 2.10). In this Easter season, we have the example of the Lord himself. His sorrowful Passion led to his glorious resurrection and ascension. The apostles mourning the death of our Lord were filled with joy on seeing him after his resurrection. If we put our trust in the Lord, especially during times of trial, he will come to our assistance with his peace and joy.

Where do we go from here?

God wills for us only what is good, not evil. We live in a broken world and we sin against each other; this is the source of the bad things we must endure. God does not abandon us but sustains us through life's chaos. We can lean on God's strength and love when our own is weak. This is the promise of Jesus' resurrection.

**Lord, grant me the grace to always put my trust
in you amid all the joys and sorrows of life,
knowing that you alone are my sure comfort.**

Acts 18.9-18 • Psalm 47 • John 16.20-23

One night the Lord said to Paul in a vision, "Do not be afraid, but speak and do not be silent; for I am with you, and no one will lay a hand on you to harm you, for there are many in this city who are my people."   *Acts 18.9-10*

God's presence and protection

God is always present to us, but sadly, we are not always aware of God's presence, nor are we always present to God. We were born into God at baptism, and this divine life grows in us and is nourished by the sacraments and prayer. The realization of this indwelling presence of the Blessed Trinity in our souls should be a great source of love, joy and peace for us, dispelling all our fears and anxieties.

The words of the fourteenth-century English mystic Julian of Norwich, in the *Revelations of Divine Love,* reinforce this conviction: "… [when] our Lord showed that I would sin, [and] I here stands for all, I began to be rather fearful. And our Lord answered 'I am keeping you very securely.' The word was said with more love and assurance and a sense of spiritual protection than I know how to tell" (Number 37).

Where do we go from here?

When troubles and darkness come, turn to God first. Commend yourself to God's protection and love, relying on the comfort of the Holy Spirit. God is with you and you need not fear; just hold on to hope and trust as you traverse the trials and sorrows that inevitably come.

Blessed Trinity, grant me the grace to become more and more aware of your dwelling within me, and through this realization, to grow in greater love and service of you and your people.

Zephaniah 3.14-18 *or* Romans 12.9-16 • Isaiah 12 • Luke 1.39-56

" **A**nd blessed is she who believed that there would be a fulfillment of what was spoken to her by the Lord."
Luke 1.45

Mary – our model in faith, hope and love

On this wonderful feast day of the Visitation of our Lady to her cousin Elizabeth, one of the joyful mysteries of the Rosary, we see how Mary, who has just conceived Jesus in her womb through faith, hurries out of charity to be of assistance to her elderly cousin, bringing Jesus to her. In like manner, Mary brings Jesus to us in all our own particular needs, and she brings to Jesus ourselves, our loved ones and those for whom we intercede. Elizabeth, through the power of the Holy Spirit, affirms Mary in her faith, hope and love, and both joyfully proclaim the praises of God, expressed in the beautiful canticle of the "Magnificat."

Where do we go from here?

Mary is our model. Her faith shows us what ours needs to be. Mary believed in the Lord's promise that what God said would be accomplished. The Scripture is filled with God's promise of faithfulness—these promises are ours. Let us, with Mary, believe that what God has promised he will do. Make a list of God's promises found in the Scripture.

**Dear Lord, help me to imitate Mary in her faith,
hope and love so that my whole life becomes
a Magnificat to the praise and glory of God.**

Acts 1.1-11 • Psalm 47 • Ephesians 1.17-23 • Matthew 28.16-20

"Go therefore and make disciples of all nations, baptizing them in the name of the Father and of the Son and of the Holy Spirit, and teaching them to obey everything that I have commanded you. And remember, I am with you always, to the end of the age."
Matthew 28.19-20

Jesus has gone before us

The beautiful prayer in Ephesians asks "that the eyes of [our] heart [may be] enlightened" to know "the immeasurable greatness of his power for us who believe" (Ephesians 1.18-19). At his Ascension, Jesus promises the eleven that he will always be with them and all his followers until the end of time. By baptism we are sealed with the power of the Holy Spirit and the indwelling presence of God: Father, Son and Holy Spirit. By grace we receive the power of God's life and the commission to share God's life, power and love with our brothers and sisters. What a tremendous inheritance is ours! To understand with the eyes of the heart is to see life from God's perspective and to live from our inner centre. Jesus has gone before us to open the way to Life.

Where do we go from here?

Do you believe in the greatness of God's power in you? Carry a short prayer in your heart during the day: "Lord, I do believe in the greatness of your power within; heal my unbelief." We need to tap into the power and greatness of the Holy Spirit dwelling in our heart. Our weakness is not greater than God's power at work in us. Let us seek in every way to live in God.

**Jesus, help me to lay hold of the inheritance
you have given me and to walk in the power of the Spirit.**

Acts 19.1-8 • Psalm 68 • John 16.29-33

His disciples said, "Yes, now you are speaking plainly, not in any figure of speech! Now we know that you know all things, and do not need to have anyone question you; by this we believe that you came from God." Jesus answered them, "Do you now believe? The hour is coming, indeed it has come, when you will be scattered, each one to his home, and you will leave me alone. Yet I am not alone because the Father is with me." *John 16.29-32*

Lord, give me understanding

The disciples are all bluster! They cry, "Yes, now we understand. It is all clear and easy." Jesus asks, "Do you really believe now?" He knows that they are not prepared for what is to come. They still think in terms of victory and success, and in a way, they are right. But God's victory is not what they expect. They will desert Jesus. Yet Jesus is not alone, because the Father is with him.

Do we not often pray and then wonder why God does not answer? Aren't we like the disciples? God does answer, but the answer is not what we expected, and often not what *we* want. The answer does not always look like victory or blessing. Jesus' death and resurrection show that, if we trust God, victory is ours unfailingly.

Where do we go from here?

What are your spiritual expectations? How do you think God should or will work in you? Are you open to the unexpected? Our expectations are always limited in comparison to God's desire to give. Begin your day without expectations and be willing to be surprised by God.

God, give me faith and wisdom to trust in your presence and your unfailing blessing in my life.

Acts 20.17-27 • Psalm 68 • John 17.1-11

"**A**nd this is eternal life, that they may know you, the only true God, and Jesus Christ whom you have sent."
John 17.3

To be Jesus for others

Jesus is the human face of God. All that he did and said revealed God's nature in human terms. Eternal life begins now through faith in Jesus and his revelation of our God: Father, Son and Holy Spirit. The kingdom of God is already present in a hidden manner in our deepest hearts. We make the kingdom present to others by doing as Jesus did: loving as God loves, not only those who love us, but also those who are far from God.

There is no greater example of love than Jesus, who laid down his life for sinners. Throughout history, Christians have laid down their lives rather than deny their faith. St. Charles Lwanga and his companions, whose feast we celebrate today, found the strength to die because of their faith in Jesus. They died forgiving their persecutors.

Where do we go from here?

The kind of knowing Jesus is talking about is the knowledge of the heart. We can know about God through study or the words of others, but to truly know God is to experience God in our lives. Eternal life is entering into the life of God. We begin now. Do you know God? Is God alive and active in your life?

Jesus, pour the love of your Holy Spirit into my heart that I may love as you did.

Acts 20.28-38 • Psalm 68 • John 17.11-19

"Sanctify them in the truth; your word is truth. As you have sent me into the world, so I have sent them into the world. And for their sakes I sanctify myself, so that they also may be sanctified in truth."

John 17.17-19

Sanctify them

The saying goes, "If you want to make God laugh, tell him your plans." As much as we would like to think that we are the captains of our own ships, the truth is that we are not finally in control. God's plan for us is echoed in Jesus' prayer—that we be made holy. Holiness is the humble recognition that we are dust and to dust we shall return. If God were to stop loving us and willing us to live, we would simply disappear like the flower that blooms in the morning and withers in the evening.

We have committed ourselves to the Lord, to trust in him for all that we need. And because he loves us, he will lead us on the right path. Sanctity is surrendering ourselves to the Lord and believing that he will always give us the grace to face whatever challenges we encounter in our lives.

Where do we go from here?

Jesus, the Holy One of God, walked the path of God's will, the way of truth, so that we would never have to walk alone. He sanctified himself so we could be sanctified. God has given himself totally to us in Jesus. In Jesus, let us totally give ourselves back to God. We have all the grace we need to do so.

Jesus, help me to follow you and to seek to walk in your ways.

Acts 22.30; 23.6-11 • Psalm 16 • John 17.20-26

Y ou show me the path of life.
In your presence there is fullness of joy;
in your right hand are pleasures forevermore.

Psalm 16.11

To know the way

The psalmist sings of the joyous path to life when we follow God in all our ways and live in God's presence. The path to eternal life is love, and our love for one another will be a visible manifestation of God. Jesus came that we might be one, as he is one with his Father in the love of the Holy Spirit. Walking in the Holy Spirit, who is the Spirit of Jesus, we find even now the source of joy and all God's good gifts, even in the midst of suffering. Like he said to St. Paul, the Lord encourages us and supports us as we keep up our courage, that we may bear witness to him in all we do. The path of life is truly filled with God's presence,

Where do we go from here?

Pray with Psalm 16. The psalms are our prayer. This psalm is a prayer for protection and is about being in God's presence, finding life and fulfillment in God. How does this psalm reflect your experience of God? What parts of the psalmist's prayer would you like to deepen in your life? Becoming familiar with the psalms is spiritually nourishing. Spend some time with them.

**God, teach me your ways.
Let your praise be ever on my lips.**

Acts 24.27; 25.13-21 • Psalm 103 • John 21.15-19

"Very truly, I tell you, when you were younger, you used to fasten your own belt and to go wherever you wished. But when you grow old, you will stretch out your hands, and someone else will fasten a belt around you and take you where you do not wish to go." (He said this to indicate the kind of death by which he would glorify God.) After this he said to [Peter], "Follow me."

John 21.18-19

Accepting help

Sometimes older folks can't do simple things with the ease they had when they were younger; they must accept the help of others. The gospel writer tells us that Jesus used this illustration to speak of Peter's death. Jesus laid it on the line, and then told Peter to follow him.

Jesus also asks us to follow him and to take on the challenges that life will bring. No matter what our age, we can never do this without the support of others. We depend on each other. Let us accept the help of our brothers and sisters, even when we think we can do it ourselves. The truth is, our self-sufficiency is an illusion.

Where do we go from here?

Often we are not comfortable letting others help us, for many reasons. Our independent mindset tells us that needing help is associated with weakness, and often it is easier and quicker to do something ourselves. The truth is we are all weak and no one is totally self-sufficient. God created us to be interdependent. Accept every offer of help today. The help is offered in love and to accept is a gift of loving gratitude to the other.

Dear God, let me be humble enough to allow others to serve me, so that I in turn may serve in love.

Acts 28.16-20, 30-31 • Psalm 11 • John 21.20-25

"**G**o to this people and say,
You will indeed listen, but never understand,
and you will indeed look, but never perceive."
Acts 28.26

Hard of hearing?

I would not like to be the messenger bearing these words, or to be the person who needed them. What do they mean? How do these words challenge us? The passage teaches us that we must learn how to listen to God's word. God will never deny anyone understanding. If we don't "get it," the problem rests in us. We do not understand or perceive when we close our hearts. If we will not listen, then God, who has given us free will, does not force us.

For someone who thirsts to understand and who waits upon God with a willingness to hear God speak, understanding will never be denied. Let us pray for God's Holy Spirit to open our hearts and minds to receive the healing God so desires to give us.

Where do we go from here?

We need to be sensitive to the things of the Spirit: attentive and alert to open our spiritual ears to hear God, to find God in all life's events. As with all the virtues, we acquire them through practice. We learn to hear the Holy Spirit by listening. Pray to hear and understand the whisper of the Holy Spirit in your heart.

**Lord, give me ears to hear and a willing and humble heart
to receive your word and to act on it.**

Acts 2.1-11 • Psalm 104 • I Corinthians 12.3-7, 12-13
• John 20.19-23

N o one can say "Jesus is Lord" except by the Holy Spirit.
I Corinthians 12.3

God dwells in us

God dwells in every Christian soul. God is closer to you than you are to yourself. Saint Thomas Aquinas tells us that it is by faith, hope and charity that God dwells in us. This gift of faith, to say and believe that "Jesus is Lord," is the Gift beyond all other gifts—God himself. When we receive the Holy Spirit in baptism, or are reunited with God through the sacrament of Reconciliation, we share in a real sense in the divine nature of God. God comes to live in us, in the entirety of our being, in the deepest part of ourselves. The gift to profess Jesus as Lord is not mere knowledge; it is to be in the most intimate relationship of our life.

Where do we go from here?

In our monastic communities, we live St. Paul's teaching on the variety of gifts at the service of the common good. Each sister is assigned the work she is to do in the community for the common good. She carries out her task using the gifts she has received from God, both natural and supernatural. We are only doing what all Christians are called to do, as St. Paul makes quite clear. To live in this way is countercultural in our competitive society. We are interrelated and called by Jesus to serve one another for the up-building of the community.

Holy Spirit, help me to become more aware of your presence within me. May I never give you cause to depart from my soul.

1 Kings 17.1-6 • Psalm 121 • Matthew 5.1-12

"**B**lessed are the poor in spirit ... Blessed are those who mourn ... Blessed are the meek ... Blessed are those who hunger and thirst for righteousness ... Blessed are the merciful ...Blessed are the pure in heart ... Blessed are the peacemakers ...Blessed are those who are persecuted for righteousness' sake ...."

Matthew 5.3-10

The desire for holiness

Have you ever had one of those days? You've made a firm resolution to stop yelling at the kids and to be more patient with your co-workers. But then the toys are all over the floor, you snap at a colleague, and you finally fall into bed at night, feeling like a failure. Jesus has some good news for you: "Blessed are those who hunger ... for righteousness, for they will be filled."

At the end of the day, it is not about what we have accomplished, but where our heart lies. Jesus takes our desire for holiness and says, "You will be filled!" He is not concerned by how much we have "failed," but by how much we desire to grow closer to him. Holiness is really about the desires of our hearts and the gift of self. Holiness is God's work in us; we just need to let God do it!

Where do we go from here?

Reflect prayerfully on the Beatitudes. Take one of the Beatitudes each day—ponder it and let it enter into your heart. What does this particular Beatitude mean to you? How can you make it a part of you? How would it change your life? Try it out!

**Dear Jesus, you know how much I want to grow in holiness.
Help me to keep this hunger for you strong,
even when I think I've failed or lost my way.**

1 Kings 17.7-16 • Psalm 4 • Matthew 5.13-1

S he went and did as Elijah said, so that she as well as he and her household ate for many days. The jar of meal was not emptied, neither did the jug of oil fail .... *1 Kings 17.15-16*

Becoming rich by giving all

The widow of Zarephath had very little, not even enough to survive. Yet when she gave all that she had, a miraculous event occurred—she suddenly had more than enough! God works like that in our lives, too. We may feel poorly equipped for what God asks of us, be it charitable works, praying for those in need, or spreading Jesus' love among those we see every day. But when we give all we have, God intervenes and gives us what we need to serve him. What would have happened if the poor widow had kept her sparse food for herself and her child? God would have provided for Elijah in another way. But without her trusting faith, could the miracle have happened for the widow? By keeping to ourselves the little we call our own, we impoverish ourselves, and little by little we starve ourselves of the love we need to live in God and share with others.

Where do we go from here?

We are made rich by becoming poor, a real and true paradox of the spiritual life. Everything we have is a gift from God. God has given to us freely and abundantly. When we give to others from God's generous giving to us, God looks at our poverty and pours out his love and gifts upon us even more lavishly. God cannot be outdone in generosity. Why don't you test the theory?

O God, help me to give generously of myself to you and the people I encounter this day. I trust you to never let my love for others run dry.

Acts 11.21-26; 13.1-3 • Psalm 98 • Matthew 10.7-13

The Holy Spirit said, "Set apart for me Barnabas and Saul for the work to which I have called them." Then after fasting and praying they laid their hands on them and sent them off.
Acts 13.2-3

Set apart for God

Like Barnabas (whose feast we celebrate today) and Saul, you have been chosen to be set apart. At your baptism, God set you apart and consecrated you for himself. At your confirmation, you enlisted in God's army, and were given the gifts of the Holy Spirit to equip you for battle. The war has been won; we know that Satan has lost and God has won the victory. Yet the battle continues as each soul must choose to whom he or she will give allegiance, and then live out that allegiance.

Barnabas and Saul were called to a specific mission by the Holy Spirit, and you are, too. You must arm yourself with prayer and fasting, that you might not be caught off guard in the fight. Above all, you must keep a quiet heart so that you can hear your commanding officer, the Holy Spirit, directing you.

Where do we go from here?

We tend to think it is the other person who has been called and set apart. No, it is you who God has chosen and set apart for a special work in the Church for the good of all. Pray to the Holy Spirit to guide you into what God wishes you to do. Have no doubt—you have been called and appointed by God.

Holy Spirit, direct me today and always as I strive to give my whole allegiance to God. Let me not be confounded by the enemy, but make me ever more faithful to your guidance.

1 Kings 18.41-46 • Psalm 65 • Matthew 5.20-26

"**F**or I tell you, unless your righteousness exceeds that of the scribes and Pharisees, you will never enter the kingdom of heaven."
Matthew 5.20

Righteousness of the heart

What a shock it must have been to Jesus' listeners to hear this proclamation! The scribes and Pharisees were exceedingly particular in obeying every least command of the law. They were scrupulously "correct." What righteousness could surpass that? The Pharisees obeyed the letter of the law, but their hearts were cold and self-reliant. They missed the whole point of all their "right" actions—love.

Jesus calls us to a righteousness of the heart based on love. This is why Jesus warns not only against murder, but also against holding anger in our hearts. What good is it to abstain from murder but to cherish murderous thoughts in our heart? The righteousness to which God calls us begins in our heart and overflows to our actions.

Where do we go from here?

All good desires and actions begin in our heart. Examine what your heart priorities are; if they are good, then your deeds will be good. It is so important to be in touch with our heart, what we put first in our life. We need to live our life from our heart and make our heart a place where God is welcome and the Holy Spirit can lead us.

O Lord, grant me the grace of a righteous heart.
Purify my intentions so that everything I do today
may be done for love of you.

I Kings 19.9, 11-16 • Psalm 27 • Matthew 5.27-32

Now there was a great wind, so strong that it was splitting mountains and breaking rocks in pieces before the Lord, but the Lord was not in the wind; and after the wind an earthquake, but the Lord was not in the earthquake; and after the earthquake a fire, but the Lord was not in the fire; and after the fire a sound of sheer silence.   *I Kings 19.11-12*

Listening in silence

Elijah found the Lord, not in the great wind or fire, but in the sound of silence. When is the last time you heard the sound of sheer silence? God's voice resonates in the silence. Real silence is not merely a lack of noise, but a quietness of heart. It is a heart that is dwelling in itself with quiet expectation, looking and listening for the Beloved's voice.

In today's world, silence and stillness are hard to find. In a doctor's waiting room, for example, if the television or radio (or both!) are not turned on, then the patients are reading magazines or playing with their electronic devices. No one sits still in silence. Yet silence is not only for cloistered nuns and monks. It is an integral part of a healthy spiritual life for everyone.

Where do we go from here?

Listen to see if you can hear the sound of sheer silence. It is God. The Trinity—Father, Son and Holy Spirit—dwells in our hearts. If we are still, we can encounter the God of our heart. We create the atmosphere of silence and God makes known his presence.

O Lord, grant me a quiet heart to hear you speaking in the depths of my soul. Help me to make the sound of silence a part of my every day.

1 Kings 19.16, 19-21 • Psalm 16 • Matthew 5.33-37

"I say to you, Do not swear at all, either by heaven, for it is the throne of God, or by the earth, for it is his footstool, or by Jerusalem, for it is the city of the great King. And do not swear by your head, for you cannot make one hair white or black. Let your word be 'Yes, Yes' or 'No, No ….'"   *Matthew 5.34-37*

Living truth

In today's reading from the Sermon on the Mount, Jesus continues to call us to a deeper following of the Law in the way we speak. Swearing distinguishes between a trustworthy statement of veracity and a falsehood. To swear is to put our stamp of validity on our statements. Christians should have no need for this, because our Christianity puts a stamp of validity on all that we say. We should, of course, be truthful at all times, and thus have no need to swear. Yet our truthfulness must go deeper than words. Jesus calls us not only to speak truthfully at all times, but, more importantly, to live truthfully. Our authentic living is the stamp of veracity for everything we say. True words flow from a true heart.

Where do we go from here?

When Jesus says let your word be "Yes, Yes" or "No, No," he is telling us that truthfulness in our words is proved by the truthfulness of our deeds. Christians are called to live the truth in love, to be whole and integrated in our person. Is what you profess with your tongue true to the reality of what is in your heart? Examine your thoughts and the movement of your heart. Do you need to change something? Ask the Holy Spirit to guide and sustain you.

**O Lord, set a guard over my mouth,
so I may always speak truthfully.**

Sunday | JUNE 15 | Trinity Sunday

Exodus 34.4-6, 8-9 • Daniel 3 • 2 Corinthians 13.11-13 • John 3.16-18

T he Lord descended in the cloud and stood with [Moses] there, and proclaimed the name, "The Lord." ... And Moses quickly bowed his head toward the earth, and worshipped.

Exodus 34.5, 8

The call to worship

Today we celebrate the mystery of the Blessed Trinity. In Exodus, God reveals himself to Moses as a merciful and faithful God, "slow to anger, and abounding in steadfast love." With the new law of grace, God is further revealed to us as a Trinity of Persons in the unity of one divine nature. At God's self-revelation to Moses, Moses quickly humbles himself before God and adores God. Moses gives us our cue regarding the proper response to God's revelation of God's interior life as a Trinity. Rather than puzzling over this immense mystery as if it is a riddle to be solved or a curious enigma to be deciphered, God invites us to humble ourselves and to worship. Our gaze should be one of awe and reverential wonder as we contemplate the ineffable mystery of the Trinity.

Where do we go from here?

Open your heart to experience a relationship with each Person of the Trinity. God our Father: picture yourself held in the arms of a loving father; rest in the image and wait upon God. The Son: picture the human face of God; Jesus, the Wisdom of God—open your heart to receive the wisdom of the Son. The Holy Spirit: the shared Love of the Father and the Son. Open your heart for an encounter with Love. Let your heart be filled with love.

O Adored Trinity! May you be praised and worshipped at all times and by all peoples and nations!

I Kings 21.1-16 • Psalm 5 • Matthew 5.38-42

"Y ou have heard that it was said, 'An eye for an eye and a tooth for a tooth.' But I say to you, Do not resist an evildoer. But if anyone strikes you on the right cheek, turn the other also; and if anyone wants to sue you and take your coat, give your cloak as well …."
Matthew 5.38-41

Generous love

When we are injured through the actions or negligence of another, a sense of righteous anger wells up in our hearts. We feel the imbalance of justice, and we want to restore this balance, often by retaliating. Yet, here is Jesus telling us not only to accept the injustice and injury but to offer the other cheek as well! Jesus invites us to love as he loves, with a heart wide open. His heart is wide open, waiting to embrace us in love. He refuses to let any amount of injustice or injury close his heart to us. He never seeks to protect himself; he thinks only of us.

To love as Jesus loves, we must think more of the other than of ourselves, not letting any amount of hurt close our hearts to our neighbours.

Where do we go from here?

If each of us thought more of others than of ourselves, everyone would be loved: such a simple equation and so difficult to make it concrete and real. Jesus is telling each one of us we have to go the extra mile. The hard truth is we are called to love not only those who love us, but everyone. We can love in this way because we have been infinitely loved by God. Reflect on how much God loves you and share that love with anyone who crosses your path.

O Lord, I offer you my heart so that you may bring your healing love to others through me.

1 Kings 21.17-29 • Psalm 51 • Matthew 5.43-4

W hen Ahab heard those words, he tore his clothes and put sackcloth over his bare flesh; he fasted, lay in the sackcloth, and went about dejectedly. *1 Kings 21.27*

The mercy of God

Have you ever noticed how harmless and insignificant sin can seem before you commit it, but afterwards, how horribly disastrous and terrible it becomes? This is a little trick of the Devil to lure us into committing sin, and then to frighten us away from seeking God's forgiveness. After all, we say to ourselves, how could God forgive such a terrible evil? But if we look through God's eyes, the situation suddenly changes. When Ahab had sinned, God was determined to unleash his wrath upon him as the just penalty for his wickedness. Yet, as soon as Ahab repented, God instantly forgave him and rescinded the punishment.

We can always trust God to ungrudgingly forgive us. God responds with overflowing mercy, eager to bring us back into friendship.

Where do we go from here?

It is easy for us to judge God by human standards—a God who doesn't readily forgive or who bears grudges or exacts his pound of flesh, because that is how we tend to be. God understands our weakness and wants to enclose us in his steadfast love and faithfulness. God wants to draw us into his truth, to help us love ourselves and others with God's mercy and steadfast love.

Most merciful Jesus, forgive me my sins and grant me the grace to rise again when I have fallen.

2 Kings 2.1, 6-14 • Psalm 31 • Matthew 6.1-6, 16-18

But I trust in you, O Lord;
I say, "You are my God." …
Let your face shine upon your servant;
save me in your steadfast love.

Psalm 31.14-16

Abiding in God's love

God calls his people to be morally upright. We witness the culture of death making inroads day by day. Stories of needless suffering, lack of respect, and destructive choices surround us, at times causing us to lose hope. Yet our standards for living should not come from our secular society. All time and this moment of history are in God's hands. Our words and our actions have the power to give life or to take it, to be honest and forthright or deceptive and misleading.

Who will abide in God's steadfast love? The one who trusts in you, O Lord. If we speak the truth from our heart and live the word in deed, we witness to Jesus, who is the way, the truth and the life.

Where do we go from here?

What measure do we use to judge life and others? The human standard we should use to evaluate what is worthy, good and just is Jesus, who is God in human condition. Our Father in heaven wanted to give us an unerring way to bring us to holiness and truth—Jesus is our way and the Holy Spirit is our teacher and comforter.

**Lord, grant me the grace to have a listening
and understanding heart.**

Sirach 48.1-14 • Psalm 97 • Matthew 6.7-15

L ight dawns for the righteous, and joy for the upright in heart.
Psalm 97.11

Walk in truth

What do we value most in life? Is it status, wealth or fame? Do we tend to identify with successful people rather than with those who are apparent failures? In our school years, did we take part in hurting others on the margins of society so that we could seem "cool"? Was climbing the corporate ladder or growing in popularity more important to us than charity?

We are followers of the Christ, who embraced cruel indignities for us. "He had no form or majesty that we should look at him, and nothing in his appearance that we should desire him" (Isaiah 53.2). So let us love as Jesus would have us love: unselfishly, compassionately and, most of all, without concern for "what people will think." Then will the healing light of the Holy Spirit dawn upon us, and the Lord will rescue us in all our needs.

Where do we go from here?

It is hard to do what is right without concern for our status, our image in society, or what others think of us. We can be concerned about these things as long as they do not take priority over what God wants of us. The will of God must be the first priority in our life from which all else flows. Ask God for the grace to live in his will. Begin today to choose to do what is honest and just, according to the teaching of the Church and the truth of the gospel. We can always fail—the important thing is to get up and continue walking in God's light.

Jesus, teach me to love as you love.

2 Kings 11.1-4, 9-18, 20 • Psalm 132 • Matthew 6.19-23

" **D**o not store up for yourselves treasures on earth, where moth and rust consume and where thieves break in and steal; but store up for yourselves treasures in heaven, where neither moth nor rust consumes and where thieves do not break in and steal. For where your treasure is, there your heart will be also.

Matthew 6.19-21

Where is my treasure?

Jesus tells his disciples not to store up earthly treasures that are fleeting and fragile. Of course, we do need to provide for our bodily needs and for our family. So what are the heavenly treasures Jesus is talking about? They are our good deeds and loving accompaniment of all who come into our lives.

Wherever my treasure is, there will be my heart. What things do I have my heart set on? What am I working for? What concerns fill my heart each day? Jesus has taught us that his Father knows all our needs and will look after us. Let us work hard, seek God, and fix our hearts on God's kingdom of love.

Where do we go from here?

Meditate on this passage from the Gospel of Matthew. What are your treasures? Where are your treasures? What does your heart desire? What are the heavenly treasures you want to store up? What are you willing to do to fix your heart on the treasures of heaven? Take time with these questions in the light of Jesus' words. Write down your findings.

Lord, in all that I do and seek to achieve for myself and for others, keep my heart fixed on you.

2 Chronicles 24.17-25 • Psalm 89 • Matthew 6.24-34

"**N**o one can serve two masters; for a slave will either hate the one and love the other, or be devoted to the one and despise the other. You cannot serve God and wealth."

Matthew 6.24

Whom do I serve?

The medieval mystic Meister Eckhart describes God's love for us as a baited hook that draws a fish to tasty bait. God opens his heart for us, and draws us by love, the bait of God's "hook." Still, some people feel that God is a restraint in their lives, a moral straitjacket that dulls the edge on life.

The key to today's reading is our capacity for choice. God does not force us to love him. God has given us a freedom that is fearful when we truly look at it. Who will I serve? Do I choose God and the treasures of the kingdom, or worldly pursuits and the accumulation of things? Where will I establish the foundation of my life? Let me choose God and his kingdom.

Where do we go from here?

Where will I establish the foundation of my life? This is really a hard question. God is willing to give me all the grace I need to become holy. But the choice is mine. So how are you choosing to live your life? All the responsibility is yours. God provides strength and grace.

**Lord, help me to serve in freedom—
to choose your way and to follow.**

Deuteronomy 8.2-3, 14-16 • Psalm 147 • 1 Corinthians 10.16-17 •
John 6.51-59

T he cup of blessing that we bless, is it not a sharing in the blood of Christ? The bread that we break, is it not a sharing in the body of Christ? Because there is one bread, we who are many are one body ....
1 Corinthians 10.16-17

May we be one

When we gather to celebrate the liturgy and receive the body of the Lord in the Eucharist, we become what we eat. Christ takes possession of us if we open ourselves to the full reality of what is taking place. In receiving the body of the Lord, we also receive all his members. We become more deeply united with Christ's members, the Church, and one with all God's children. Jesus teaches us in the gospels that we are to love one another; that is his purpose in dying for us: to reunite us as one body, again moving together toward the kingdom of his Father. Jesus promised when he returned to the Father to send the Holy Spirit to teach us how to love one another.

Where do we go from here?

Receiving Jesus in the Eucharist is a sign of our unity with the Church and with one another. We are the Body of Christ united in the Holy Spirit. That is why the gospel tells us that if there is a lack of forgiveness in our heart, someone whom we are at odds with, or even one who feels at odds with us, we should seek to be reconciled before approaching the table of the Lord. God in Jesus loved and forgave us while we were yet sinners. We are called to do the same for one another.

**Jesus, help me to listen to the guidance of
your Holy Spirit dwelling in my heart.**

2 Kings 17.5-8, 13-15, 18 • Psalm 60 • Matthew 7.1-5

"Do not judge, so that you may not be judged. For with the judgment you make you will be judged, and the measure you give will be the measure you get. Why do you see the speck in your neighbour's eye, but do not notice the log in your own eye?"
Matthew 7.1-3

Do not judge

An ancient practice handed down in the monastic life is to be attentive to our thoughts. Our thoughts can disrupt our peace of mind and heart, and encourage us to think ill of our neighbour, or they can lift us into God. Jesus reminds us today that our thoughts are what should concern us more than anything. Our rash judgments of others, if not stopped and quickly replaced with good thoughts, can lead us far away from the path Jesus intends us to follow. If we deal first with the speck in our own eye, our vision will be clear to see the goodness in others. Attentiveness to the thoughts we entertain can teach us so much about our path to conversion.

Where do we go from here?

It is a sobering thought to hear that the measure we give will be the measure we get. God pours out on us his gifts in lavish measure. As disciples of Jesus, we are called to pour out our gifts, unstintingly, in imitation of God's generosity. We limit God's generosity to us by not being generous with others. A selfish and miserly attitude actually changes us, narrowing our spirit and our capacity for receiving God's gifts. God's desire is to be generous, but if the cup of our spirit is full, there is no room for more.

Lord, lead me in your ways, that I may give glory to you and serve you woleheartedly.

Isaiah 49.1-6 • Psalm 139 • Acts 13.22-26 • Luke 1.57-66, 80

The Lord called me before I was born,
while I was in my mother's womb he named me.
He made my mouth like a sharp sword,
in the shadow of his hand he hid me …

Isaiah 49.1-2

I have chosen you

This selection from Isaiah is one of the four "servant songs" that the Church has always applied to Jesus as Messiah. In today's liturgy, on the feast of John the Baptist, the Church applies this text to John's vocation, which he received from all eternity. John is the great precursor, called to announce the presence of the long-awaited Messiah. He was the voice of God for the people of Israel.

Each of us can also say, "The Lord called me before I was born." God created each of us as a unique individual with a special mission to witness to the presence of Jesus. We make Jesus known in our words and in the way we live, doing good, listening compassionately, being a sign of God's steadfast love.

Where do we go from here?

God calls us as friends to be servants to others. We are in God's service, following the example of Jesus, who came to serve and not to be served. We cannot live by the great "me" philosophy of our modern culture. We are members of the body of Christ and as such we exist toward the other.

Dear Jesus, help me to fulfill the commission you have given me to be a sign of your loving and healing presence.

2 Kings 22.8-13; 23.1-3 • Psalm 119 • Matthew 7.15-20

"You will know them by their fruits. Are grapes gathered from thorns, or figs from thistles? In the same way, every good tree bears good fruit, but the bad tree bears bad fruit. A good tree cannot bear bad fruit, nor can a bad tree bear good fruit."

Matthew 7.16-18

The fruits of holiness

Jesus gives us a very good rule of thumb for discerning his presence in our hearts. What are the fruits of my way of living? If my life is firmly established in Jesus, then I will do the works Jesus did: being compassionate and merciful, loving others and praying for them, forgiving others as God has forgiven me in Jesus.

Forgiveness is the greatest measure of the fruits of my life in Jesus. If I can forgive as God has forgiven me, the reign of God has taken possession of my heart. Forgiving love is the great sign of God's presence in the world, and a certain sign of the gift of the Holy Spirit producing the fruits of holiness in my heart.

Where do we go from here?

How do I live my life? This is what judges me before God. It does not mean I will not fail in my desire to do good, or not sin. What is important is how I am living my life in its totality and fundamental intention. Continue to fill your heart with good desires, especially the desire to be in God's will and to love as God loves. Our deeds flow from the seeds of the desires we plant in our inner spirit.

Lord, teach me to forgive others as I have been forgiven.

2 Kings 24.8-17 • Psalm 79 • Matthew 7.21-29

"Everyone then who hears these words of mine and acts on them will be like a wise man who built his house on rock. The rain fell, the floods came, and the winds blew and beat on that house, but it did not fall, because it had been founded on rock. And everyone who hears these words of mine and does not act on them will be like a foolish man who built his house on sand. The rain fell, and the floods came, and the winds blew and beat against that house, and it fell—and great was its fall!"

Matthew 7.24-27

The Lord is our sure foundation

Hearing the words of Jesus is the foundation of our life in God. Hearing is much more than using our ears to hear the sound. By hearing his word, Jesus means letting the word enter into our hearts so that it changes our life. If we hear with our hearts, Jesus promises we will be wise, and our life in God will be built on unshakeable rock. When the Word truly enters into our hearts, then our choices will lead to good works that will manifest the presence of God to others.

Where do we go from here?

Hearing the words of Jesus with the ears of our heart always bears fruit in good deeds. It is never enough for us to store up all kinds of spiritual treasures for ourselves if we do not share them with our neighbour—only then can we call ourselves Christian.

Lord, let me hear with my heart, and manifest your love and forgiveness to everyone.

Deuteronomy 7.6-11 • Psalm 103 • 1 John 4.7-16 • Matthew 11.25-30

" **C**ome to me, all you that are weary and are carrying heavy burdens, and I will give you rest. Take my yoke upon you, and learn from me; for I am gentle and humble in heart, and you will find rest for your souls. For my yoke is easy, and my burden is light."
Matthew 11.28-30

Come to me

This feast of the Most Sacred Heart of Jesus celebrates God's love for us. Jesus' heart is the human heart of God, loving us with an eternal and faithful love. So we can take Jesus at his word, and come to him with our tiredness, our discouragement and our heavy burdens. He has already transformed our burdens and our weariness by carrying them to the cross. Let us find our rest from all life's burdens in Jesus. Let us walk in the light of the Lord and live in the power of the Holy Spirit.

Where do we go from here?

The heart is the symbol of love. Jesus' heart pierced on the cross is the symbol of God's love made visible for us. All creation came forth from the intimate love of the Trinity. In the beginning the Father spoke a Word and then breathed on everything that God had made and life began. How much does God love you? The loving and pierced heart of Jesus tells you.

**Lord, I give you this day's burdens and sorrows;
transform them into love.**

Isaiah 61.9-11 • 1 Samuel 2 • Luke 2.41-51

I will greatly rejoice in the Lord, my whole being shall exult in my God; for he has clothed me with the garments of salvation, he has covered me with the robe of righteousness, as a bridegroom decks himself with a garland, and as a bride adorns herself with her jewels.
Isaiah 61.10

My soul proclaims the greatness of the Lord

Mary's Magnificat echoes this joyful text from the prophet Isaiah as we celebrate the feast of the Immaculate Heart of the Blessed Virgin Mary. God adorned her with the garment of salvation to prepare her for the task of motherhood. In her womb, she nurtured Jesus, our Saviour and our hope. At the right time, she brought forth abundant life and healing for all peoples and nations.

God gives each of us the grace we need for the task that has been prepared for us, for all eternity. Let us learn to sing with Mary God's praise, and to magnify God with our lives. God can do wonderful things in us, if we, like Mary, say "Yes."

Where do we go from here?

Every year, the day after the Feast of the Sacred Heart, we celebrate the feast of the heart of Mary. Mary's heart was so empty and pure. She gave everything to God so that the Spirit of God could come upon her and she could give the Son of God a human body. Mary was the most beautiful of all God's creatures. Her humanity is the perfect example of the work of the Holy Spirit in a human heart and the pattern for our spiritual journey. Let us ask Mary to mother us into the total gift of ourselves to her Son.

Here I am, Lord. Send me.

Acts 12.1-11 • Psalm 34 • 2 Timothy 4.6-8, 17-18 • Matthew 16.13-19

I have fought the good fight, I have finished the race, I have kept the faith. From now on there is reserved for me the crown of righteousness, which the Lord, the righteous judge, will give me on that day ....   *2 Timothy 4.7-8*

To fight the good fight

Today we celebrate the feast of St. Peter and St. Paul. These two great pillars of the Church are paradigms for the work of grace in their diverse lives and in us. Jesus called each of them, knowing both their strengths and their weaknesses. Peter was an impetuous and blustering man who jumped into the fray before he realized what his actions meant. Yet he was a man of deep love, who, by denying Jesus, learned the meaning of forgiveness. Peter's sin and Jesus' steadfast love made him a man of compassion and stability. St. Paul was a man of great fervour, zeal and commitment to what he considered to be true. Jesus used the zeal of this enemy of the early Christians to spread the good news of the gospel to the Gentiles. The stories of Peter and Paul show that Jesus takes us as we are and transforms our lives into something beautiful for God.

Where do we go from here?

St. Peter and Paul, both weak and fallible men who followed the Lord, fought the good fight and completed the race. God asks you to do the same through living out your Christian commitment in your daily life. I met a woman once who I truly felt was a saint. She radiated God and I felt humbled in her presence. Live in a way that someone can say, "I just saw Jesus."

**Lord, fill me with the strength and
power of your love to serve.**

Amos 2.6-10, 13-16 • Psalm 50 • Matthew 8.18-22

A scribe then approached and said, "Teacher, I will follow you wherever you go." And Jesus said to him, "Foxes have holes, and birds of the air have nests; but the Son of Man has nowhere to lay his head."

Matthew 8.19-20

The rewards of discipleship

The gospel does not tell us whether the scribe could accept the price of discipleship. Initially, new enterprises can seem exciting and interesting, and we are enthusiastic. Our enthusiasm in following Jesus is tested by the endurance we need for the task. To follow Jesus means to live as he did: to care for others, to be compassionate, to give ourselves unstintingly. Are we ready?

In the gospels, Jesus is crystal clear about what discipleship will ask of us. The rewards are great: freedom, joy and peace in the gift of the Holy Spirit. Can I see others, poor and rich alike, with the eyes of Jesus, and love them and serve them with his love? God will provide the grace—one day at a time.

Where do we go from here?

Have we ever said to Jesus, "I will follow you wherever you go"? I think we can say it if we say, "Jesus, give me the grace to follow you wherever you go today." Jesus always tells us how it will be and then asks, "Are you still willing?" We are afraid of our weakness, that we won't have enough strength or courage for the task. We won't, but Jesus does. Step out, forget yourself, trust Jesus and give it a try.

Jesus, I rely on the gift of your Holy Spirit and the power of grace to complete the task of discipleship.

Amos 3.1-8; 4.11-12 • Psalm 5 • Matthew 8.23-27

"**W**hy are you afraid, you of little faith?"
Matthew 8.26

Do not be afraid

Amos asks the people why they are so blind to the message of God spoken through the prophets. God is very present to them, and God wants to act on their behalf. They have no difficulty reading the signs of nature and interpreting them. If the lion roars, they know that prey is in sight.

The tempest episode in the gospel is a good illustration of the difficulties presented by a weak faith. Jesus chides his intimate friends for the "little faith" they express. They ought to be reading the signs of God's presence among them. In a world that is often divided in terms of the secular and the sacred, we may struggle to find avenues for communication with God.

But when we are surrounded by people of great faith, we can more easily discern God's presence in nature and in events.

Where do we go from here?

How can I strengthen my faith today? Why not read one of the documents of the Church? For example, read the Vatican II document on the liturgy, *Dei Verbum* (found online). It will most certainly deepen your grasp of the liturgy and enrich your faith-filled participation in it. Celebrating the Eucharist is the heart of our Christian life. Jesus gives himself daily as food for the journey.

In and through your presence, Lord, help me to pour the balm of prayer on the deep wounds of your people, trusting in your healing and forgiveness.

Amos 5.14-15, 21-24 • Psalm 50 • Matthew 8.28-34

Hate evil and love good, and establish justice in the gate.
Amos 5.15

Be just and do good

Amos calls the people to conversion. He came at a time of plenty and prosperity, but warned the people of the trouble ahead. Deportation, famine and exile will put an end to their complacency. They can still avert this, if they will only open their lives to conversion. Conversion will influence the manner of God's coming.

In the gospel, the demons recognize Jesus and ask, "What have we to do with you, Jesus?"—as if to say, "Leave us alone." But Jesus has no difficulty triumphing over the demons. He has more difficulty with the local inhabitants. They fail to recognize the Saviour. The road to conversion is open to them. They refuse to take it. One day this rejection will be translated to the cross.

Where do we go from here?

Am I complacent about my life in God? Is everything going so well that it seems I can do it on my own? Give thanks to God for all the good things in your life, but never forget to pray for strength in the times of trouble. Inevitably they come. If we trust in the Lord, hardship gives us a sense of who is really keeping things in order: God. A simple formula for life: Give thanks for all blessings; pray for God's aid in times of trial; trust in God's presence with you in all the circumstances of your life!

Lord, help me to recognize your call to conversion and to open my heart to your love, so that I may be like those trees planted by streams of water.

Ephesians 2.19-22 • Psalm 117 • John 20.24-29

Y ou are citizens with the saints and also members of the household of God. … you also are built together spiritually ….
Ephesians 2.19, 22

Living stones

God continues to build his household. God simply replaces the team
of builders with Christ and the Apostles. The Church is a temple and
dwelling: solidly founded, yet unfinished. It is the personal work of
Jesus, but he needs the collaboration of the faithful. This image of the
household of God gives Paul an opportunity to speak of the Church
as the temple and the new dwelling place of God.

To unbelievers, Christ has disappeared, but his followers continue to see him as a living person. This does not imply merely a vision
of his physical presence, but a true understanding of who Jesus is.
With St. Thomas, we too can cry out, "My Lord and my God!" Jesus
tells Thomas that the day will come when people will see with the
eyes of faith and believe, and he called these people blessed.

Where do we go from here?

There is a spiritual bond among the members of Christ's body,
the Church. We are part of the communion of saints. We are the
pilgrims on the way toward eternal life. Today we are building the
body of Christ by our good and practical deeds of love. Do some
volunteer work for the Church: offer to be a reader or minister of
hospitality at Mass. Be kind and helpful to someone, perhaps at the
store, thus showing Christian love in the wider community.

**United to you, O Christ, we pray that all we do and suf-
fer brings nearer that final peace between God and God's
people, so that we may all be one in your household.**

Amos 8.4-6, 9-12 • Psalm 119 • Matthew 9.9-13

W hy does your teacher eat with tax collectors and sinners?"
Matthew 9.11

Eating with sinners

Matthew gave a feast, and many publicans and sinners were present. Jesus' response to the Pharisees is that he had not come to call the just but the sinner to repentance.

Jesus' mission was to go where needed. He was not saying that some people were so good that they had no need of anything he had to offer; still less was he saying that he was not interested in good people. He came to invite people who are very conscious of their sin and in deep need of a saviour. We are all in need of Jesus.

Where do we go from here?

Am I aware of my need for Jesus and my responsibility to love as he loved me? Where am I needed? How can I reach out to the poor and marginalized? Is there someone of your acquaintance whom you find unlovely? Go out of your way to make him or her feel welcome and special. We all need to feel special and loved. If everyone thought of the other, no one would ever be lonely. It is love that will change our world. Do your part to make love a more common commodity.

**Having received your healing forgiveness, may I
in turn be a source of pardon and compassion to others.**

Amos 9.11-15 • Psalm 85 • Matthew 9.14-17

"**N**ew wine is put into fresh wineskins ...."
Matthew 9.17

....

Preparing for the Messiah

The discipline imposed by Jesus on his disciples scandalized the crowds because it did not resemble that of other rabbis. In the Old Testament and in Judaism, the practice of fasting was associated with waiting for the coming of the Messiah. The disciples were already living with the Messiah. When the "Bridegroom" is gone, the followers of Jesus will have a much deeper meaning for their fasting, uniting this act to the redemptive sacrifice of Christ. In Jesus' parable about the old and new wine, he does not make a value judgment about the superiority of the old wine to the new. What is stressed is the incompatibility of the old and the new; they cannot be joined at the cost of losing both. We cannot compromise to the point where everything is lost.

Where do we go from here?

In the workplace, in discussions, we do need to negotiate and to compromise. Can we compromise on everything? It is something to ponder. Flexibility is a good gift. We do need to listen to the other, but we cannot compromise our faith in its essentials. Reflect; are there areas where you have gone too far in compromising? The answer is to live the truth in love. Jesus was firm on certain truths while always loving those whom he encountered.

Help me, Lord, to abstain from sin, and strengthen my heart to carry out your commandments.

Zechariah 9.9-10 • Psalm 145 • Romans 8.9, 11-13 • Matthew 11.25-30

J esus said, "I thank you, Father, Lord of heaven and earth, because you have hidden these things from the wise and the intelligent and have revealed them to infants ....
Matthew 11.25

God's Spirit gives understanding

In Romans 8, Paul teaches that the Spirit of God dwells in us. He says that to live in the flesh is to seek sovereignty, much like Adam did when he disobeyed. To live in the Spirit is to be obedient to the ways of God. Life in the Spirit is closely associated with the resurrection of Jesus.

In Matthew's gospel, Jesus thanks the Father for his mission to the little ones. Then he extends an invitation to them. The simple, the childlike and the "poor in spirit" are disposed to accept Jesus. We know Jesus through faith. Jesus does not condemn cleverness but the pride that can close our hearts to the truth of the word of God. Jesus gives knowledge and understanding to anyone who is humble and trusting enough to receive them.

Where do we go from here?

"Life in the Spirit" has a nice ring to it. Do you live your life in the Spirit? Pray for the Holy Spirit to be poured out on you—every day. Allowing the Spirit of God to direct you is to be free, joyful and alive to all good things, peaceful and full of love. Sounds pretty good to me. Is it true? Yes, it is!

O Holy Spirit, grant me the grace of belonging entirely to you, heart, soul and body.

Hosea 2.14, 15-16, 19-20 • Psalm 145 • Matthew 9.18-26

" **I** f I only touch his cloak, I will be made well."
Matthew 9.21

To believe

The woman suffering from hemorrhages had great faith in the power of Jesus to heal her. She did not approach him directly. She believed that only touching the "tassel" of his cloak would be enough to receive his healing. She would also avoid contaminating him.

According to the Law, her disease made her, and anyone who came in contact with her, "unclean." Jesus knew that someone had touched him and that power had gone out from him. Her need touched his compassionate heart. The woman in the gospel is saved because of her great faith.

Where do we go from here?

Do you believe in healing? Do you believe in the power of prayer? So many people in our world are bent over with suffering, oppression, poverty and cruelty. Pray to God for healing in these terrible situations. Look around. Is there someone close at hand whom you can help to have a better life? I know of a group of women who walk the streets of Vancouver at night to help the street people. They bring hope and dignity.

God of mercy, look kindly on me in my suffering.
Ease my burden and make my faith strong
so I may always have great trust in you.

Hosea 8.4-7, 11-13 • Psalm 115 • Matthew 9.32-38

"The harvest is plentiful, but the labourers are few ...."
Matthew 9.37

To labour for the kingdom

Jesus is aware that a large number of people are ready to receive the gospel; they are like a vast field of grain ripe for the harvest. Many labourers are needed, and he sets about selecting twelve of his disciples who will work with him to gather in the harvest.

It was in view of this great need that Jesus decided to send his Apostles forth on a missionary journey, a journey that would be a foretaste of the great mission they would bear in the world after his ascent into heaven. By their way of life, their proclamation of the good news, and through the power of the Spirit, they would make Jesus known. But he first impressed on them the need to pray for workers in his service, to reap the harvest of souls.

Where do we go from here?

Pray for missionaries, for vocations to the priesthood and religious life. Encourage young men and women to dedicate their lives to God for the sake of the kingdom. Such lives are a necessary witness to the kingdom of God. Did you ever consider volunteering for work in the missions for a short or longer period? Take the challenge! Our shared vocation is to make Jesus visible in the world by the way we live.

**Bless me, Lord, with a missionary heart,
a great desire to share your thirst for the salvation of all.**

Hosea 10.1-3, 7-8, 12 • Psalm 105 • Matthew 10.1-7

"**A**s you go, proclaim the good news, 'The kingdom of heaven has come near.'"
Matthew 10.7

Send me

Jesus now feels it is time to select from among his disciples those who will share his missionary journey. To make this important decision, he spends the whole night in prayer in a place of seclusion. The next morning, he gathers his followers and chooses twelve. These twelve will be known as "Apostles," which means "to be sent." These will be his personal companions, and soon he will send them out to proclaim the good news. They will go out to the "lost sheep of Israel." It took persecution to make Christians go forth from Jerusalem and spread the gospel to the Gentiles, as St. Paul was already doing.

We, too, are sent to preach the good news of the kingdom—even more, we are sent to be that good news. Jesus still seeks out those who will follow him more closely and will work to spread the Good News.

Where do we go from here?

We do not need to go to a foreign land to be a missionary. There are so many people all around us who are poor and in need. Poverty can come in many forms. Open your eyes today to recognize your poverty and the poverty of your brothers and sisters. Do not hold out a helping hand in pity, but as one who shares their condition.

**Bless the families, Lord, who foster vocations
to the mission fields.**

Hosea 11.1, 3-5, 8-9 • Psalm 80 • Matthew 10.7-15

"**A**s you go, proclaim the good news …. Cure the sick, raise the dead, cleanse the lepers …."
Matthew 10.7

Do the works of the kingdom

"The coming of the kingdom" must be proclaimed. Jesus imposes on his disciples the counsels he taught in the Sermon on the Mount. They are to leave all to follow him. He wants their style of life to be an embodiment of the word they proclaim: not just to talk to people about Jesus Christ, but also to show him to them. He promised them no material rewards, but gave them the grace of faith. Now they, in turn, were to be the means of taking this gift to others, and to bestow it as freely as it had been given to them.

Where do we go from here?

The Apostles were sent to give freely what they had received. Are you willing to give without any return in gratitude? It is easy to give to those who are grateful and appreciative, but Jesus asks more. In Luke 14.12-14, Jesus says that when you give a banquet, don't invite your rich friends but invite the poor, the crippled and the lame, because they cannot repay you—wait for your payment, which will be given by the Lord. Our way of giving and the example of our life make Jesus visible. At biblegateway.com, look up the word "give" in the gospels. God gives so freely to us.

Jesus, be the inspiration and strength of all those who work in your name and spread your kingdom.

Hosea 14.1-9 • Psalm 51 • Matthew 10.16-23

"**D**o not worry about how you are to speak; … for it is not you who speak, but the Spirit of your Father speaking through you."
Matthew 10.19-20

The gift of the Spirit

Jesus uses the image of the wolf and the sheep to teach the Twelve that their mission will encounter opposition and persecution. In fact, these will be a stimulus for the spread of the Good News they preach. The presence of Jesus in the world challenges all people.

The gift of the Spirit will transform their preaching into witness. The Spirit will help them to be strong and effective witnesses to the kingdom. Like the Apostles, we have the great gift of the Holy Spirit, who gives us the ability to fulfill our duties, our mission. The Holy Spirit is there in all our needs. Let us open our hearts to this grace.

Where do we go from here?

Are you aware of the gift of the Spirit you carry in your heart? Without a doubt, that gift is present within you. Believe it and pray for a deeper awareness of the power you have in the Spirit to transform yourself, the community, the Church and the whole world. You can make a difference! Do it. Today is the feast of St. Benedict, a man of the Spirit and a man of peace. He is a paradigm of how much the Lord can do through one person.

O Lord, give your people dedication to the Father's will, and the courage they need to embrace the sacrifices involved in living their vocations.

Isaiah 6.1-8 • Psalm 93 • Matthew 10.24-33

"So do not be afraid; you are of more value than many sparrows."
Matthew 10.31

....

Fear not

The Lord does not minimize the dangers that will await his followers. There will be discrimination, torture and death. But Jesus takes the example of one of the most common little creatures. He reassures his followers that God watches over all, even the sparrow. How much more will God watch over his friends? Nothing can happen to them without God's leave. God will be with them in their trials.

Jesus assures us of his faithful presence. In the eucharistic celebration, we come to realize just what that means. Here we celebrate Christ's victory of love and the proclamation of his kingdom.

Where do we go from here?

Let the liturgy make a difference in your life. On Sunday, don't just sit passively in the pew—participate. Listen attentively to the word of God and bring a phrase or thought away with you to think about; discuss the readings and the homily together as a family. How will the Word make you different? It has the power to do so. If you can add the daily celebration of the Eucharist to your schedule, it will help you in day-to-day living.

Lord, let us share in your victory.
Grant peace between all peoples.

Isaiah 55.10-11 • Psalm 65 • Romans 8.18-23 • Matthew 13.1-23

For as the rain and the snow come down from heaven,
and do not return there until they have watered the earth,
making it bring forth and sprout ...
so shall my word be that goes out from my mouth ....

Isaiah 55.10-11

God's word is fruitful

Thank you, living and eternal God, for the great love you have shown to your children in all times. Thank you also for comparing your love to a farmland that produces its fruits when it is watered well by rain. You tell us that the word you send to us will achieve the end for which it was sent. You seem to disregard the fact that you have given us free will, and, just as too much rain can ruin a crop, so our unwillingness to cooperate can hinder the fruitfulness of your word. But your love finds a way to make your word come true for your children—not just those who lived before the advent of Jesus, but for us today, too.

Where do we go from here?

God's word will not return empty. What seeds do you think the word of God is planting in your heart right now? God is asking you something: are you responding? Listen to your heart. Make time in your life for reading the Scriptures. Begin with the gospel of Luke. Read a little each day and think about its message. What is God asking you?

**For this, O God of Love, I praise you;
I love you and thank you.**

Isaiah 1.10-17 • Psalm 50 • Matthew 10.34–11.1

"For I have come to set a man against his father, and a daughter against her mother .... Whoever loves father or mother more than me is not worthy of me ...." *Matthew 10.35, 37*

Priorities

The divisions Jesus speaks about in the gospel are a reminder to me that suffering and hardship, conflict and division are inevitable in this life. Even Jesus had to embrace them. God's merciful love and blessings are granted to those who are willing to take up their cross daily and humbly follow Jesus. When I place God first in my life, I am in right relationship with God and with others. By offering God all my words, thoughts and actions, I can not only endure my own trials, but I can help others in their struggles. Together we can praise and thank God for the strength and comfort God offers us at all times, even during hardships and trials.

Where do we go from here?

How do I deal with the hard moments of life? Do I think God has forgotten me? That God does not care or isn't doing his job? Our gift of memory enables us to hold together the times of darkness and light. In the times of light, we can remember the grace of God's strength sustaining us in our times of darkness. The alternating patterns of light and darkness in our life can bring us to a confident trust that God is never absent, but is near in whatever circumstances we find ourselves. We can share this confidence with others.

Jesus, help me to trust in you as I unite my sufferings to yours, and humbly and gratefully carry my own cross for love of you.

Isaiah 7.1-9 • Psalm 48 • Matthew 11.20-24

Then he began to reproach the cities in which most of his deeds of power had been done, because they did not repent.
Matthew 11.20

The challenge of the gospel

In our readings for today, there seems to be very little by way of good news. Isaiah speaks of the kings of Judah, Aram and Israel, and the danger they pose for the House of David. He and his people are filled with fear for themselves and for Jerusalem. The Lord, however, reassures them: "Pay attention and keep calm. Do not be frightened ...." At the same time, they cannot be complacent, for they are further told, "If you will not take your stand on me, you will not stand firm."

The gospel details a refusal to repent. In what ways do I need to repent? Am I willing to move beyond my comfort zone in order to serve God and others? Am I faithful in fulfilling the gospel precepts in my life?

Where do we go from here?

What is your comfort zone in serving others? Are you someone whom others can ask for help? A friend I know, when asked for help, stops whatever she is doing to assist me, and she always does this with a smile. The next time someone asks you for help, do it. The doing takes less time than talking about all the reasons you are too busy. St. Bonaventure gives an example of living the gospel of love.

Through the intercession of St. Bonaventure, whose feast we celebrate today, may we stand firm before God in sincerity and truth.

Isaiah 10.5-7, 13-16 • Psalm 94 • Matthew 11.25-27

"**A**ll things have been handed over to me by my Father; and no one knows the Son except the Father, and no one knows the Father except the Son and anyone to whom the Son chooses to reveal him."

Matthew 11.27

Learning to pray

Jesus speaks to his Father: God the Son speaks to God the Father and calls him Lord of heaven and earth. Heaven and earth are so well represented in this prayer of Jesus. Jesus is also teaching us how to pray by his example. He praises his Father for the good things he has done on earth. He does not ask for favours for himself or for the people he knows. Rather, his prayer is one of praise to his Father. What a powerful example for our own prayer. We need strong faith to be able to pray like Jesus. We also have to learn to notice the good things God does on earth, and, like Jesus, praise and thank our heavenly Father for his love and constant care.

Where do we go from here?

Are you a grumbler or are you someone who sees the good side of things? It is more healthy, both physically and spiritually, to be upbeat. Today, make a list of all the good things and all the blessings in your life. Say a prayer of thanksgiving to God, and thank your family and friends for their love and goodness. A grateful heart is a blessing to everyone.

I praise and thank you, Father in heaven. Make me your loving child and teach me to pray as Jesus did. Amen.

Isaiah 26.7-9, 12, 16-19 • Psalm 102 • Matthew 11.28-30

"**C**ome to me, all you that are weary and are carrying heavy burdens, and I will give you rest."
Matthew 11.28

....

Bearing our burdens

This favourite passage from Matthew is a source of comfort and encouragement in the midst of the stress and challenges of our busy lives. The image of a yoke probably is not familiar to most city dwellers. Perhaps imagining two people pushing a stalled car to safety off a busy highway might bring the meaning to life. We need to acknowledge our weakness and accept the help of others. So often when we are overburdened, anxious, hitting our limits, we try to go it alone.

We turn everywhere except to God. Even to pause for a few moments in the midst of our daily storms to fix our eyes on Jesus can change our perspective dramatically. A little quotation sums it up well: "Work time for prayer into your day, and your day will work out better."

Where do we go from here?

Can you accept help from others? Accepting help from someone is a gift, a way of saying, "I trust you and need you in my life." Loving means being vulnerable and needy; it allows others to be co-workers with us. We are all members of one body in Jesus. Our goal is not self-sufficiency but interdependence. Allow someone to help you today—even if you can do it yourself.

**You are with me, Lord, in every moment of my day, but
I am not always with you. Only with your presence and
help can the burdens and cares of my day be lived fruitfully.**

Isaiah 38.1-6, 21-22, 7-8 • Isaiah 38 • Matthew 12.1-8

" **G** o and say to Hezekiah … I have heard your prayer, I have seen your tears."
Isaiah 38.5

Trust in the Lord

Hezekiah is mentioned in the Second Book of Kings as the king who did what was right in the sight of the Lord. Throughout his reign in Jerusalem, he trusted in the Lord and kept his commandments. The Lord was with him, and wherever Hezekiah went, he prospered. When he became sick and was at the point of death, he prayed and the Lord heard him.

Today the Lord invites us to have confidence in his mercy and love. Like that of Hezekiah, our prayer is an expression of our relationship with God. In fact, our life itself is a prayer before God. Our compassionate and forgiving God knows our struggles and failures in life, our joys and sorrows, aspirations and hopes. God is always ready to help and to embrace us whenever we call upon God with all our hearts.

Where do we go from here?

Do you sometimes feel God does not understand you, see your tears or hear your pleading? Life deals us some pretty hard blows. Continue to pray and renew your trust in God's love. Like the image of God in the familiar story of "Footprints in the Sand," God never walks away from us. We need to stay put. In your prayer, use the image of Jesus tenderly carrying you in his arms. Allow God's love to enfold you. Abide in his love.

**Lord Jesus, help me to know your infinite mercy,
so that I, too, may become a bearer of your mercy
to my brothers and sisters.**

Micah 2.1-5 • Psalm 10 • Matthew 12.14-21

"**B**ut the Pharisees went out and conspired against him, how to destroy him.   *Matthew 12.14*

God's servant

Nothing Jesus did or said was right in the eyes of the Pharisees. Jesus, aware of their hostility and plan to kill him, remained courageous and determined. He lived according to God's purpose and agenda rather than his own. In Jesus, the prophecy of the Suffering Servant is fulfilled: the loving, humble and gentle teacher has come to bring the light of truth. He is God's justice, and in him, the redeeming love and mercy of God is made manifest.

The way to glory in God's kingdom is through the cross. Jesus calls us to be kind and compassionate toward others, to show understanding to those who are weak or discouraged, and to show encouragement and hope to those who are hopeless.

Where do we go from here?

Pray to the Holy Spirit for the discernment to understand God's will in your life. Think about ways you can make a difference at home, at church, in the workplace. Make a list and move forward in putting your list into practical actions. Take one thing at a time; when we try to do everything, we often do nothing. Be modest in your plans. Step by step, perform some small act each day to make a difference. God will smile.

Lord, make me an instrument of your hope, so that through the love you have given me, I may encourage those who have no hope.

Wisdom 12.13, 16-19 • Psalm 86 • Romans 8.26-27 • Matthew 13.24-43

"**A**t the harvest time I will tell the reapers, Collect the weeds first and bind them in bundles to be burned, but gather the wheat into my barn."

Matthew 13.30

Judge not

Harvest time is the time for judgment, and only God has the right to judge. Yet how quickly we judge each other. We often label people as "good" or "bad" the minute we meet them. We start processing the details of their appearance, their clothes and manner of speaking. Then we share our assessments and judgments with others. It is so easy to do. Jesus urges us to rise above such attitudes and to treat others with loving respect. Like Jesus, we are to love unconditionally. Let God be God! God alone can see the motives and intentions of the heart.

Where do we go from here?

Every human being is precious in the eyes of God. Do I have a list of criteria for assessing people? Is it based on very superficial standards, such as appearance, popularity, beauty or status? Dare to look deeper. See the beauty that lies at the core of every human heart. Ask yourself, "What is special about this person?" Reach out to someone today. Introduce yourself to someone new at church.

**Judgment belongs only to you, Lord God.
Keep my heart and mind pure, lest I judge others.**

Micah 6.1-4, 6-8 • Psalm 50 • Matthew 12.38-42

"**A**n evil and adulterous generation asks for a sign, but no sign will be given to it except the sign of the prophet Jonah."
Matthew 12.39

The sign of Jonah

This is another test for Jesus. The sign of Jonah: what is it? Jonah, against his will, was sent to call the people of Nineveh to repentance and to tell them of God's mercy. He refused, going in the opposite direction and trying to escape from God. God went to great lengths to bring him back—even had him spend three days in the belly of a whale! This is a symbol of conversion, a time when we surrender to God's ways in our life. During that time, Jonah was totally at God's mercy, and it was only when his heart was purified that God "spewed" him out to do God's work. Jesus is telling the Jews that he is the Great Sign. He is God's mercy incarnate, and they do not recognize him. They do not let him touch their hearts or their lives.

Where do we go from here?

There are times when running away seems the best of all options. But there is no running away from God. "Where can I flee from your spirit?" (Psalm 139) When life becomes burdensome, it is then we should run toward God, who is always our refuge and our strength. Are you facing a difficult situation or a time of grief? Take time to bring it to God, and pray for wisdom and comfort. God is greater than any problem we can bring to him.

Lord, open my eyes to see you in the signs you give me every day. Open my ears to hear your call to conversion and repentance today.

Song of Songs 3.1-4 or 2 Corinthians 5.14-17 • Psalm 63 •
John 20.1, 11-18

> found him whom my soul loves.
> *Song of Songs 3.4*

Finding Jesus

In the midst of the summer's heat, it is quite natural to want to quench our thirst with a cold, refreshing drink. Our bodies speak to us of our needs, and we instinctively respond. Mary Magdalene reminds us of our spiritual needs: to seek the One whom our hearts desire and to fill our souls with the love of Jesus. Our response will lead us first to the cross, then to the empty tomb, and ultimately to our heart's desire in the resurrected Christ. We cannot cling to him, but we must announce him to the world: "Go and tell my disciples: 'I am ascending to my Father, and your Father, to my God and your God.'"

Where do we go from here?

Can you share your faith with others? We so easily share our hobbies—golfing, fishing, cooking—with friends and acquaintances. It is much harder to share things close to our hearts. Every day brings us opportunities to witness to others in small and unobtrusive ways about the comfort, strength and happiness that being rooted in Jesus brings. Take one of those opportunities today to talk about God's love.

Lord, give me courage to announce, "I have seen the Lord!"

Wednesday | JULY 23

Jeremiah 1.1, 4-10 • Psalm 71 • Matthew 13.1-9

" Ah, Lord God! Truly I do not know how to speak, for I am only a boy." But the LORD said to me, "Do not say, 'I am only a boy'; for you shall go to all to whom I send you, and you shall speak whatever I command you …."

Jeremiah 1.6-7

No excuses: I am with you

In this text we have the call of the prophet Jeremiah. God often encounters reluctance when the prophets receive their initial call. The source of Jeremiah's fear and reluctance is the sense of his inadequacies. God accepts no excuses! When God calls, he gives the gifts needed to fulfill the task and promises to be with the prophet, but that doesn't mean it will be easy. God calls each one of us for a task and God knows what we are capable of with his grace. God knows us even before we were formed in our mother's womb and tells us not to be afraid.

Where do we go from here?

Reflect on and pray with Jeremiah 1.1, 4-10. The text addresses so many things we need to bolster our courage. God knows what he is doing when he calls us to a ministry in the church or to bear the cross in our life. Don't say I can't do it—God says you can! Leap into God's will and begin the task, holding firmly to God's word and promise. The Almighty can do great things in us.

God, let me keep my gaze fixed on your promise and not on my weakness. Your grace is sufficient.

Jeremiah 2.1-3, 7-8, 12-13 • Psalm 36 • Matthew 13.10-17

" or to those who have, more will be given, and they will have an abundance; but from those who have nothing, even what they have will be taken away." *Matthew 13.12*

The kingdom of heaven

Jesus chose disciples with whom he could share the knowledge of the kingdom of heaven, and through them, could make it known to the whole world. He did not choose them because they were intelligent and able to comprehend the mysteries of God's kingdom. They were simple people with humble lives. Yet Jesus saw in them an eagerness to know him and a willingness to give up what they had to follow him and be part of his life.

As followers of Christ, we also have been given the gifts and wisdom to fulfill our mission, in our homes and work, in our communities and societies. When we spend time with the Lord in prayer, when we give ourselves in the service of others or when we do God's will, the Lord will reveal himself to us and will bless us abundantly.

Where do we go from here?

We need to spend time with a friend so that our relationship grows and deepens. Our relationship with God is the same. We need time to listen to God speaking to our hearts and revealing his presence in our life. It is important to set aside time for prayer in our day: perhaps early in the morning before the day starts, or in the evening when our day is done. Have a regular schedule of times set aside to meet God.

Lord Jesus, thank you for calling me to participate in your mission. May I become generous in giving myself to the service of your Church and in building up your kingdom.

2 Corinthians 4.7-15 • Psalm 126 • Matthew 20.20-28

J esus answered, "Are you able to drink the cup that I am about to drink?" They said to him, "We are able." He said to them, "You will indeed drink my cup, but to sit at my right hand and at my left, this is not mine to grant, but it is for those for whom it has been prepared by my Father."

Matthew 20.22-23

Drinking the cup

Jesus tells James and John that if they wish to follow him, they will drink the cup that he will drink. The second letter to the Corinthians tells us we hold this treasure in earthen vessels: the earthen vessels of human living. Jesus' daily loving presence allows us to share this cup by all that comes into our lives: the death of a loved one, sickness, financial worries, the daily concerns of living. Let us believe and trust in Jesus, and carry the needs of our suffering world in our hearts.

Where do we go from here?

James and John don't really understand what they are asking. They do drink the cup Jesus drank after the resurrection and the sending of the Holy Spirit. The Holy Spirit equips us to be disciples of Jesus in the ordinary and extraordinary circumstances of our life. Every time you face a challenge or difficult situation today, pray to the Holy Spirit to guide you and give you the courage to move forward. God has promised to help! Remind the Lord that you are taking him up on the promise.

**Spirit of Jesus, fill my heart with your love,
that I may share this love with all I meet each day.**

Sirach 44.1, 8, 10-15 • Psalm 132 • Matthew 13.16-17

"**B**ut blessed are your eyes, for they see, and your ears, for they hear."

Matthew 13.16

I hear

An old Slovak proverb says, "God gave us two gates on our mouth: our teeth and our lips. He gave us one gate on our eyes: our eyelids. But he didn't give us any gate at all on our ears." We are great talkers, but most of us are not very good listeners. I heard a priest say once that the real generation gap is not that we cannot talk to each other, older and younger, but that we do not listen to each other.

Listening is the key in any human relationship, and listening is very important in our relationship with God. We are blessed that we have ears to hear the gospel proclaimed and preached. Are we bearing fruit in loving relationship with God? If not, maybe it is time that we open our ears to listen and receive the word of God in our hearts.

Where do we go from here?

Today we celebrate the feast of Saints Joachim and Anne, the parents of Mary. They were upright people and lovers of the Lord who listened intently to God. Their parenting and example formed Mary to listen and say yes to God. Are you a good listener, or do you only seem to listen, just waiting for your chance to talk? Today, take time to be silent and listen to God intently. And take time to really listen to a brother or sister in compassionate love. Develop a habit of listening! It takes practice.

Mary, our Mother, you knew how to listen. We ask your intercession to help us to listen and be receptive to God's word, that it may bear fruit in our lives.

I Kings 3.5-12 • Psalm I 19 • Romans 8.28-30 • Matthew 13.44-52

" **G** ive your servant therefore an understanding mind to govern your people, able to discern between good and evil ...."
I Kings 3.9

An understanding heart

If only we could ask for an understanding heart and always do what is right. If only we could be like Saints Basil and Gregory, who, rather than compete with one another in their studies, sought to help the other "do better" and be first. "Their rivalry was not subject to envy. Rather, it consisted not in seeking the first place for oneself but in yielding it to the other, for each looked on the other's success as his own." If only.... Our world is filled with so much violence, competition, envy and selfishness. Can we make a difference? Can we allow the other to be first? If only we might ask for an understanding heart to do what is right....

Where do we go from here?

We live in a competitive world. God's world view is not competitive, but is about unity and giftedness. Each one of us has been given a gift for the service of all. One gift is not better than another but is suited to the individual—all the gifts are needed to make the body of Christ whole. Ponder the difference between giftedness and competition. What gifts do you have for the service of the common good? Are you using them well? Have you bought into the mindset of getting ahead at any cost? Ask God for an understanding heart. May "if only" become the truth of the way you live.

**Lord, help me to let go of envy and rivalry,
and seek to cooperate with the unfolding of your plan
for me with an understanding heart.**

Jeremiah 13.1-11 • Deuteronomy 32 • Matthew 13.31-35

He told them another parable: "The kingdom of heaven is like yeast that a woman took and mixed in with three measures of flour until all of it was leavened." *Matthew 13.33*

Hidden in Christ

You see bread rising and expanding when the yeast is mixed with the flour. The yeast is not visible once it becomes one with the flour. It works from within, a powerful, hidden work. Jesus tells us this is like the kingdom of heaven in this world. The kingdom is growing and expanding in the hearts of believers who are one in the Holy Spirit. In union with God, they become the hidden leaven by which the kingdom expands and grows among peoples and nations. When Jesus comes again, he will proclaim and manifest all that has been hidden. The growth of the secular society with its culture of death can discourage us, but we know Jesus has conquered. And we are the hidden leaven expanding the kingdom of God, unseen but powerful and relentless in its work.

Where do we go from here?

Believers are a hidden leaven. This means we work to make God visible, not ourselves. The one sent to proclaim God's presence is not the one at centre stage. Jesus was the good news that God is among us. Am I willing to be a hidden leaven, or do I like the limelight? It is something to think about. Where is the focus of my service and of my sharing? A good test is whether I am willing to give without any return.

Jesus, I believe in your victory over sin and death.

Jeremiah 14.17-22 • Psalm 79 • Luke 10.38-42

"**M**artha, Martha, you are worried and distracted by many things; there is need of only one thing. Mary has chosen the better part, which will not be taken away from her."

Luke 10.41-42

One thing necessary

In our Christian journey, no matter what our calling—single, married, lay or religious—these two elements emerge: practical deeds of service and contemplation. Necessary practical tasks need to be done, whether it's earning a living or caring for family, along with the great privilege we have of listening to God's word speaking to our hearts.

We do not live by bread alone. We also need spiritual food to nourish our souls. The temptation is to try to live as if our spiritual side did not exist. Sometimes even good things can fill up our lives to the point that we neglect our souls. God's gifts to us (family, friends, jobs, abilities) are not given for us to abandon a close walk with Jesus. Our task is to keep all in balance.

Where do we go from here?

Keeping everything in balance is not always easy. For most of us it is easier to "do" than to "be." We need regular times in our day when we tap into our Source, God. It is essential to take time to be silent, to pray, to read the Scriptures and then to listen to God. Informing our faith through study is also important in order to nourish it. Read the Vatican II document *Lumen Gentium* (found online) to nourish your faith.

Lord, help me to balance my life: to seek first the Kingdom of God and to realize that "there is need for only one thing." Help me to put my energy where you want it to be.

Jeremiah 15.10, 16-21 • Psalm 59 • Matthew 13.44-46

"The kingdom of heaven is like treasure hidden in a field. ... the kingdom of heaven is like a merchant in search of fine pearls ...."
Matthew 13.44-45

Possessing a treasure

The kingdom of heaven, the life of the Trinity that Jesus came to bring, cannot be seen in our daily reality except with the eyes of faith. When we discover and experience this hidden treasure and pearl of great price—eternal life in God—it becomes the deepest longing of our hearts. It is the guiding star that leads us through life until we reach its fullness in God. The price of this hidden treasure is saying "yes" to all that comes into our life each day. The opportunities, the encounters and the challenges are to be met with the faith, trust and love received from Jesus. Are we willing to pay the price?

Where do we go from here?

Each day brings us challenges and opportunities that must be met with faith. We are fragile, but God gives us strength. Begin the day with a prayer of loving trust in Jesus' accompaniment during the day, and frequently look inward to refocus yourself in God dwelling in your heart. The frantic pace of life often causes us to overlook God's presence manifested throughout our day. Living a calm, focused life in God affects and changes us; it sends out ripples, shaping the whole universe, creating harmony and peace.

Jesus, each day you show me the price of this treasure.
Purify my heart in my "yes" to you.

Jeremiah 18.1-6 • Psalm 146 • Matthew 13.47-52

The vessel he was making of clay was spoiled in the potter's hand, and he reworked it into another vessel, as seemed good to him. Then the word of the Lord came to me: Can I not do with you, O house of Israel, just as this potter has done? says the Lord. Just like the clay in the potter's hand, so are you in my hand, O house of Israel. *Jeremiah 18.4-6*

God's clay

When preparing to become a contemplative religious sister, I was given a practice to help me stay in the presence of God. At intervals during the day, I was encouraged to speak a short prayer. After reading the potter and the clay story, I recalled one such gem that expresses a profound truth of who I am and who God is: "Lord God, I acknowledge your supreme dominion over me and my total dependence upon you." God is the potter and we are the clay. If we willingly surrender ourselves to God, as the clay gives itself to the potter, we begin to realize who we are and who God is.

Where do we go from here?

The secret to being present to God throughout a busy day is using an inner Scripture phrase or word to refocus your spirit. If things aren't going well, pause a moment and say inwardly, "God, be merciful to me." Is your day going really well? Pause and say in your heart, "I thank you, God, for your presence to me," or say the name of Jesus at intervals during the day. It is something we can all do—it all happens in the heart.

"Take, Lord. You have given all to me; to you I return it. Do with it what you will." (St. Ignatius of Loyola)

Jeremiah 26.1-9 • Psalm 69 • Matthew 13.54-58

I f you will not listen to me, to walk in my law that I have set before you, and to heed the words of my servants the prophets whom I send to you urgently—though you have not heeded—then I will … make this city a curse for all the nations of the earth.

Jeremiah 26.4-6

Trust in the Lord

After Jeremiah speaks his prophecy, everyone panics, insisting that he must die. They are not listening to God's promise of love and fidelity that underpins his foreboding words. In our lives, we are not called to respond to God's word in a reactionary way, following the urges of the flesh. We are called to respond to it with the obedience of faith (see Romans 1.5; 16.26; Catechism of the Catholic Church no. 143), listening attentively to our Divine Lover, who wants only what is best for us, and speaks of evil only so that we may be spared from it. The Lord will sustain us in times of adversity in our faithfulness to discipleship.

Where do we go from here?

The Holy Spirit dwelling in our hearts is always prompting us to walk in God's ways. It is all very practical. We walk in the ways of God by choosing every day to do what is loving, to respect each person we meet, to be just and fair in our dealings, to be honest and truthful in small as well as in great things. Test yourself today. The Catechism of the Catholic Church is a wonderful tool for deepening your faith. Why not begin reading it, and form a discussion group with friends?

Lord, help me always to trust in your providential love, so that in obedient faith I might never abandon you out of fear.

Jeremiah 26.11-16, 24 • Psalm 69 • Matthew 14.1-12

Do not let the flood sweep over me,
or the deep swallow me up,
or the Pit close its mouth over me.

Psalm 69.15

Lord be with me

When we ask God to deliver us from suffering, we are really asking God to draw us to himself, to give us the grace to surrender to his will, and to see things from his vantage point. The psalmist praises God, despite his many grievances, because he knows that "all things work together for good for those who love God, who are called according to his purpose" (Romans 8.28). In this life, suffering is unavoidable. But we must recognize it as the suffering of death leading to life in God, for which we must "sing praise with all our skill" (Psalm 47.8).

Where do we go from here?

We live in a broken world, and suffering comes to all of us, whether we are following Jesus or not. God has promised to be with us during these times by his love and grace. We need to hold tight to that promise and trust God's loving presence in our life. When you find yourself in impossible situations, tell God about it and call upon his sustaining power. God has promised to be with us. We can hold God to that promise.

**Loving Father, help me to always turn to you
in my suffering, and see in it your gracious invitation
to rejoice in new life.**

Isaiah 55.1-3 • Psalm 145 • Romans 8.35, 37-39 • Matthew 14.13-21

Who will separate us from the love of Christ? Will hardship, or distress, or persecution, or famine, or nakedness, or peril, or sword? ... No, in all these things we are more than conquerors through him who loved us.

Romans 8.35, 37

We are conquerors

In this passage, Paul tells us not to be overly worried about the hardships we encounter, because in Jesus, we are conquerors. How can this be? St. Paul shows us that the only condition for God's love is our own reciprocation, our willingness to receive it. We cannot be separated from the love of Christ by any worldly or even spiritual power. God will never withdraw God's love from us. When we patiently endure the trials and sufferings of this world by the grace of God given to us in Christ, we are victorious, because whatever assails us is nothing compared to Jesus' love in us. We are more than conquerors, because we have already won the prize—God himself.

Where do we go from here?

Do you believe you are a conqueror? That nothing can separate you from Jesus' love? Look at the example of the saints. St. Paul is a wonderful example of how God's grace pursues us and strengthens us to meet every kind of adversity. Nothing can separate us from Jesus if we cling to him. Read St. Paul's letter to the Romans, Chapter 8: reflect on it, pray over it and look for ways to make the teaching a part of your life.

Lord Jesus, I love you.

Jeremiah 28.1-17 • Psalm 119 • Matthew 14.22-36

But when the disciples saw him walking on the sea, they were terrified, saying, "It is a ghost!" And they cried out in fear.
Matthew 14.26

God among us

Jesus came to show us who he is and what we could become. While the disciples struggle in their boat, Jesus leaves them to their own devices and spends hours in intimate conversation with his Father. When he sets off across the lake, he unabashedly makes use of his divine nature to walk on the water in front of them all. When Jesus reproaches Peter for his littleness of faith, he does so as a loving father would chide a child knowing that the child can do much better. Peter is still looking to the earthly, natural consequences and not to heaven, his final goal.

Where do we go from here?

St. John Vianney, whose feast day is today, is a powerful example of how God's grace can transform us. He did not do well with his studies in seminary; he almost failed to be ordained, and initially was denied the faculties to hear confessions. God knew better! By the grace of God, he became a renowned confessor. God can do great things in us and through us. Think of Mary's Magnificat: "God who is mighty has done great things for me."

St. John Vianney, pray for me, that I might recognize that my treasure is not on earth but in heaven.

Tuesday | AUGUST 5

Jeremiah 30.1-2, 12-15, 18-22 • Psalm 102 • Matthew 15.1-2, 10-14

Why do you cry out over your hurt? Your pain is incurable. … I am going to restore the fortunes of the tents of Jacob, and have compassion on his dwellings. … And you shall be my people, and I will be your God. *Jeremiah 30.15, 18, 22*

Healing

All God's people have been healed of an "incurable wound." The wound is original sin; the remedy is baptism, and in the sacrament of reconciliation, we are healed of the suffering and wounds of our sins. When God speaks of the atrocity of Israel's sin through his prophet Jeremiah, God is not relaying a message of despair. This is something God's people need to hear: in human terms, the situation is hopeless. If it were not for the unfathomable love of the Redeemer of Israel, all would be lost. Christ instituted his Church, the great hospital for the spiritually sick, even unto death, to give us the same message of hope.

Where do we go from here?

Hope is one of the theological virtues we receive at baptism. We are strengthened by hope, through the light of the Holy Spirit, to keep our eyes fixed on Jesus and the promise of eternal life. We are sustained by hope in all the circumstances of life, and we know God supports us beyond our meager strength to endure. It is wonderful to know that God gifts us with whatever we need to follow Jesus. We are never without help; we never have to do it alone! Count on it!

Lord, save me from my sins, and fill me with the hope of your resurrection.

223

Daniel 7.9-10, 13-14 or 2 Peter 1.16-19 • Psalm 97 • Matthew 17.1-9

T he mountains melt like wax before the Lord,
before the Lord of all the earth.
Psalm 97.5

Stand in awe before the Lord

On today's feast, this psalm does fitting homage to God's indescribable majesty. The psalmist has probably never actually seen mountains melt like wax, but he knows that, in the presence of the God of Israel, all creation trembles in awe. God is Being Itself, and all creation receives its being from God. When Jesus is transfigured on the mountain and reveals himself as God, Peter, James and John do not understand, though they see it with their own eyes. Jesus reveals his glory and the glory we will share. The words of the psalmist become almost incomprehensibly delirious with joy, pointing to the great glory they cannot contain but must proclaim.

Where do we go from here?

Jesus' transfiguration, which the Church celebrates today, is always a sign of the hope to which we are called. The Transfiguration gospel is also used on the second Sunday of Lent. It always surprises me that we have just begun Lent and God wants to encourage us. Whenever we hear this gospel, we can rejoice in God's plan for our life. Sit down today and outline a plan of how you are going to put God into the plan of your day, today and every day.

**Jesus, you still have many things to tell me.
Open my mind and heart to listen.**

Jeremiah 31.31-34 • Psalm 51 • Matthew 16.13-23

[J]esus] turned and said to Peter, "Get behind me, Satan! You are a stumbling block to me; for you are setting your mind not on divine things but on human things."
Matthew 16.23

To repent

When Jesus calls Peter "Satan," he is not equating him with the devil. Peter is called an "accuser" or "adversary" (from the Hebrew *satan*; see Job 1–2) for trying to deter Jesus from doing his Father's will. When Jesus tells Peter, "Get behind me," he is not renouncing the one he just made head of the Church. Rather, it is a call to repentance, to turn and stop trying to overrule his Master's teachings with those that come from "the will of the flesh" (John 1.13). Jesus tells him to "get behind": that it is better to follow in order to better lead. As I hear this call to repentance, how is the Lord asking me to "get behind" him?

Where do we go from here?

What things do I need to change in my life in order to follow Jesus? What events or circumstances that affect my life can be changed? We all need to take Jesus' call to repentance as a personal responsibility. The sacrament of reconciliation is God's gift in which we can meet Jesus and be healed; it is a source of ongoing spiritual growth.

**Lord, I cannot detect all my errors.
From hidden faults, acquit me. (Psalm 19.12)**

Nahum 1.15; 2.2; 3.1-3, 6-7 • Deuteronomy 32 • Matthew 16.24-28

Look! On the mountains the feet of one who brings good tidings, who proclaims peace!
Nahum 1.15

The gift of peace

Peace always comes at a price. The Good News is that victory is ours: will we take it? In today's gospel, Jesus tells us to take up our cross daily, in whatever form it comes, doing violence to our sinful passions and desires. The Lord, however, has compassion on his servants "when he sees that their power is gone" (Deuteronomy 32.36), and is crucified in their place. Jesus gains the victory in us by his power, knowing that we could never do it on our own. How can we proclaim the message of Christ's peace to someone today?

Where do we go from here?

Some people have an aura of peace and calmness about them. St. Dominic de Guzman, whose feast we celebrate today, was such a man. He was so loving and joyful that people were drawn to him, and he then brought them to Jesus. Do people feel drawn to you because of your life in Jesus? Ask Jesus for a loving and joyful heart. A kind word and a smile can transform a gloomy day.

Lord, help me to take up my cross and follow you, so that in perfect joy I may proclaim your peace to all I meet.

Saturday | AUGUST 9

Habakkuk 1.12–2.4 • Psalm 9 • Matthew 17.14-20

T he Lord is a stronghold for the oppressed,
a stronghold in times of trouble.
Psalm 9.9

God, my rock

It is easy to speak of God as "rock," "stronghold," "fortress," but what do we really mean when we say that? The most obvious answer is that God is there for us when we need him. Today's readings reveal much more about this aspect of our loving God. They show us that God does not move or change. Even when things seem hopeless, God assures us that God is still there, preparing for our redemption. Even when we behave like the same "faithless and perverse generation" of Matthew's gospel, God still shows tender concern by healing and saving us.

Where do we go from here?

We all have those days when nothing seems to go right and the best solution would be going back to bed! Begin the day with a prayer of thanksgiving. Think of three things you are grateful for and hold them in your heart as you begin the day. During the day, review some of the positive things that have come your way, and again thank the Lord. Develop a habit of gratitude, and rejoice in the Lord always.

**Jesus, my stronghold, help me to trust in your promise
as I await your redemption.**

I Kings 19.9, 11-13 • Psalm 85 • Romans 9.1-5 • Matthew 14.22-33

I have great sorrow and unceasing anguish in my heart. For I could wish that I myself were accursed and cut off from Christ for the sake of my own people, my kindred according to the flesh.

Romans 9.2-3

Meeting God

Paul suffers so much when God's chosen people, Israel, do not hear the message of his preaching. He knows, of course, that there is still hope for the Jews, but his heart cries out with longing for God's promise to be fulfilled. As Jesus goes about his earthly ministry, he reveals himself to be at once the long-awaited Messiah come to set his people free, as well as someone far beyond all their hopes and expectations. Elijah waits for God on the mountain, and when God finally arrives, the "sound of sheer silence" is too much to bear. We, too, will meet God in the sheer silence. Will we hear God's voice? Let us prepare our hearts by silent listening.

Where do we go from here?

We all share St. Paul's anguish at times—for a loved one whom we want to help, or perhaps a family member who is sick, away from the Church, or without work. We need to persevere in prayer and in hope, trusting these dear ones to the Lord. God's promise does not fail. This is our hope. Do not let go of the promise. Persevere in prayer.

**Lord God of hosts, I have been zealous for you.
Help me to see you as you truly are.**

Ezekiel 1.2-5, 24-28 • Psalm 148 • Matthew 17.22-27

"**G**o to the sea and cast a hook; take the first fish that comes up; and when you open its mouth, you will find a coin; take that and give it to them for you and me."

Matthew 17.27

God of surprises

In the questions Jesus asks Peter, he sets up a parallel between God the Father, the king of heaven and earth and ruler of the Temple, and the "kings of the earth." Jesus is free from the Temple tax, because he is Son of the Father, the one for whom the tax is being collected. It seems Peter has already forgotten the heavenly message of Christ's Transfiguration: "This is my Son, the Beloved." He apparently also does not understand what he has just been told a few moments ago about Jesus being killed and raised. So Jesus in his mercy sends Peter a "loaded" fish. How's that for a sign? Our God is a God of surprises! Let us take on the expectation and wonder of children.

Where do we go from here?

Do you seek signs of God's presence in your life? The sign of God's presence is your believing heart, your presence at the Eucharist year after year, times of prayer, and your perseverance in seeking the Lord. The sign of God is not in the "big bang" moments, but in the quiet faithfulness of following Jesus in the humdrum moments of the day. Stop to listen: God is speaking. Do not miss the quiet, still Word of love.

**Lord, may you give me the true sight
and clarity of vision afforded by faith,
and use even my blindness to your greater glory.**

Ezekiel 2.8–3.4 • Psalm 119 • Matthew 18.1-5, 10, 12-14

O pen your mouth and eat what I give you.
Ezekiel 2.8

To be found

The message of today's readings is threefold: we must become like little children to enter the kingdom of heaven; the word of God is sweet; and we are each entrusted with the mission of safeguarding the faith of our brothers and sisters, in that order. To be able to taste the sweetness of God's word, we must become humble like a child and "eat" what God gives to us. Thus, having tasted and digested the Word, we are able to speak that word to others, so that they might not be lost if they have gone astray. The word of God needs to enter our hearts enabling us to proclaim the good news.

Where do we go from here?

Open your mouth and eat what I have given you to eat. We eat the body of Jesus in the Eucharist. It is food that transforms us by taking us into Jesus, into the life of God. The word of God in the liturgy is meant to enter into our hearts. It is Jesus speaking to us. Before going to Mass, read and then reflect on the Scripture readings. What phrases jump out at you? What challenges you? Take the challenge seriously.

May I be humble and simple as a child, dear Jesus, to savour and delight in your word! May my soul find its rest in you, and so draw others to you in your glory.

Ezekiel 9.1-7; 10.18-22 • Psalm 113 • Matthew 18.15-20

W ho is like the Lord our God, who is seated on high, who looks far down on the heavens and the earth?
Psalm 113.5-6

Jesus is God's nearness

Instead of remembering that God "is seated on high," it seems sometimes as though God does not exist at all, or we forget that God is the All Holy One. The really wonderful thing is that God looks down on us, and also became one of us. We must be careful never to water down either aspect of God—God's radical transcendence or God's radical immanence—for they rely on each other. God became human to transform our human nature into God's divine nature. We do not see God's transcendence the way God does. The love of God that characterizes God as wholly, radically other makes God radically immanent to each of us. Jesus is our model of being like God, striving for an ever-greater holiness that will bind us all the more to our brothers and sisters.

Where do we go from here?

Does God seem very far away? The truth is that God is never far from any of us. Take time today to think about how much you are loved and cherished. Pray to the Holy Spirit for the gift of discernment and the humility to receive insights into what is wounded and in need of healing. Faith gives us a wonderful advantage in interpreting both the joys and the sorrows of living. God in Jesus wants us to know him, to be taught by the Holy Spirit, and to be brought into the infinite love and goodness of God.

God of heaven and earth, make your holiness manifest in me, that all might see your saving power in Christ Jesus.

Ezekiel 12.1-16 • Psalm 78 • Matthew 18.21–19.1

"You wicked slave! I forgave you all that debt because you pleaded with me. Should you not have had mercy on your fellow slave, as I had mercy on you?" *Matthew 18.32-33*

Be merciful

What we learn from this parable is how serious it is not to forgive our brother or sister. It is to reject the forgiveness and mercy Jesus offers us by his death on the cross. Our Lord died for us precisely so that we might be restored to the fullness of the image and likeness of God in which we were created. This means offering ourselves unreservedly to our neighbour, especially by forgiving all their transgressions against us, unconditionally, holding nothing back, so that we might truly accept the glorious sacrifice Jesus first made for us, unconditionally, holding nothing back.

Where do we go from here?

St. Maximilian Kolbe, whose feast day is today, is an example of what it means to lay down our lives for others as Jesus did. We can follow his example by daily forgiving the weakness of others and their offences. How many times do we have to forgive? Without measure. The ability to forgive is the sign of the Holy Spirit's presence within us. Forgiving is the sign of love. Is there someone whom you need to forgive? Have you been carrying resentment or a grudge against one of your brothers and sisters? Does what they did seem unforgiveable? God does not think so. Extend mercy and forgiveness to someone today.

St. Maximilian Kolbe, pray for me, that like Jesus, I might offer myself without reserve or condition to all of my brothers and sisters in gratitude for his great gift.

Revelation 11.19; 12.1-6, 10 • Psalm 45 • 1 Corinthians 15.20-26 • Luke 1.39-56

F or as all die in Adam, so all will be made alive in Christ.
1 Corinthians 15.22

Mary, a praise of God's glory

Because our Blessed Mother was preserved from original sin from the moment of her conception through the grace bestowed upon her in her mother's womb, she was likewise preserved from death. Her earthly life ran its course, to be sure, but her body and soul are even now united in glory with the Most Holy Trinity. She is already fully "alive in Christ." When we consider Mary's Assumption in light of this reading, we see how her glory is always God's glory and vice versa, so intimately united are they. It is no wonder, then, that God finds no greater praise in any of God's creatures than in humble Mary, the lowly handmaiden through whom God chose to make known the hidden ways of God, that we might be made alive in Christ.

Where do we go from here?

Am I alive in the Spirit? Is following Jesus a source of joy for me? Today, rejoice in being a Christ-follower, a disciple of Jesus. Joy is a gift of the Holy Spirit, which we received at baptism—activate it! Share your joy with others. Our Christian faith is our greatest treasure. The warranty is without limits and is eternal.

Holy Mary, Mother of God, on this feast of your Assumption, pray for us poor sinners, that as in Adam we have all died, so in Christ we may all be made truly alive.

Ezekiel 18.1-10, 13, 30-32 • Psalm 51 • Matthew 19.13-15

W hy will you die, O house of Israel? For I have no pleasure in the death of anyone, says the Lord God. Turn, then, and live.

Ezekiel 18.31-32

....

Delighting in God

This reading from Ezekiel may sound harsh at first. Perhaps it would sound better if we saw in it a heartbroken Lover, begging his beloved to quit their destructive behaviour and turn instead to Life. Then the message in today's first reading becomes more obvious: our salvation is dependent on the decisions we make to choose or to reject God in our lives.

God wants us to choose him. An even deeper, more intimate message is that God takes pleasure in us. We see the same thing in today's gospel when Jesus, who is usually busy teaching, reproving, healing or prophesying, takes time to bless the little children. What a beautiful image of God's pleasure in us!

Where do we go from here?

Choose life! Hearing the word of God and putting it into practice is to choose life. Take one of Jesus' words in the gospel and put it into practice. Choose a challenging one and spend the day saying yes. We become virtuous by doing, not by theorizing.

With all my heart I seek you, O God. Do not let me wander from your commandments, so that I may live, and let my only delight be in you. (See Psalm 119.10.)

Isaiah 56.1, 6-7 • Psalm 67 • Romans 11.13-15, 29-32 • Matthew 15.21-28

"Lord, help me." He answered, "It is not fair to take the children's food and throw it to the dogs." She said, "Yes, Lord, yet even the dogs eat the crumbs that fall from their masters' table."

Matthew 15.25-27

A banquet

Many hear Jesus speak, and they witness the miracles he performs, but they do not accept him or his teachings. Yet a Canaanite woman recognizes him and addresses him as Lord, Son of David. She asks for the healing of her daughter who is tormented by a demon. Seemingly rebuffed, her response impresses Jesus, and he commends her great faith. An outsider discerns the worth of table scraps while those with an invitation to the banquet (see Luke 14.16-24) decline the invitation.

Where do we go from here?

Would you be satisfied with table scraps? Can you persevere in the face of a seeming rebuke? Jesus truly thirsts for us. He longs to shower us with his blessings, but he will not impose himself. He waits for us. God wants to give to you abundantly all the gifts of the Spirit. Open your mind and heart to receive. Name two ways that God is waiting for an answer from you, waiting for you to respond.

O Lord, help me to recognize when I am settling for scraps, and grant me the grace to hunger for more.

Ezekiel 24.15-24 • Deuteronomy 32 • Matthew 19.16-22

Y ou were unmindful of the Rock that bore you;
you forgot the God who gave you birth.
Deuteronomy 32.18

Remembering God

I could not wait to get my first job. I equated it in many ways with freedom. If I had my own income, I wouldn't have to run to my parents for my needs (which were really just my wants). At one point, I even suggested to them that I could survive on the standard tax deduction allowed per child if they wanted to turn that over to me. For some reason, I equated extra spending money with the provision of all that would be needed, totally forgetting necessities such as shelter, food and transportation. Worse yet, in this desire for independence, I did not even factor in the most important of needs: home, family and love. In essence, I forgot my responsibility to my family. Independence became my idol. My family deserved better. So does God.

Where do we go from here?

Our society defines freedom as being without restraint, doing what is good for me. In fact, these are good working definitions for selfishness. St. Paul teaches us that "For freedom Christ has set us free" (Galatians 5.1-3). When Christ makes us free, then we are truly free. Jesus expects us to use the gift of freedom to serve others in love. Take time to meditate on chapter 5 of Galatians.

**Lord, help me recognize the idols I have substituted for you,
the one true God, and grant me the grace to return to you
with my whole heart.**

Ezekiel 28.1-10 • Deuteronomy 32 • Matthew 19.23-30

" I f you wish to be perfect, go, sell your possessions, and give the money to the poor, and you will have treasure in heaven; then come, follow me."
Matthew 19.21

....

True riches

By the world's standards, amassing a fortune is both a goal and an important measure of success. Being wealthy is a responsibility to share our blessings with others, an opportunity to be aware of the needs of others and to be generous in providing for those who are less fortunate. However, if there is a "disconnect" between wealth and charity, we put ourselves in a perilous position. In our pride over our achievements, we may become blind to the needs of others and to our own shortcomings. We begin to believe that money is a tool that not only can buy us happiness, but can even pay our way out of difficult situations. Our true riches are in heaven. It is far better to be poor in this world, for the sake of the kingdom, and rich in the next. God has promised. Who am I to argue?

Where do we go from here?

Jesus tells us that of those who have much, much will be expected. That "much" refers not only to money, but also to the gifts of nature and grace that we have been given. They are to be put at the service of others. Am I a writer? Then I can share good words with others. Am I strong? Then I can help those who are weak. Whatever I am good at belongs not only to me, but to my brothers and sisters also. I have nothing that I have not received.

Lord, all things are a gift from you. Help me to use my riches wisely by using them in your service.

Ezekiel 34.1-11 • Psalm 23 • Matthew 20.1-16

For thus says the Lord God: I myself will search for my sheep, and will seek them out.   *Ezekiel 34.11*

Lost and found

As a child, I had an uncanny knack for getting lost, most often whenever we would travel seven miles into the city for Saturday shopping. Something would catch my eye, and before I knew it, strangers surrounded me and I had lost sight of my family. The worst incident came when I went with my uncle into Detroit for the wake of Cardinal Mooney. I got separated from my uncle, so I walked up and down the streets, sure that I would find his car. When that failed, I turned myself in to the "lost and found" at the Cathedral. This was truly a prophetic experience. Lost as a child, I was carried by a priest into the Cathedral of the Blessed Sacrament. Lost as an adult, I was led to the Blessed Sacrament. God truly did shepherd me. Thanks be to God!

Where do we go from here?

Do I feel lost? That is a good sign, because it is the first step to being found. If I do not know I am lost, then I have no need to be found. In what ways do I feel lost or alienated? What do I think are the solutions? Begin asking the questions so that you can find the answers. The Holy Spirit is the best guide. Pray for understanding. It is a very practical first step. And then listen, and believe an answer will come. The next essential step is to act on what God is asking.

Lord, many have strayed and are lost.
In your great mercy, through the intercession of St. Bernard,
whose feast we celebrate today, bring them home.

Ezekiel 36.23-28 • Psalm 51 • Matthew 22.1-14

"For many are called, but few are chosen."
Matthew 22.14

To be chosen

Early in my journey back into the Church, after more than twenty years away, I went on pilgrimage to Medjugorje. Our Lady was still appearing to several visionaries daily. When I arrived at the church, a small crowd had formed at a side door, and a young man was selecting who would go in. Not knowing what this was all about, I just stood back and waited—wanting to be picked but not sure for what. I remember thinking that God would have to take care of it. The young man made his final selections, went in and closed the door. Suddenly it reopened, and the few of us still remaining were invited in. The young man was one of the visionaries. Although I felt and saw nothing, I was being inwardly transformed. It began with that initial trust in God's providential care.

Where do we go from here?

Jesus says to each of us, "You have not chosen me, but I have chosen you." Jesus has chosen me—he has a purpose for my life. We are chosen to make the journey, stretching us to our full human potential as lovers of life, beauty and truth. We encounter God in the places where we live our life and among the people we rub shoulders with. The great challenge is learning to be happy in and find God where we are at this moment. We are all prone to the "if only" doldrums. God uses everything in our life to bring us to holiness—everything can be recycled for eternal life.

**O Lord, grant me the grace to hear your call
and the disposition of heart to be chosen.**

Ezekiel 37.1-14 • Psalm 107 • Matthew 22.34-40

For he satisfies the thirsty,
and the hungry he fills with good things.
Psalm 107.9

....

God hears our prayers

One of the greatest sorrows of many who come asking for our prayers is that they have family and loved ones who have not only left the Church, but no longer believe in God. It is particularly painful when they recognize that their witness has been less than stellar. Some express a sense of helplessness and a fear that time for conversion is running out. So, what can we do? There is only one answer. Pray. Our job is to prepare the soil with prayer so that it may be receptive and bear great fruit. Then let God do the rest. For God "satisfies the thirsty and the hungry he fills with good things."

Where do we go from here?

Today we celebrate the Queenship of Mary, the Mother of Jesus, who intercedes for her children. She can show us how to be faithful disciples of Jesus. Like Mary, each of us has been called in a unique way to follow Jesus. What is your call? To become involved in Church ministry, to serve the poor, or to be a prayerful presence in the world pointing to Jesus? How are you meant to minister to others?

Mary, our Queen and Mother, pray for us and for all those we love, that we may hunger for the good things of God.

Ezekiel 43.1-7 • Psalm 85 • Matthew 23.1-12

" The greatest among you will be your servant. All who exalt themselves will be humbled, and all who humble themselves will be exalted."

Matthew 23.11-12

Glorify the Lord

One day as I was on my way to pray before the Blessed Sacrament, I was stopped to address a problem one of the sisters was having with a malfunctioning piece of equipment. After a few minutes of examination, I saw that the wires were incorrectly connected. When I arrived in chapel, I spent the first few minutes congratulating myself for my "brilliance" at recognizing the problem so quickly and fixing it. Then, realizing what I was doing and remembering why I had come in the first place, I apologized to the Lord for my self-centredness and asked forgiveness. How absurd it was to have come to glorify the Lord by singing my own praises! I would far rather hear the Lord call me a good and faithful servant than hand him a resumé telling him why I qualified as one.

Where do we go from here?

We are not humble in order to be exalted! It just doesn't work that way. We are humble because that is the truth. No matter what our position or how important we may be, in the sight of God we are totally dependent on grace. We are also dependent on one another—no one is totally self-sufficient. This is a cause for joy: we do not have to do it alone! Allowing someone to help us gives dignity to the other. Let someone help you today—it is a gift. If you don't want help, you probably need it.

**Lord, forgive me for the times I come to you
with my mind full of distractions and my heart full of self.**

Isaiah 22.15, 19-23 • Psalm 138 • Romans 11.33-36 • Matthew 16.13-20

"**F**or who has known the mind of the Lord? Or who has been his counsellor?"
Romans 11:34

Who is in charge?

How many times have I tried to tell God my better way of doing things, or rationalized my behaviour because what God wanted didn't seem reasonable anymore? Yes, I have tried before to be that counsellor, not that I know the mind of God … or maybe I do.

I think I give God a chuckle. How could my plan possibly be better than God's? God's wisdom resides in the Church. The keys were given to Peter. No amount of creative reasoning will put them into my hands. Speak, Lord, your servant is listening.

Where do we go from here?

Let us pray for the light of the Holy Spirit to "know the mind of the Lord" in our life, and seek the counsel of the Spirit, that we may walk in God's way. Jesus tells us in the gospel that he sends the Spirit into our heart so that we may understand all he has taught. Listening and the willingness to be small and open as a little child are essential for our life of faith. Think of the beautiful example of St. Thérèse of Lisieux and her "little way."

Help me, O Lord, to recognize your voice when those to whom you have given authority speak in your name.

2 Thessalonians 1.1-5, 11-12 • Psalm 96 • Matthew 23.13-22

"But woe to you, scribes and Pharisees, hypocrites! For you lock people out of the kingdom of heaven."   *Matthew 23.13*

Learning curves

Hypocrisy evokes a strong response of indignation. Jesus warns us to observe what the Pharisees have to say, but not to follow what they do. The moral message of the hypocrite loses its force when the hypocrisy is brought to light; hence, damage is done by those who profess one thing while doing another.

A word of caution is needed. Am I holding others to a standard that is impractical or unjust? For example, one day I was a laywoman, the next I was dressed in a religious habit. I needed time to develop new ways of speaking and acting in harmony with my new way of life. The habit did not come with the automatic installation of wisdom and virtue. What it does signify is a desire to grow in both. Thank God for learning curves!

Where do we go from here?

If you find yourself surrounded by hypocrites, it is probably because you are projecting. An important lesson of the spiritual life is that the only person I can change is myself. So get on with it! Usually when we work on changing what is wrong with us, we do not have time or energy to try to change others. Another wonderful principle of the spiritual life is this: at least once a day, laugh at yourself. It is a very healthy exercise.

Dear Lord, with my prayers, help me to assist those striving to be closer to you, and let others be patient with me as I journey toward you.

2 Thessalonians 2.1-3, 14-17 • Psalm 96 • Matthew 23.23-26

S o then, brothers and sisters, stand firm and hold fast to the traditions that you were taught by us, either by word of mouth or by our letter.   *2 Thessalonians 2.15*

Stand firm

From the outset, the Church had to address errors introduced by those who misinterpreted teachings or events, whether innocently or maliciously. The letter to the Thessalonians was written to counter misconceptions concerning the second coming of Christ, which some were maintaining was imminent.

Preoccupation with the second coming continues to this day, with some people going so far as to predict the exact date and hour. The folly of this becomes clear as that day passes with no results. This leads to ridicule, and, more seriously, to a falling away from true faith. It is important for us as Christians to "stand firm and hold fast to the traditions that you were taught by us." As Catholics, we can be sure we are on firm ground if we follow the teachings of the Church.

Where do we go from here?

God is eternal and we are creatures of time, but we do have an eternal moment in which to serve: now. The past is gone. I cannot retrieve it; I can make amends and learn from it. I cannot know what tomorrow will bring; I can plan for it and then let it go. I exist and live and love and serve only in God's eternal "now." Think about it.

**Lord, you promised that you would not leave us orphans.
Grant that we may remain obedient to the shepherds
you have left us to lead us safely back to you.**

2 Thessalonians 3.6-10, 16-18 • Psalm 128 • Matthew 23.27-32

K eep away from believers who are living in idleness and not according to the tradition that they received from us.
2 Thessalonians 3.6

To work for God

Most of us have very little tolerance for "deadbeats," whether it is someone who avoids financial obligations or one who manages to avoid work. Paul is addressing an even bigger problem: those who have strayed from the Truth passed on to them and who believe the second coming of Christ is at hand. Why work? Why be productive if it is all going to end soon anyway? Not only were they in error, but also they were adversely influencing others.

I once met someone who accumulated a massive credit card debt because of the belief that a cataclysmic event was imminent. The debt would be of no consequence once the disaster occurred. That erroneous belief led to severe financial hardship for the whole family, not to mention the moral implications. Disaster did occur, but not the one anticipated.

Where do we go from here?

St. Monica, whose feast day is today, is a great example of persevering prayer. For years, she prayed for her son, the great St. Augustine, without seeing any change. God did hear her prayer and took note of her tears. Are you praying for someone special? Do not lose hope. Know that your prayers are not wasted. God will apply them at the proper time.

Dear Lord, through the intercession of St. Monica, lead all those for whom we pray away from error and into the fullness of Truth.

I Corinthians 1.1-9 • Psalm 145 • Matthew 24.42-51

K eep awake therefore, for you do not know on what day your
Lord is coming. *Matthew 24.42*

The Lord is coming

I probably should not admit this, but I am not particularly keen on
suffering. However, that fear is not as intense as the fear of dying
suddenly and having the sisters make sense of what I have managed
to fit into my monastic cell (from the Latin *cella*, meaning a small
chamber). At least if I have a long enough illness, I may be able to
trim things down to a more manageable (read: "less embarrassing")
state. I'm hanging on to scraps of paper with names and phone numbers of people whose names I no longer recognize, just in case they
are important for me to have, since I probably should remember
who they are.

All this concern for the material state of my cell: I pray that my
soul is in better shape than that.

Where do we go from here?

Until God started nudging his heart, the great St. Augustine, whose
feast we celebrate today, spent many years caught in the cycle
of self-gratification and pleasure and unhealthy relationships. He
knew he needed to change; his response was "yes, but not yet."
His heart was cluttered with fears and unrest, needing to be emptied and swept clean by the Holy Spirit. Our sense of dissatisfac-
tion is often the prompting of the Holy Spirit to seek something
more. St. Augustine reminds us that nothing is impossible for God.

**Lord, St. Augustine came to know that you are
all that matters. Through his intercession,
may I be found ready when you come.**

Jeremiah 1.17-19 • Psalm 71 • Mark 6.17-29

The king was deeply grieved; yet out of regard for his oaths and for the guests, he did not want to refuse her.
Mark 6.26

....

Addictions

If I were to come up with a recipe for disaster, one that could ruin many lives, I do not think I could do better than King Herod. Take one part alcohol, one part loosened tongue and add a double measure of pride, and you've got the makings of trouble. While we may not be in a situation where someone loses her head because of our imprudence, I am not so sure that the outcome will not be as deadly. How many lives have been lost due to drinking and driving?

How many friendships, marriages and families are destroyed by alcohol and loosened tongues? How many reputations have we tarnished or seriously compromised with our gossip? A good formula is to stop, to think and to pray that the Lord will be with you to deliver you (see Jeremiah 1.19).

Where do we go from here?

We need to pray earnestly about those things in our lives that hold us in bondage. Possessing everything we want is not always what gives us happiness; having more or having in excess can deter us from enjoying or appreciating true happiness. Do you know someone struggling with addiction? Pray for them earnestly; encourage them to seek help and support them by your love.

Lord, in your righteousness deliver me and rescue me; incline your ear to me and save me. (Psalm 71.2)

1 Corinthians 1.26-31 • Psalm 33 • Matthew 25.14-30

"Then the one who had received the one talent also came forward, saying, 'Master, I knew that you were a harsh man ... so I was afraid, and I went and hid your talent in the ground.'"

Matthew 25.24-25

Take the risk

I can relate all too well to the servant who took the one talent and hid it in the ground. To invest the sum would have meant that he was taking a risk that might lead to a loss. Better, therefore, to hide it away than to have to face the master later.

Our faith is like that, too: living it to the fullest means you might have to take the risk of being ridiculed, even despised for standing firm and loyal to the teachings of the Church. To compartmentalize our beliefs by not taking them into the public square is to fail to witness to the beauty and truth of our faith. To say it is a private matter is to effectively bury it. To be a Christian means committing to a way of life permeated by Jesus and formed by his teaching.

Where do we go from here?

Having the courage to take risks and to visibly live our Christian commitment by the ways we choose to shape our lives is life-giving. Fear of standing out or being different often holds us back. How much time do you spend thinking about how others see you in ratio to thinking about how God sees you? We need to live from our centre, to be who we are and give our unique contribution without fear. The only important question is "Am I doing what God asks?" God will sustain us by God's grace.

Dear Lord, help me to grow rich, and to be an effective witness to the beauty of your Truth, to the joy of a life lived in you.

Jeremiah 20.7-9 • Psalm 63 • Romans 12.1-2 • Matthew 16.21-27

F or you have been my help,
and in the shadow of your wings I sing for joy.
Psalm 63.7

The shadow of God's wings

One day at Morning Prayer, we were chanting Psalm 63. I glanced up at the crucifix hanging over the organ. The overhead lights cast a shadow of the outstretched arms of Christ on the cross that very much resembled the wings of a bird in flight. It was then that I realized that to be in the shadow of his wings was to be stationed at the foot of the cross. It is by means of that cross that we become disciples of Jesus.

Despite my human weakness, I know that the foot of the cross is where I need to be, and that the Lord will always be there as my help. From there, in the shadow of his wings, I sing for joy.

Where do we go from here?

The Spirit of the Lord hovered over the beginning of all creation. The Spirit of the Lord hovered over Mary to bring about the new creation. The Spirit of the Lord hovers over each of us to guide us into becoming a new creation for God and a light for our brothers and sisters. Each of us has been called by God to be filled with the Spirit. Today, say "yes" to receive the fullness of God's loving presence.

**Thank you, O Lord, for your life-giving sacrifice
on the cross and for the shelter it provides those who
take refuge in its shadow.**

1 Corinthians 2.1-5 • Psalm 119 • Luke 4.16-30

Your commandment makes me wiser than my enemies,
for it is always with me.
Psalm 119.98

....

God's commandment: love

This verse from Psalm 119 reveals something very important about God. God's commandment makes the psalmist wise because it is always with him. It is in God that "we live and move and have our being" (Acts 17.28). We rely on God's wisdom. This is why Paul preaches the "holy folly" of the cross, which demonstrates not human wisdom, but "the power of God" (1 Corinthians 2.5). God's commandment teaches us how to love, how to become like the Father, in his Son, through the Spirit. Does it not follow, then, that we would have all things besides? (See Romans 8.32.)

Where do we go from here?

Wisdom is a gift of the Holy Spirit. We receive the seven gifts of the Holy Spirit at baptism and in the sacrament of confirmation to enable us to live God's very life. These gifts are basic to our faith. Can you name all seven? Look up the meaning of the gifts of the Holy Spirit in the *Catechism of the Catholic Church* online (no. 1303). The fruit of wisdom is love. God gifts us with God's love, enabling us to love others without measure.

**Jesus, Son of God, help me to listen to the voice
of the Father as you did, even unto death.**

1 Corinthians 2.10-16 • Psalm 145 • Luke 4.31-37

I n the synagogue there was a man who had the spirit of an unclean demon, and he cried out with a loud voice … "I know who you are, the Holy One of God." But Jesus rebuked him, saying, "Be silent, and come out of him!"
Luke 4.33-35

Drawn to Jesus

Why is there a demon in the synagogue, and why does it seem he is trying to pick a fight with Jesus? You can tell he's afraid. In Jesus' time, if you knew someone's name, you had power over him. In desperation, the demon tries his only weapon: "I know who you are, the Holy One of God." It does not work. This scene in the synagogue is not mere happenstance. The Spirit of God (who is ever present with Jesus, as is the Father) is constantly vigilant, overseeing his beloved creation to preserve and sustain it. In God's provident love, it seems as though this demon was drawn to Jesus expressly for the purpose of manifesting Jesus' power and liberating one of his beloved sons. We are constantly being drawn unawares into his loving arms.

Where do we go from here?

It is a gift to recognize who Jesus is. Who is Jesus for me? We can find the answer to that question in prayer. By setting aside times for prayer and for silent listening, we develop a relationship with Jesus. We learn to follow Jesus and to be transformed by our prayer conversation with him. Jesus promises we will find joy and peace in him. Trust in this promise and make time in your day to be with the Lord.

Loving Jesus, help me to let myself be drawn by your healing power, especially when I feel most helpless, unloved and afraid.

I Corinthians 3.1-9 • Psalm 33 • Luke 4.38-44

So neither the one who plants nor the one who waters is anything, but only God who gives the growth.
I Corinthians 3.7

God gives the growth

When Paul says this, it is not to strip us of all dignity, for our dignity is inherent in our participation in Christ. St. Paul talks about the significance of each member of Christ's Body having their own unique, necessary function (1 Corinthians 12). He is trying to teach the Corinthians a lesson, to help them realize that their "jealousy and quarrelling" are not of God but "of the flesh." Do we find ourselves tempted to jealousy because someone seems to enjoy greater privileges, instead of giving thanks that we are members of Christ's Body with our own unique gifts? God's grace accompanies each of us. God is not glorified by anything I have accomplished but because I allowed God to accomplish it in me. If I am not receptive to God's work, how can I possibly blame anyone else?

Where do we go from here?

Factions never give life. Jealously and quarrelling bring division and rivalry. God has created each of us uniquely special, endowed with our particular strengths and gifts of love to create harmony among people. Rather than looking at what someone else has, give thanks to God for who you are and all that you can accomplish with God's help.

All-powerful Creator, grant me the grace I need to recognize the marvellous work you are doing in and through me so that I might rejoice exultantly.

1 Corinthians 3.18-23 • Psalm 24 • Luke 5.1-11

Who shall ascend the hill of the Lord?
And who shall stand in his holy place?
Those who have clean hands and pure hearts …

Psalm 24.3-4

Rejoice in God's gifts

How should we feel when we read these words? Intimidated because our hands and hearts might not be pure enough to stand before God? Pleased at "making the cut" because we manage to get to church occasionally? Rather, we should rejoice in the gift of faith and grace that our good Lord has given us. We should stand in perfect awe of God's majesty, for "the earth is the Lord's and all that is in it," including our very selves. This does not mean we are not responsible for keeping our hands clean and our hearts pure. It means that, while we must participate in the effort, God is the one who actually gets the job done. However, as this psalm affirms, when we "seek the face of the God of Jacob," God gets to work on us, and for that we can stand in humble amazement.

Where do we go from here?

Who will climb the mountain of the Lord? It is simple: those who seek God. If we seek God, we will find God. God is not hiding; God wants to be found. Remember the story of Genesis! God was not hiding from Adam and Eve. They were hiding from God. What is causing you to hide from God? Seek the Lord; seek to do what is necessary to have God as part of your life. You will find yourself sitting on God's mountain, surrounded by beauty.

God of Jacob, may I be ever mindful that you are my mighty king and I am your treasured possession, your beloved child.

1 Corinthians 4.1-5 • Psalm 37 • Luke 5.33-39

"Y ou cannot make wedding guests fast while the bridegroom is with them, can you? The days will come when the bridegroom will be taken away from them, and then they will fast in those days."

Luke 5.34-35

The bridegroom

When Jesus schools the scribes and Pharisees, he is not trying to teach them how to repair garments or properly store and drink wine. His point is that they do not recognize who he is. "Look at me," he seems to say. "I am the Bridegroom whom you have been awaiting so long! Rejoice while there is still time!" The parable he tells points at their blindness. Jesus also implies that their ways are innovations deviating from God's plan, and these have blinded them to who he is. He does not denounce the necessary disciplines of fasting and prayer, but insists that they must be practised in accord with right reason and prudential judgment—according to God's will and for God's glory, not their own.

Where do we go from here?

The truest fasting is fasting from harsh words or unkind judgments. Jesus came among us precisely to take upon himself human love and compassion, our human weakness and the effects of sin and death itself. Our imperfections cannot separate us from God. Nothing can separate us from God's love. In our turn, we want to bear the burdens of our brothers and sisters in love as Jesus bore ours.

Lord, when I remember my sins and how they have estranged me from you, help me, in virtuous obedience to your voice in the Church, to turn again to you in fasting and prayer.

I Corinthians 4.6-15 • Psalm 145 • Luke 6.1-5

We have become like the rubbish of the world, the dregs of all things, to this very day. I am not writing this to make you ashamed, but to admonish you as my beloved children.

I Corinthians 4.13-14

....

Beloved children

In today's first reading, Paul admonishes his "children," because they have become glutted on their apparent successes. He reminds them that they have nothing that they did not first receive, and so have no reason to boast. As he compares his situation to theirs, he says, "Be imitators of me."

We are called to offer our lives in sacrifice for the spread of God's kingdom: an offering pleasing to God that will bear fruit through the Holy Spirit. We wait in faith for the fruit to ripen and the kingdom to be manifest. Our task is only to be faithful.

Where do we go from here?

Scripture is like a mirror reflecting truth. Your continued interaction with the word of God—taking it in, memorizing it and allowing it to interact with your thoughts, memories and desires—brings true self-understanding and conversion. Faithfulness to the power of God's word will transform your mind and heart. Through the word, we can bear fruit and be faithful in our following of Jesus.

Crucified God of Love, teach me to be faithful to you in loving sacrifice so that my life may bear much fruit for the sake of the gospel.

Ezekiel 33.7-9 • Psalm 95 • Romans 13.8-10 • Matthew 18.15-20

Love does no wrong to a neighbour; therefore, love is the fulfilling of the law.
Romans 13.10

Love is the fulfillment of law

If fulfilling the law is as easy as remembering to love, why do we have so many laws? God is love. What should our love be? Jesus is our model of God's love. He emptied himself (Philippians 2.7) in order to show us the true face of our God, who is love. When we empty ourselves, we surrender ourselves in trust. God provides us with laws and guidelines so that we know how to love in deed and in truth; it is God's Holy Spirit who is always guiding us.

Where do we go from here?

Jesus is our example for loving. He altered the second commandment, "Love your neighbour as yourself," by telling us to love one another as he loves us. The New Testament tells us what it means to love as Jesus loves. It is to do what the Father in heaven tells us, and to allow the Holy Spirit to guide us. Christian love is expressed in practical deeds. The test of our love for God is how much we love our brothers and sisters. If someone comes to you in need today, find a way to help.

Sweetest Mary, my Mother, help me to love as Jesus loved, as you loved, so that I might be restored to the image and likeness of God in which I was made.

Romans 8.28-30 or Micah 5.2-5 • Psalm 13 • Matthew 1.1-16, 18-23

I will sing to the Lord,
because he has dealt bountifully with me.
Psalm 13.6

Rejoice in our salvation

Today we celebrate the Nativity of the Blessed Virgin Mary. Considering the innocence of our Blessed Mother, who was and remained sinless from her conception, and then the native innocence of other babies and children, there seems to be some kind of gap. As we mature, we tend to lose that innocence. Mary is our model of receptive openness to God's grace. She knows that this Saviour whom she bore is faithful to his promise of healing mercy and salvation. She rejoices, because salvation was hers from the beginning, but even more so, her joy is complete because that salvation came to all of creation.

Where do we go from here?

Mary's mission was to give birth to the Word of God through the power of the Holy Spirit. It was by grace she was able to achieve God's purpose in her life. Each of us receives a divine call that can change not only us as individuals, but our world, our time, our workspace and our small part of creation. This is our profound Christian hope as disciples. What purpose does God wish to achieve through you?

Dear Blessed Mother, help me to see how bountifully the Lord has dealt with you, so that in you, I might recognize that I, too, have been made a new creation in Christ.

I Corinthians 6.1-11 • Psalm 149 • Luke 6.12-19

A nd all in the crowd were trying to touch him, for power came out from him and healed all of them.
Luke 6.19

The tender power of God

It is no coincidence that this account of healing follows Jesus' choosing his apostles.

Jesus spent the night in prayer with his Father before choosing the apostles so that he might share that divine intimacy with us through their ministry. Jesus continues to heal and teach us through the ministers of the Church, and through all of our brothers and sisters who go forth in the strength of the sacraments. Let us remember in a special way our pope and all of the Church's servant-leaders.

Where do we go from here?

What can I do to make the Church more visible as a community of love, as a place where the gospel teaching of Jesus invites people to "come and see" why these Christians love each other so much? How can I make my parish a place of welcome? It is easy to complain about the way things are in my parish and to expect things to be different, instead of being part of the reason why things are changing. Get involved. Help people to feel welcome and loved. Invite friends to help you.

Lord, fill your Church with the Spirit to continue Jesus' ministry of healing and forgiveness.

1 Corinthians 7.1, 17, 25-31 • Psalm 45 • Luke 6.20-26

T he present form of this world is passing away.
1 Corinthians 7.31

I am with you

When Paul wrote to the Corinthians, Jesus' return was considered imminent. They needed to know what to do to be ready for his coming. Jesus has not yet come again in glory, but he does come for each one of us at the end of our life. Now is our time to serve and to grow in God's love, the arena where we prepare for eternal life. What do I need to do to be ready? How is my life shaped to God's glory, to being a praise of the God who is so near? Let me walk each day in the light of the Holy Spirit.

Where do we go from here?

We do not like to think about death. Our culture avoids it. Yet as Christians, death is not the end but the beginning. We walk with Jesus and, like Jesus, should fix our eyes on where we are going, our completion in eternal life. We need to share our hope by the way we live our life. Pray to the Holy Spirit to increase your love for God and for your brothers and sisters so that love will blossom one day into the joy of eternal life. How do you view death? Is it a fearful thing or a doorway into the fullness of life?

**Lord, help me to be faithful in all circumstances
so that I may use every possible opportunity to glorify
your holy name with all I am and have.**

Thursday | **SEPTEMBER 11**

1 Corinthians 8.1-7, 11-13 • Psalm 139 • Luke 6.27-38

S earch me, O God, and know my heart;
test me and know my thoughts.
See if there is any wicked way in me,
and lead me in the way everlasting.

Psalm 139.23-24

You know me

Psalm 139 is a beautiful hymn to the ineffable mystery and intimacy of God, an intimacy that is even greater than that of a mother and her child. The psalmist knows that to live a righteous life, he must ask for wisdom and knowledge from God, who knows him better than he knows himself. When left to our own devices, most of us breeze through life assuming we are basically good. God, who defines the standard of true goodness, knows better. I need to allow the Holy Spirit to shed light on every corner of my inward spirit so that I might be healed of sin. Let us ask God constantly for light and guidance, trusting always in God's mercy.

Where do we go from here?

Nothing can be hidden from God. God knows my inmost being. God sees the deepest truth of who I am to be in God's love. Pray to see how God sees you; begin the process of becoming a new creation. Forming new habits changes our behaviour. In what areas of your life do you feel that you need to change? Choose one habitual action that you would like to change. Work at it daily and resolve to persevere. God's grace will heal and transform you.

Even before a word is on my tongue, O Lord, you know it completely. If I have strayed from the path you have set before me, in your mercy draw me back into your love.

1 Corinthians 9.16-19, 22-27 • Psalm 84 • Luke 6.39-42

"**C**an a blind person guide a blind person? Will not both fall into a pit? A disciple is not above the teacher, but everyone who is fully qualified will be like the teacher."

Luke 6.39-40

How am I blind?

It is easy to understand Jesus' words in this gospel as condemnation for putting ourselves above others. Perhaps, instead, it is simply Jesus telling us that God sees everything; we must depend on God for guidance. Our light and understanding comes from God. Let us live in dependence upon this light, and see with God's vision. The beautiful and awesome thing about this is that, by God's divine life given to us in the sacraments, God shines God's light through us. If we abandon ourselves wholeheartedly to God's grace, we "will be like the teacher," and become a light to others.

Where do we go from here?

How do we know if we are blind? Are there things you do not want to face about yourself? This could be an indication of something you do not want to see—a kind of blindness. Take a criticism someone has shared with you about yourself. Instead of ignoring or rejecting it, take time to reflect on it. Is there truth in it? An honest and humble dialogue with our perceived weakness or lack can be an important opportunity for growth in our spiritual life.

Father, shed your light on my ignorant blindness, and through the grace of the sacraments, help me always to illumine the path of others by pointing back to you.

1 Corinthians 10.14-22 • Psalm 116 • Luke 6.43-49

Y ou cannot partake of the table of the Lord and the table of demons. Or are we provoking the Lord to jealousy? Are we stronger than he?

1 Corinthians 10.21-22

Faith and culture

In modern living, we experience a struggle between faith and culture. Martyrdom is not an immanent likelihood in our Western culture, but the Church is nonetheless persecuted through society's hatred of its morals, the culture's refusal to accept its standards of decency, the difficulty within ourselves of being true to the gospel. We need to recognize who we are as beloved children of God. We are Christ's body, the visible presence of his love. Our firmness of faith and love for one another give witness to God's presence among us.

Where do we go from here?

Our decisions determine how the story of our lives will unfold. God leaves us free. Morality concerns what we have in our hearts. We live a moral life by the choices that turn us to God. When we choose wrongly, God does not abandon us but knocks gently on the doors of our hearts for entrance. Our sinful choices do not thwart God's plan but only slow our spiritual growth. God is ever ready to forgive our sins. God's forgiveness does not change God; it changes us. Our life in God is a win-win situation. Here is a spiritual barometer: What desires fill your heart?

O God, you see all things and sustain them in your love; give us the strength to love without measure.

Numbers 21.4-9 • Psalm 78 • Philippians 2.6-11 • John 3.13-17

He humbled himself and became obedient to the point of death—even death on a cross. *Philippians 2.8*

Mad love

Everything is a free, gratuitous gift of our merciful God. The prodigal love of our Saviour, the God who is unthinkably, madly inebriated with love for us, obediently embraced death that we might have abundant life. Christ "emptied himself" (Philippians 2.7) and was obedient to the will of his Father. In the Blessed Trinity, we find our example of true love—a total outpouring of love.

Where do we go from here?

The cross is the sign of God's gift of reconciliation. God so loved us that God sent Jesus to lift our burdens and heal our brokenness. We can claim that great gift by opening the doors of our hearts to grace and following Jesus. Jesus emptied himself as an example of how we are to live and to love one another. We activate this gift by asking the Holy Spirit to fill us with God's love, to love our brothers and sisters. It is in God's grace that we are able to love unstintingly. Try today to love beyond your own ability by opening your heart to God's love. Jesus has promised us the gift of the Holy Spirit. Remind him, and then let go of the selfish, self-serving love that is getting in the way.

Dear Jesus, Prodigal Love made human, in your great desire for me that led you in obedience to ignominious death on the cross, transform my love for my brothers and sisters into a self-emptying love.

Hebrews 5.7-9 • Psalm 31 • Luke 2.33-35 or John 19.25-27

I trust in the Lord ....
My times are in your hand;
deliver me from the hand of my enemies and persecutors.

Psalm 31.6, 15

Love's price

When we consider the sufferings of Jesus and his mother, we find a paradox. Did not Christ know he would rise again? Yet he suffered. Did not Mary trust perfectly in God's all-embracing providence? She suffered, too. We do not prove our faith in God through a life without suffering, but by turning to God with loving trust. At the foot of the cross, Mary abandoned herself totally into the hands of God, with utmost confidence that she would be delivered from all her foes. In surrendering her son to the Father's will, Mary abandoned the "worthless idol" of self-interest and rejected even the rights of her maternity. Her spirit was invincible, but because her heart was that of a loving mother, it broke when the soldier's lance pierced the one she had surrendered: her Son.

Where do we go from here?

During times of hardship, reflect on the sorrow Jesus and Mary, his mother, endured. Jesus suffered everything we will ever suffer—including abandonment—so that we will never suffer alone. The suffering and sorrows of life are a part of our human condition. God sustains us. Are you facing a difficult situation? Entrust it to Mary's loving and maternal heart: Mary, who held the body of her dead Son in her arms for our salvation and healing.

**Mary, my Mother, help me to turn
to my compassionate God in faith, hope and love.**

I Corinthians 12.12-14, 27-31 • Psalm 100 • Luke 7.11-17

For just as the body is one and has many members, and all the members of the body, though many, are one body, so it is with Christ.

I Corinthians 12.12

One body

One of the greatest joys of our monastic life is the choral office, raising our voices in praise and worship at numerous times throughout the day. But as any choir director can testify, the quality of the end result improves with practice and rehearsal. Voices must blend together and be in tune with the instruments lest the result be discordant and unpleasing to the listening ear.

So it is with the praise and prayer we as the Church offer to God. Might it not be more pleasing to God when our prayers are offered from hearts that are in unity and harmony? Each member has a role to play, a part to sing, so that the resultant prayer and praise make beautiful music for the Lord. Let us each concentrate on our part by living our lives in God's presence.

Where do we go from here?

St. Augustine tells us to sing a new song, and that new song is our common praise offered to the Lord. Our spirits are united in one song, producing a joyful song of praise to God. Our lives are united in one purpose of love and desire, giving the new song its structure and visibility. Individual prayer is important for our becoming one with God. Our common prayer and sharing together, the sacraments, are also important to make Christ visible in a praying community.

Lord, help us to be in harmony, one in mind and heart, as we offer you our prayers and praise.

I Corinthians 12.31–13.13 • Psalm 33 • Luke 7.31-35

A nd now faith, hope, and love abide, these three; and the greatest of these is love.
I Corinthians 13.13

Gift of love

Very few words are as misunderstood in the modern world as the word "love." To a believer, love (charity) is a desire for what is good, and to love is to desire what is good for another. The ultimate good is God, who is love (1 John 4.16). Paul goes on to describe love. It is patient, kind, not jealous or boastful or arrogant or rude. It doesn't insist on its own way, nor is it irritable or resentful. It rejoices in what is right, not in what is wrong.

We are all called to love, and I can honestly say that I desire others to know and experience the ultimate Good, who is God. My love is far from perfect—Paul's list offers many challenges. The best I can say is that I love my neighbour as myself, because I want us all to grow in perfect love, to come to know and love God for all eternity.

Where do we go from here?

Read and reflect on I Corinthians 13, St. Paul's description of charity. It is not enough simply to read it; working on each verse, we need to put it into practice in our daily lives. This text is life changing and life forming. It holds the secret of loving as God loves. Take the challenge.

**Help me, Lord, to accept your gift of love
and to grow to perfect love.**

I Corinthians 15.1-11 • Psalm 118 • Luke 7.36-50

I f we say that we have no sin, we deceive ourselves, and the truth is not in us. If we confess our sins, he who is faithful and just will forgive us our sins and cleanse us from all unrighteousness.

I John 1.8-9

....

God is faithful

There is a tendency today to downplay the significance of sinfulness or even to recognize its existence. Some years back, a woman shared her concern about her husband, who had not gone to confession in nearly two decades. When she encouraged him to do so, he responded that he had not sinned. While that may be true, it is far more likely that he stopped recognizing the occasion of sin.

Many remedies for empty churches have been proposed; most deal with issues related to the priesthood. Could it be that our churches are not full because Christ came to call sinners and we no longer relate to the salutation?

Where do we go from here?

Sin diminishes us and makes us so much less than we are meant to be; it has a devastating effect in the world, on others and on ourselves, also. Perhaps we do not reflect enough upon the fact that the one who sins is diminished. Sin is not creative, and it takes away our freedom. Our origin in God means that our being and our actions are associated with our divine origin. God's goodness and love are the criterion for human happiness. It is a gift of the Holy Spirit to be aware of our shortcomings. Take one thing you want to change in yourself and begin working on it today.

Lord, heal me, for I have sinned against you. (See Psalm 51.4.)

I Corinthians 15.12-20 • Psalm 17 • Luke 8.1-3

I f there is no resurrection of the dead, then Christ has not been raised; and if Christ has not been raised, then our proclamation has been in vain and your faith has been in vain.

I Corinthians 15.13-14

Jesus has risen

Every now and then, someone will state that their faith would not be shaken if Christ had married and had children, or even if he was not God. Here St. Paul tells us emphatically that our faith should be shaken if Christ was not raised from the dead.

Christ's mission as God and man was to bring salvation to us, redemption for our sins. He did this by offering himself as a sacrifice. That sacrifice was offered on Calvary when he died once and for all on the cross. By his resurrection, Christ overcame death and opened heaven for us. If this did not happen, then we remain in our sinful state, with no hope for eternal life. Yes, we should care that Christ rose from the dead: our future, our very lives depend on it.

Where do we go from here?

Jesus has risen, indeed! Alleluia! Everything is different. Then why does everything seem the same? We can see the difference in the joy and freedom of the saints. We can also perceive the difference in those people we know who have given over their lives to Jesus—they have a joy, a serenity and a selfless giving that can only be fully explained by grace. We are the witnesses to the something "new" that has happened. Share your faith, hope and joy today with someone. Jesus has risen.

Lord, thank you for your gift, the promise of eternal life.
Let your sacrifice for me not be in vain.

I Corinthians 15.35-37, 42-50 • Psalm 56 • Luke 8.4-15

"These are the ones who, when they hear the word, hold it fast in an honest and good heart, and bear fruit with patient endurance."

Luke 8.15

Follow God's path

In her diary, St. Faustina describes a vision of two roads (#153). One road was broad, beautiful and joyful, ending in a precipice, which was the abyss of hell. The second path was narrow and strewn with rocks and thorns, a road of suffering and tears, ending in a beautiful garden. All those who entered the garden immediately forgot their sufferings.

We are on a journey. We have come from God and we are meant to return to God for eternity, but in order to attain eternal life, we must ensure that the Word falls on a fertile path, so that we have the strength and grace to travel the rocky road. How do we prepare the soil so that the Word may take root? By prayer and the sacraments. We cannot make this journey without God's help; let us pray constantly that our hearts might be receptive to God's grace.

Where do we go from here?

The martyrs whose feast we celebrate today, St. Andrew Kim and companions, are an example of the good seed of the Word falling on fertile ground. Their joyful surrender of their lives is a testimony of God's sustaining presence. Jesus is God among us; through the power of the Holy Spirit, God continues to be intimately part of our lives.

Lord, may your Word take deep root in my heart so that I may follow you and not be diverted from the path to eternal life.

Isaiah 55.6-9 • Psalm 145 • Philippians 1.20-24, 27 • Matthew 20.1-16

"These last worked only one hour, and you have made them equal to us who have borne the burden of the day and the scorching heat."

Matthew 20.12

Mercy upon mercy

Today's readings speak of mercy, and culminate in the parable of the labourers in the vineyard. Like those who were hired early in the morning, we are adept at noting what others have and at wanting the same for ourselves. If "A" leads to "B," then everyone doing "A" should get "B." How many times did I compare myself to others, expecting the same recompense and complaining if I found that someone got something I did not? How radical to think that latecomers should receive the same wages as those who worked longer hours. But that is what mercy is about: full measure, flowing over. So our challenge is to rejoice not only that we were hired, but also that we will have companions who are hired on after us!

Where do we go from here?

Have you ever said, "It's not fair; why do some people seem to have so much?" Take a few minutes today to list all you have to be grateful for—beginning with the gift of faith that sustains you. Apparent success and adulation are not always the best measure of happiness. Our greatest earthly treasure is being surrounded by those whom we love and who love us.

Lord, give me the grace to rejoice that your mercy extends so widely and is without limits.

Proverbs 3.27-34 • Psalm 15 • Luke 8.16-18

"Then pay attention to how you listen; for to those who have, more will be given; and from those who do not have, even what they seem to have will be taken away." *Luke 8.18*

Give back to God what is given

Each week, the Sister charged with planning the liturgy for that week assigns various ministries to us. Someone presides at the Liturgy of the Hours; some are called upon to accompany us at the organ; chantresses, readers, acolytes and more need to be designated. Each ministry is a gift to us, since it is a small offering we can give back to the Lord.

Surprisingly, there are times when not seeing your name on the list of duties is perceived as a blessing. Worse yet, sometimes I have grumbled inwardly when unexpectedly given a ministry on a week I thought I had off. It is then that I realize that it is God's gift I am failing to use. By God's grace, may I joyfully and freely give what I have received.

Where do we go from here?

God's gifts grow greater and more abundant in the giving! Try it and see if it is not true. As an old saying goes, God cannot be out-done in generosity. Take time to reach out to someone: to show loving-kindness and to offer a helping hand where it is needed. Use your time and energy for others unstintingly today. Today is our time for doing. We can always rest tomorrow. It's something to think about!

Lord, may I never reject the opportunities you send me to serve you, and let me not forget that in serving others in your name, I serve you.

Proverbs 21.1-6, 10-13 • Psalm 119 • Luke 8.19-21

> have chosen the way of faithfulness;
> I set your ordinances before me.

Psalm 119.30

The way of faithfulness

What does it mean to choose the way of faithfulness? The psalmist answers that it is to follow God's commandments. God's law is not there to curb our freedom but to set us free from slavery to sin. Are God's commands difficult to follow? Yes, they can be, because our wounded human nature does not like to be restrained, and often we prefer doing what we want, when we want. But God's grace is always there as our help.

John Paul II, in reflecting on Pilate's question to Jesus—"What is truth?"—suggests it was about Pilate's personal relationship with truth, an attempt to escape the voice of conscience. Do we not continue to do the same? But rather than questioning the meaning of truth, we have chosen to redefine it: "That's your reality, not mine."

Where do we go from here?

Have you ever, like Pilate, asked for a definition of truth? Did you want an answer? Sometimes we ask, not really wanting to know the answer, so that we do not have to change. Do you ever find yourself longing to be different but not wanting anything to radically change? The trouble is, God does tend to be radical. The Greek word for "change" is *metanoia*, which means a change of mind: to repent, along with the determination to put the new way of being into action.

Through the intercession of St. Pio of Pietrelcina, whose feast day is today, lead me, O Lord, to the fullness of truth. Help me to follow your law.

Proverbs 30.5-9 • Psalm 119 • Luke 9.1-6

Remove far from me falsehood and lying; give me neither poverty nor riches; feed me with the food that I need, or I shall be full, and deny you, and say, "Who is the Lord?"
Proverbs 30.8-9

Sufficient

How well God knows the human heart. Everything in moderation, right? Super-sized food orders, "extreme" vacations—even our vocabulary gives us away. How many people do you know who are ready to say, "I have enough, thank you very much"? Generally, we always want more than we have. If I only had a little more, I could pay off my bills … I could get a better car … I could finally take a vacation … I could help someone in need. The list goes on. When we do get that little more, we find that once again we need just a little more. We seem to be held hostage by our wants and desires. There is only one thing that we really should desire without limit: the One who is without limit.

Where do we go from here?

The prayer of Proverbs begins with a desire to be delivered from falsehood and then given daily sustenance: truly a trusting request of faith in God's providence. In the gospels, we are told to give and we will be given in abundant measure. God is prodigal; not only will God give us what we need—at times something different than what we think we need—but God will give us more than enough to give to others of the lasting treasures of the kingdom. Read chapter 6 of Luke's gospel, slowly and prayerfully.

**Give us this day, O Lord, our daily bread
so that we may be filled with your riches.**

Ecclesiastes 1.2-11 • Psalm 90 • Luke 9.7-9

Herod said, "John I beheaded; but who is this about whom I hear such things?" And he tried to see him.
Luke 9.9

Encountering Jesus

Now and then you meet someone who will go to great lengths to get their way. It can mean bending the rules or crossing the line of legality. When they have acquired what they sought, they are quite content for the end to justify the means. Contrast this with God, who will not force himself upon us. More awesome yet is how God can use what we give him, flawed as it might be, and use every situation for our spiritual good. God can make use of the evil we do or the wrong intentions with which we do good to unite us more closely to him.

Herod was curious to see Jesus. If only his heart had been open to the grace of an encounter with Jesus. Let us not waste our opportunities. Let us be open to the grace of transformation.

Where do we go from here?

Who is this Jesus? Who is Jesus for me? Do I allow my Christian faith to shape my life, my relationships? What are the character and quality of my thoughts? How do I deal with the many thoughts that pass through my mind, sorting them out and deciding whether to accept or reject them? To do so enables me to reflectively shape my existence according to God's plan.

**Lord, make use of the little I give you
to lead me wholeheartedly back to you.**

Friday | **SEPTEMBER 26**

Revelation 7.9-17 • Psalm 124 • 2 Corinthians 4.7-15 • Luke 9.23-26

But we have this treasure in clay jars, so that it may be made clear that this extraordinary power belongs to God and does not come from us.   *2 Corinthians 4.7*

To live our faith

One marvels at the courage, strength and depth of faith of the Canadian martyrs, whose feast we celebrate today. I more readily relate to the denial of St. Peter than to the courage of the martyrs. In the initial zeal that accompanies our conversion, we are filled with great desires to witness to our faith, even to die for it. Then, as time goes on and that fervour dissipates, we realize that we are having trouble living the faith, let alone dying for it. One young woman described this best when she stated that it was easier to die once than to live in humility. Living for our faith requires a daily dying to self. What a radical contradiction to society's current emphasis on self-actualization and self-fulfillment. Thankfully, if we submit to God's action in us, we can exhibit heroic virtue and become spiritual martyrs.

Where do we go from here?

It is always good to remind myself that I am the clay vessel that carries God's life. My weakness should not surprise me. It does not surprise God. My failure to follow Jesus brings me face to face with my fragility, teaching me that only by grace am I able to become holy. God only waits for me to ask for all I need to enter into God's will. Pray to overcome what holds you back from doing the Father's will, and during the day, renew your surrender to the Holy Spirit and your trust in God's saving action in your life.

Lord, grant me the grace to be a good witness.
Help me to die to self so that I might live for you.

Ecclesiastes 11.9–12.8 • Psalm 90 • Luke 9.43-45

et your work be manifest to your servants,
and your glorious power to their children.
Let the favour of the Lord our God be upon us,
and prosper for us the work of our hands ....
Psalm 90.16-17

Prosper our work

Our true work is our work for the kingdom of God. Everything else we do, though important for the here and now, will pass away; only the work of the Lord will remain. We celebrate the feast of St. Vincent de Paul today. God truly prospered the work of Vincent's hands, and we, his children in the Spirit, continue to benefit by his life and his self-giving. In the name of Jesus, he ardently loved and served the poor.

Where do we go from here?

The example of the saints shows us what God can do with someone who allows God's love to be made perfect in him or her. St. Vincent was an ordinary man who said yes to God, and then was able to accomplish marvellous works. Jesus promised us that we would do the works he did through the power of the Holy Spirit. Give your life to the Lord today, and ask him to empower you to do the works of God.

Jesus, I give my whole life to you to do God's work.

Ezekiel 18.25-28 • Psalm 25 • Philippians 2.1-11 • Matthew 21.28-32

" **A** man had two sons; he went to the first and said, 'Son, go and work in the vineyard today.' He answered, 'I will not'; but later he changed his mind and went. The father went to the second and said the same; and he answered, 'I go, sir'; but he did not go. Which of the two did the will of his father?"   *Matthew 21.28-31*

Our "yes"

Despite being brought up in a Catholic household with strong parental witness to the faith, I did not take long to break my word to the Lord. "Yes," I had said. I truly did want to belong to the one, holy, catholic and apostolic Church. So many options opened to me once I left home. Many of these were not in conformity with the teachings of the Church, but they were attractive to a young, impressionable college student. Yet God's grace is never far away and God's mercy is freely given if we but ask. How wonderful when we are given another chance. Even if we turn away from all the sins committed, we shall surely live; we shall not die (see Ezekiel 18.25).

Where do we go from here?

Second chances are wonderful things. If we stop to look back on our spiritual journey, it is filled with second chances. The entire Old Testament, a history of our journey with God, is a story of second chances. God wanted to write a book that would clearly show us God's ever-renewed mercy in the face of our broken promises. All the great men and women of the Bible, carefully chosen by God, were sinners. God knows us and sees what we can become by the power of grace. God renews God's love for us every day: let us renew ours.

Help me, Lord, to be faithful to my word.

Revelation 12.7-12 or Daniel 7.9-10, 13-14 • Psalm 138 • John 1.47-51

And he said to him, "Very truly, I tell you, you will see heaven opened and the angels of God ascending and descending upon the Son of Man."

John 1.51

....

Sent from God

The word "angel" means messenger. The angels are emissaries from God to bring us a word from God and to help to bring about its fulfilment.

Michael, Gabriel and Raphael, whose feast the Church celebrates today, all had special missions. Michael was faithful to God and was sent to fight Lucifer, the devil. Michael continues to help humankind in the battle against the evil one. Gabriel was sent to Mary to announce the coming of the Saviour. And Raphael heals Tobias of his blindness, and guides the journey of his son. The angels come at the bidding of the Son of Man to help us to journey to God.

Where do we go from here?

Actively seek a relationship with the angels, these powerful emissaries of God. Ask them for their help on your journey to holiness. Pray that they help you to have peace in this world. Peace begins in our hearts and ripples out to cover the earth.

**Fill my heart with peace, O God,
and may your angels guide me on my way to you.**

Job 3.1-3, 11-17, 20-23 • Psalm 88 • Luke 9.51-56

W hen the days drew near for him to be taken up, he set his face to go to Jerusalem.
Luke 9.51

The hard road

When Jesus' time drew near, he steadfastly faced the task of his death for our sake. All of today's readings are about suffering, and from a human perspective, they are rather gloomy. Today's saint, St. Jerome, is also a rough and ready character, quite irascible. It just shows that saints can be made from sinners like you and me. St. Jerome loved Jesus and was always struggling with his character faults—and Jesus loved Jerome. St. Jerome once told God he had nothing to give him, and asked, "What can I give you, Lord?" And God replied, "Give me your sins."

Where do we go from here?

St. Jerome spent his whole life studying Scripture, and through him we have the Vulgate translation of Scripture. Today would be a fitting day to resolve to become more familiar with the whole Bible. Perhaps buy a study edition of the Bible with introductions and footnotes; join a Bible study group in your parish; read the Bible as a family and discuss it together. The word of God reveals to us who God is and who we are.

Through the intercession of St. Jerome, may I offer all that I am to the Lord and let God work miracles.

Job 9.1-12, 14-16 • Psalm 88 • Luke 9.57-62

"Look, he passes by me, and I do not see him;
he moves on, but I do not perceive him."
Job 9.11

....

I am with you always

What we hear from Job in this first reading is a common lament. In moments of awareness, I realize that God did approach me, but I did not notice God's presence. How often I become so absorbed in my problem, my pain, my joy, that I forget that God is with me in that experience.

God has told us, "I am with you all days, even to the end of the world," and that really means all days, even today, even now. As we grow in holiness, we will become more and more aware of the precious moments when we can invite God into the details of our daily lives, where God truly wants to join us.

Where do we go from here?

I am called to holiness. This seems a pretty tall order. And yet, this is what the Christian life is all about. What does it mean? It means inviting God into my life, recognizing God's presence in my heart and in others. The best definition of holiness is learning to live in love, and it is manifested by my concrete love for my family, friends and neighbours. So let us invite God into the details of our daily lives, listen to God's voice and follow Jesus in this moment, during this day, and always.

Lord, please help me to be aware of your companionship in each moment of my life.

Thursday | **OCTOBER 2**

Exodus 23.20-23 • Psalm 91 • Matthew 18.1-5, 10

I am going to send an angel in front of you, to guard you on the way and to bring you to the place that I have prepared.
Exodus 23.20

"All night, all day, angels watching over me, my Lord"

In infinite mercy and loving kindness, God recognizes our weakness and confusion in life. Like the tender Father that God is, God does not ignore this defect in us, but gives us each a special help to guide us through life. Today is the feast of the Holy Guardian Angels. The guardian angel that God has sent you is a beautiful and unique creation whose mission it is to keep you from harm in all the dangers you encounter, and to show you the way in all your doubts and difficulties. If you are attentive to your angel's protection, you will notice that there have been many occasions when you were guided away from some harm or prevented from entering a problematic situation.

Where do we go from here?

Let us thank the Lord for our guardian angels, and remember to call on them each day to lead us to the presence of our loving God. We are on a journey; our guardian angels help us to our destination of eternal life. Pray to your guardian angel to help you to be attentive to God's presence.

Angel of God, be with me this day, and guide me into the presence of our Father in heaven.

Job 38.12-21; 40.3-5 • Psalm 139 • Luke 10.13-16

Y ou knit me together in my mother's womb.
I praise you, for I am fearfully and wonderfully made.
Psalm 139.13-14

The Lord's response to my praise

Your Creator is the same One who planned and drew into existence the mighty galaxies, and who devised the means by which various sounds weave together to form music. The amusing kitten at play and the mighty intellect of an Einstein are products of the same Divine Wisdom. And all of that expertise was used in forming you. Through your existence, God says, "I lovingly chose the colour of your eyes, the shape of your nose, the stature of your body, your temperament. I picked out the talents and gifts I would bestow on you, and wove all of them into your personality with the utmost care, along with a multitude of spiritual gifts. You are special to me. I have never duplicated your combination of qualities, nor will I ever make another exactly like you. You are the only one who can give me glory in the precise way that is possible for you. You are very precious to me."

Where do we go from here?

Take a moment to be consciously in your body: feel your feet planted on the ground; think about your unique existence. We have received all good things from God. Think about the things you like to do, the things you are good at doing. These are the particular gifts God has given you, along with a capacity to do and be so much more. Our sins and failures obscure the depth of our goodness as God-images. When we are in touch with our inner goodness, then we will be able to find that goodness in others.

Dear Lord, thank you. I am wonderfully made.

Job 42.1-3, 5-6, 12-13, 15-17 • Psalm 119 • Luke 10.17-24

"**N**o one knows who the Son is except the Father, or who the Father is except the Son and anyone to whom the Son chooses to reveal him."

Luke 10.22

....

Jesus shows us God

God in himself is unknowable by mere mortals. And yet we love God. How can we love someone we do not know? Jesus comes to our rescue here. By becoming human, Jesus made God knowable to us in the flesh. As we study and contemplate the Scriptures, we learn who Jesus really is. As we become more intimate with Jesus, he can choose to reveal the Father to us so that we can know the Father, too. If we prepare ourselves for receiving this knowledge, Jesus will teach us the intimate love of his (and our) Father.

Where do we go from here?

St. Francis rejoiced in God's presence everywhere. He praised the sun and moon, the grass and the flowers, the blue sky. St. Francis found God especially in the hearts of the poor. Jesus came to bring hope to the poor, the unloved, the outcast and the sinner. St. Francis followed Jesus, and became poor for his sake and to better serve all those who were close to Jesus' heart. Today, in some small way, let us follow the example of St. Francis. Seek reconciliation with someone who has offended you or whom you have offended.

Jesus, help me to open my mind and heart to receive from you a greater realization of who the Father is.

Isaiah 5.1-7 • Psalm 80 • Philippians 4.6-9 • Matthew 21.33-43

Do not worry about anything, but in everything by prayer and supplication with thanksgiving let your requests be made known to God. And the peace of God, which surpasses all understanding, will guard your hearts and your minds in Christ Jesus.   *Philippians 4.6-7*

Take everything to the Lord

To worry is to fret or suffer mentally about what will happen if someone doesn't intervene. We casually tell a friend, "Don't worry. Everything will be fine." Often, what we mean is "Forget it; don't think about the problem." But St. Paul advises, "Yes, do think about it and talk about it with the Lord." Discuss with him the problem and the possible solutions or consequences. But be sure that, as you ask him to give you the answer or solution, you also thank him for taking the matter into his hands. This, Paul tells us, will bring us peace—the peace of God, which surpasses all understanding.

Where do we go from here?

Doesn't everyone want to find peace? Peace in our workplace, peace with others and peace in our hearts? The peace that passes understanding is God's gift, and it begins in our hearts. God's gift of peace is not dependent on the circumstances of our lives, or even on the absence of upheaval. Jesus said, "My peace I give to you." The peace of Christ is the fruit of the Holy Spirit dwelling within us. We prepare our hearts for peace by diligently seeking God in times of turmoil. Prayer is a very practical exercise.

Jesus, I bring this very important situation to your loving care. Please use your wisdom and love to solve the difficulty. And thank you for doing it your way.

Galatians 1.6-12 • Psalm 111 • Luke 10.25-37

"What must I do to inherit eternal life?"
Luke 10.25

What must I do?

The question asked of Jesus by the lawyer is one that we all ask at various stages of our spiritual development. We first must examine our lives in the light of the commandments. Besides keeping the letter of the law, do I act by its spirit as well? I may not have physically killed someone, but have I murdered a reputation, or hindered someone from attaining a goal that he or she is pursuing? The commandments function on many levels at which I can avoid forbidden actions or fulfill the law's requirements. When I say I am obeying the commandments, Jesus suggests that I consider charity, love of God and especially love of neighbour. Do I really love with all my heart, soul, mind and strength? The totality of my love for God will be shown in the expressions of love for my neighbour.

Where do we go from here?

What are the desires that fill my heart? Is eternal life among the top ten? Do I understand that how I live my life now is shaping my life for eternity? My desires for God, for goodness, for prayer, and my yearning to become whole and free, are signs of the work of the Holy Spirit. Make a list of your inner priorities. Then pray over each one and ask the Lord what they mean. Use that list to understand where you are in following the Lord.

Jesus, shed your light on my life, and show me what changes I must make to have eternal life with you. Grant me the grace and strength to follow the lights you give me.

Galatians 1.13-24 • Psalm 139 • Luke 10.38-42

God, who had set me apart before I was born and called me through his grace, was pleased to reveal his Son to me, so that I might proclaim him among the Gentiles ...."

Galatians 1.15-16

Eternally chosen

In today's reading, Paul is defending his apostleship, but even more, he is wonder-struck that he has been given this grace in the first place. He does not feel worthy, because he persecuted the Church of God. Yet God loved him, chose him from all eternity and abundantly poured out God's grace upon him. Paul's cause for wonder is threefold: his unspeakable call from God; the inconceivable realization that Jesus is the Son of God; and, finally, his unheard-of commission to hand on to others what had been given to him. Is it not the same for each of us? We, too, have been chosen, loved individually and personally by God. We also know Christ as our Lord. And we, too, small as our own part may be, have been entrusted with a unique, unrepeatable mission in life.

Where do we go from here?

You are God's chosen, God's beloved—and precious. Each of us has been entrusted with a unique mission. We need to activate God's choice. You can do this first through prayer to the Holy Spirit to discern how God wishes to use you. Start each day with a prayer of discernment, because you are daily commissioned anew. Then follow through with practical deeds that show forth the face of Jesus, the presence of love in the world. In this job, there is no vacation time, but the bonuses are out of this world!

Lord Jesus, grant me grace to realize your love for me.

Galatians 2.1-2, 7-14 • Psalm 117 • Luke 11.1-4

" **L**ord, teach us to pray ...."
Luke 11.1

The gift of prayer

What is prayer but the profound awareness that God is our Father? That is why, when Jesus teaches us to pray, he brings us into his own relationship with the One who loves us. We call this One "Father."

The Father is greater than we are, and so must be honoured, respected and obeyed. The Father is tender and loving, powerful and protecting, and so we are safe, abounding in all goods bestowed, shielded from all that could harm us. And when we fail, as we are prone to do, the Father gathers us anew in strong and loving arms.

Where do we go from here?

Let us entrust ourselves to God, our loving Father. God cares for us, and is closer to us than we are to ourselves. Whatever the storms of life, we need have no fear, for God, our Father, is with us. Jesus has promised this. We can ask for what we need, and our Father in heaven hears us. God's love is a security no one can take from us.

Lord, show me the Father and it will be enough for me.

Galatians 3.1-5 • Luke 1 • Luke 11.5-13

"How much more will the heavenly Father give the Holy Spirit to those who ask him!"
Luke 11.13

Come, Holy Spirit

There are many passages in Scripture that offer directives on prayer. This one assures us that our prayer will always be answered. Not sometimes, or maybe, but always. The key to understanding is in the gift bestowed: the Holy Spirit.

To pray is to enter that world where the Holy Spirit resides in the deepest recesses of the human heart. Prayer then becomes hunger and thirst for the fulfillment of God's will in us and all around us. Sometimes we demand and persist, and sometimes we wrestle within ourselves with God. Yet, we are assured that such prayer is always answered. Always the answer is the peace we find in understanding that "for those who love God, all things work together for good."

Where do we go from here?

God always hears our prayer to receive the Holy Spirit. Jesus tells us so in the gospels. Jesus told the disciples he must go away to send the Holy Spirit to them. The Holy Spirit plants Jesus' teaching in our heart—we carry the words of Jesus within us. The Spirit guides us in following Jesus. We carry in our hearts the same Holy Spirit who transformed the lives of the saints. We need only be receptive to be transformed in love.

Lord Jesus, help me to understand.
Show me how to entrust my life to your loving care.

Friday | **OCTOBER 10**

Galatians 3.6-14 • Psalm 111 • Luke 11.15-26

I will give thanks to the Lord with my whole heart ....
Psalm 111.1

Thanksgiving

We all have much to be grateful for—family, friends, home, life itself. How often do we think of the greater gifts like faith and grace and the promise of the Spirit? Both of today's readings set our sights on Christ lifted up on the cross: Christ became a curse for us, Paul says, lifted up in weakness, weighed down by the burden of our humanity. A strong man, Jesus says, despoils the devil of his prey, ourselves. Let us be grateful for this gift of grace. Let us bow down in worship before so great a mystery. Let us gratefully take up our own crosses so that Jesus' sacrifice may not be in vain.

Where do we go from here?

Gratitude is the mark of a contemplative. To be grateful is to recognize how we have been gifted. Everything we have is a gift of God. Our gratitude reminds us of our need of God, and gratitude to our brothers and sisters reminds us of our need for others. The word *Eucharist* means thanksgiving. Jesus nourishes us with his life as often as we receive the Eucharist. Take time to notice the little things you receive today, and say thank you. Gratitude lightens and renews our hearts.

Lord Jesus, thank you for all you have given me.
Never let me be separated from you.

Galatians 3.22-29 • Psalm 105 • Luke 11.27-28

In Christ Jesus you are all children of God through faith.
Galatians 3.26

Children of God

What does it mean to be a child of God? For Paul, it means the astounding reality of being gathered up and adopted into the very family of God, nobility so great that it could never have been hoped for or even imagined. And this is all the more astounding because there is no way it can be earned or merited by human achievement. It is a pure gift of grace poured out on us in Christ Jesus. This means that every other distinction among us is blurred and brought to naught in light of our relationship to God. It means there is no longer male or female, black or white, rich or poor. It means living in the "obedience of faith," that is, becoming Christ-like, transformed into God's image: patient, kind, compassionate, all-embracing and forgiving.

Where do we go from here?

We are all children of one Father. God's plan is that we will all be united one day in God's presence. Is there prejudice in your life? Do you prefer associating with some people rather than others? In heaven, such distinctions will not be possible. Begin living in the kingdom of God, the kingdom of love, and eternal life will already have begun. This is something to take seriously.

Jesus, meek and humble of heart, make my heart like yours.

Isaiah 25.6-10 • Psalm 23 • Philippians 4.12-14, 19-20 • Matthew 22.1-14

"The kingdom of heaven may be compared to a … wedding banquet …."

Matthew 22.2

The wedding feast

What more joyful celebration can there be than a wedding? So then what are we to understand in this parable?

First of all, the kingdom of heaven is truly a wedding between God and humankind; it is the covenant and promises brought to fulfillment and eternally ratified in Jesus. Second, the joy of this union will be beyond measure for God and for us: rich food, singing and dancing, all tears banished, all suffering and pain forgotten. But third, the gift demands a response. Obligations are laid upon us and we are accountable to the One who issues the invitation. The price of entry is the wedding garment of charity. God must be able to recognize the likeness of Jesus in us.

Where do we go from here?

Jesus says to seek first the kingdom of God and all else will be given to us. Is the kingdom of God my first priority? People pursue whatever is most important to them. How do God and the things of God fit into my agenda? When I am in God, everything else is in right order. It is something to think about.

Jesus, may I become like you in all I think and say and do.

Galatians 4.22-24, 26-27, 31–5.1 • Psalm 113 • Luke 11.29-32

"This generation is an evil generation; it asks for a sign …."
Luke 11.29

Jesus, our sign

Solomon and Jonah are legendary in Jewish folklore: Solomon as the epitome of wisdom, Jonah for his miraculous escape from the belly of the whale. Jesus far surpasses them both. How is it that the crowds cannot see and cannot understand? Jesus does not rebuke them because they ask for a sign; rather, it is because they fail to see the sign so evident before them. They fail to recognize God's presence in their midst, healing their ills, forgiving their sins, showing the way to life. They thirst for what cannot satisfy. Jesus praises the Queen of the South and the people of Nineveh, because they realized their emptiness and opened their hearts for what only God can give. And what of us—do we fix our gaze on God's gift in our midst? Or are we, too, like querulous children, imposing our wills on God?

Where do we go from here?

What is the sign that Jesus is in our midst? The sign of Jonah is symbolic of the resurrection. The whale could not hold Jonah, and the tomb could not hold Jesus. In the gospels, Jesus tells us that the one sign of his presence in our lives is our love for one another. How is your love for your brothers and sisters manifested in your life?

Lord Jesus, bring me to the truth of your presence among us.

Galatians 5.1-6 • Psalm 119 • Luke 11.37-41

"Give for alms those things that are within; and see, everything will be clean for you."
Luke 11.41

....

Faith working through love

The Pharisees of Jesus' time were overly concerned with external appearances. Taking pains to look holy, they exaggerated the importance of ritual observances. Self-righteous and proud, they put their faith in their own accomplishments. Jesus shows a new way: self-emptying in place of self-importance; faith working through love, as Paul says. Looking to God instead of to ourselves is deep cleansing for our hearts, making us whole. Give alms, Jesus says, and all will be made clean for you. Give away what you have received and you will be filled with more. This kind of faith works through love. It cannot exist without love: God's love, freely given, and our love, a faint echo. Love is faith's crown, its fulfillment and the measure of our fidelity.

Where do we go from here?

God asks each of us to open our hearts to the purifying and cleansing love of the Holy Spirit. We need to take seriously that we are called to be holy. We do not want to *look* good but rather to be good to the core of our being. This means a change of life, taking up our crosses and following Jesus. Are you ready? Give your inner spirit in prayer as alms for the poor in need of God's love and mercy.

**Lord Jesus, teach me your own self-emptying,
self-sacrificing love.**

Galatians 5.18-25 • Psalm 1 • Luke 11.42-46

T he fruit of the Spirit is love, joy, peace, patience …. There is no law against such things.

Galatians 5.22, 23

The gospel in a nutshell

Throughout the New Testament, indeed throughout the whole of Scripture, we find these nuggets of pure gold that contain the entire message of Jesus in a nutshell. This passage from Galatians is one of them. Let us look deeper. First, this is an image of God: gentle, kind, faithful and forbearing. Our human destiny is set before us as well: we are to become like God, displaying toward one another the identical qualities we discover in God. Grace, too, is revealed: unmerited, undeserved, a pure gift of God. Following the Spirit's lead, a new vision of peace and justice opens before us. And finally, we need only say "no" to our earthbound desires, to cleanse the inside of the cup, as Jesus says, and to crucify our evil desires, as Paul tells us.

Where do we go from here?

Reflection and discernment are an important part of our spiritual growth. For human wholeness, we need to take time to step back from all the things we do, and just "be." This is difficult in our busy, noisy society. Are you comfortable in taking time to do nothing, to be silent, to take a quiet, solitary walk or just to sit on a rock? For how long? Try going outside and sitting down to reflect on who God is and who you are, and then just be still. Can you do this for 10 minutes? It is a good habit to cultivate. Reflect on chapter 5 of Galatians.

**Lord Jesus, cleanse my heart
so that I may be pleasing to you.**

Ephesians 1.1-10 • Psalm 98 • Luke 11.47-54

"**W**oe to you lawyers! For you have taken away the key of knowledge …."
Luke 11.52

....

The key of knowledge

Our gentle Jesus—so compassionate to the sick, the poor, sinners—loses all patience with leaders puffed up with their own self-importance. Blind guides, he calls them, whitewashed tombs, brood of vipers. They are useless at best, filled with the decay of death and, worst of all, they are dangerous. Knowledge and understanding are the keys that open the doors of our hearts to God. Jesus condemns the scribes and Pharisees, because as leaders, they ought to have been the first to recognize God at work in him. Failing that, the door to life and happiness remains closed to them. They have rejected the key.

Where do we go from here?

It is how we think and what we love that determine our next steps and move us to action. We approach God by the renewal of our minds, a change in thinking and an increase in loving. It is important to be honest about our motives and to seek what God desires for us. We prepare our minds for understanding God by examining our desires with radical self-honesty. Go deeper than a list of faults. Look for the reasons why you desire certain things.

**Lord Jesus, grant me the grace to see clearly,
to judge wisely and to love tenderly.**

Ephesians 1.11-14 • Psalm 33 • Luke 12.1-7

I n Christ we have … been destined … so that we … might live for the praise of his glory.

Ephesians 1.11, 12

Our destiny

Paul's encounter with the Risen Christ on the road to Damascus shattered the blindness of his heart, revealing to him the unfathomable love of God. In that light, a whole new world opened to Paul, a world in which God's entire plan of salvation from the beginning of time to its end was laid out: all of it is encapsulated in Christ.

What does that mean for us? It means that every person is called, chosen, loved, blessed and destined in Christ to be a child of God, a member of God's own family. Words cannot even begin to describe the riches and glory prepared for us in Christ.

Where do we go from here?

What, then, is our destiny? To what are we called? We are called to joy beyond all telling. Our eternity will be a hymn of thanksgiving, never ceasing in praise of God's grace given to us in Christ. We begin now by praising God in prayer, in liturgy and in our daily lives as we follow Jesus. Direct your inner spirit to God often each day

**Lord Jesus, small as my life is, I give it all to you.
Thank you for the gift of yourself to me.**

2 Timothy 4.9-17 • Psalm 145 • Luke 10.1-9

O nly Luke is with me.
2 Timothy 4.11

The evangelist Luke

In his gospel, Luke cites many sources as eyewitnesses. Paul must have been among the most important. His years travelling with Paul would have given experiential meaning to the words Luke places on Jesus' lips. In today's gospel, for example, Luke would have seen for himself the fields ripe for harvest, and he would have known the Lord's own yearning for more workers. With Paul, he also would have experienced being a lamb among wolves. He knew poverty in travelling without provisions, and he knew riches in sharing the bread of those to whom they ministered. He would have tasted the Lord's own peace, so evident in his gospel.

Where do we go from here?

And what about us? Is the gospel alive in our own lives, as it was in Luke's? Do we support and comfort our friends in their suffering, as Luke did with Paul? Loving Jesus sets us on fire to follow his example to serve our brothers and sisters in love. Ask God how to pray for others and use your God-given gifts to help them. Then you will be a witness of Jesus.

Lord Jesus, make the gospel alive for me.
Let me comfort others as you comfort me.

Isaiah 45.1, 4-6 • Psalm 96 • 1 Thessalonians 1.1-5 • Matthew 22.15-21

[Jesus] said to them, "Give therefore to the emperor the things that are the emperor's, and to God the things that are God's."
Matthew 22.21

We belong to God

Human life cannot be sustained without food, rest and shelter. But their rule over us is not absolute. It lasts only for a time. It cannot fully satisfy. Our first and final allegiance is to God. The true coin of our life is stamped with the very image of God. God's name is written on our forehead and in our hearts. We are God's handiwork, the crown of creation. We belong to God.

Jesus' message is clear: there are obligations and responsibilities laid upon us in this life. In the fulfillment of these, the most precious coin of our existence finds its purpose and is given back to God.

Where do we go from here?

Sort out the good and bad influences in your life, and, relying on God's grace, change what leads away from God. We belong to God. Read the gospels daily; study and pray with one gospel at a time until they are very familiar. They are the blueprint for following Jesus.

My Jesus, may your will be fulfilled in me.
May I omit nothing that is pleasing to you.

Ephesians 2.1-10 • Psalm 100 • Luke 12.13-21

"**F**riend, who set me to be a judge or arbitrator over you?"
Luke 12.14

Jesus' pure heart

Today's gospel episode offers us a glimpse into the integrity and purity of Jesus' own heart. Too often throughout the gospels, Jesus is heckled and criticized by his opponents or baited by their pretense of sincerity. Not often is he facilely admired as in this passage. Yet in either case, whether provoked or flattered, Jesus steers a straight course. His gaze is fixed on God alone. No self-interest tarnishes his heart. He cares neither for personal revenge nor for a position of honour among his followers. Instead, he uses this instance of misunderstanding to further clarify and broaden his message: avoid greed in all its forms.

Where do we go from here?

We are so easily enticed by wealth, honour, power and pleasure; how difficult is this struggle. Our society canonizes getting ahead and succeeding, no matter who gets hurt in the process. In a world where the dignity of each person is not respected, where the goods of the earth are not shared, we have injustice, poverty and oppression. Jesus calls us to a different path—one of love and respect for every person. Expand your capacity to love, and make it show in practical deeds.

Help me, my Jesus. Never permit me to be separated from you.

Ephesians 2.12-22 • Psalm 85 • Luke 12.35-38

"**B**e like those who are waiting for their master to return from the wedding banquet ...."
Luke 12.36

....

The daily wedding banquet

The themes of the wedding banquet and a marriage bond are frequently used throughout both the Old and New Testaments to describe our relationship to God. Usually we think in terms of the future, of eternal happiness. But here, Jesus tells us, the wedding has already taken place, and we should be waiting for the master's return, not only at the end of time but daily. The wedding banquet is the paschal mystery, the marriage of God and humankind effected eternally on the cross. It belongs to us, then, to make this grace operative in our own lives, watching and waiting, faithful to the grace of each passing moment. And if we do recognize God's presence in our lives, Jesus assures us, he himself will serve us; that is, he himself will carry our cross and bear our burdens with us.

Where do we go from here?

Throughout his earthly life, Jesus gives us an example of humble service to our brothers and sisters. Make a list of ways you can serve. Jot down some of the opportunities you have missed. Each day be alert to ways you can put yourself at the service of a brother or sister. Perhaps someone needs a ride or an invitation to lunch.

Lord Jesus, keep me faithful.
May I see your will in every moment of my life.

Ephesians 3.1-12 • Isaiah 12 • Luke 12.39-48

O f this gospel I have become a servant according to the gift of God's grace that was given me ….
Ephesians 3.7

....

Doing God's work

Each of us has been given a share in God's own work of creating and redeeming the world. Ours may be but a minor note, struck only once in the great symphony of God's love that surrounds us, but without it there is a void, a vacuum, that no one else can fill.

Thus the meaning of Jesus' stern words in the gospel and his praise and gratitude for that servant who fulfills the task assigned to him or her. What is this task? Basically, it consists in becoming the person God created me to be, nothing more. It means humbly and confidently accepting God's plan for my life, whether great or small, and doing God's will, trusting the unseen purpose. It means patience and fidelity, kindness and generosity. It means getting up again after a fall, asking pardon when needed and beginning anew.

Where do we go from here?

Our memory is a bank of God-encounters. God gave us the gift of memory to hold fast the remembrance of his gifts. We can bring up all those gifts of hope and joy and love during our times of darkness. They are a testimony to God's constant faithfulness and accompaniment. Out of your God experience share your hope with others.

**Lord Jesus, help me to trust your plan in my life.
I place my life at your service.**

Ephesians 3.13-21 • Psalm 33 • Luke 12.49-53

"Do you think that I have come to bring peace to the earth? No, I tell you, but rather division!"
Luke 12.51

The peace of Christ

Peace! It is our greatest treasure and Jesus' promise to us: "Peace I leave you, my own peace I give you." But here Jesus warns us he brings not peace, but division. Just as we will not find life unless we lose it, so deep abiding peace will not be ours without a struggle.

True peace, the peace of Christ, is neither passive nor weak but dynamic, springing from courage and the fire of love that brought Jesus to the cross. True peace, the peace of Christ, is a holy warfare. It means taking up the sword of the Spirit and facing the demons in our own hearts. There can be no compromise with sin or selfishness. True peace, the peace of Christ, is born of sacrifice. The peace of Christ makes all suffering sweet, every weakness strong.

Where do we go from here?

We all want peace, but we want it ready-made, without a hassle. Union with God in our daily living produces happiness and security, peace and joy, a joy that is deeper than any sorrow. The resurrected Jesus said to the apostles, "My peace I give you." Life did not get any easier for them, but they were filled with the joy and peace of the Spirit. God's peace is deeper than the chaos of life. We still must face the chaos, but we will be fortified!

Jesus, fill me with your peace. Be my strength in temptation, my consolation in sorrow.

Ephesians 4.1-6 • Psalm 24 • Luke 12.54-59

"You know how to interpret the appearance of earth and sky, but why do you not know how to interpret the present time?"
Luke 12.56

The sacrament of the present time

Every moment of life, every happening, every person we encounter, is a sign, a sacrament of God's presence. The joy of family and friends; the simple comfort of home-cooked food; the beauty of a sunset and the laughter of children—do we think to include our God in the song of praise that springs from the deepest recesses of our hearts? God is always with us, but we are not always with God. We fail to discern God's presence hidden beneath the veil, the sacrament of our ordinary human lives.

Where do we go from here?

God is with us in this present moment—in every present moment of our lives. Do you realize when you are hurt or sad that God is with you, carrying you through the rough patches of life? Do you remember God in the good times and give thanks? Interpret every event from God's perspective, and then you will be reading the signs of the times.

**Jesus, remain with me always,
and may I remain always with you.**

Ephesians 4.7-16 • Psalm 122 • Luke 13.1-9

S peaking the truth in love, we must grow up in every way into him who is the head, into Christ ….
Ephesians 4.15

. . . .

Life in Christ

Today's readings offer a beautiful compendium of the Christian life. First, the gospel reminds us we have a task to fulfill. We are expected to bear fruit; an account will be required of us. Then Ephesians tells us what that task is: we are to become the Body of Christ. Time is given to us, a process of development as we are transformed from being unruly children into mature adults who sincerely care for one another. We may be the eye that sees or the lowly foot, but whatever our gift, it belongs to the whole Body in Christ.

Where do we go from here?

Speaking the truth is not an easy task. We want to be liked, and we don't want to upset others, especially if they do not want to hear the truth. Speaking the truth in love makes it even more complicated. It cannot be a matter of telling someone off, or telling them the truth in anger. Speaking the truth in love must flow from concern for the other and from love. Truth-speaking also requires courage and the guiding presence of the Holy Spirit.

**Jesus, take my hands, my heart, my all.
Do with me as you will.**

Exodus 22.21-27 • Psalm 18 • 1 Thessalonians 1.5-10 • Matthew 22.34-40

" Y ou shall love your neighbour as yourself."
Matthew 22.39

....

The mystery of charity

Love of God and love of neighbour—these two commandments are one. They cannot be separated. One is the measure of the other; lacking one leaves the other empty, devoid of meaning. Gazing into God in prayer, we begin to see humanity through God's eyes: God's love for us, even to dying on the cross; God's plan for our happiness; God's compassion for our frailty, our brokenness. And we are led to imitate our Father, our Saviour.

Shifting our gaze to our neighbour in light of God's love, we may see the beauty of the human person, too often disfigured by sin or suffering. Caring for our brother or sister is an act of service to God. This is a great mystery that demands our full attention.

Where do we go from here?

In the gospel text, we are told that we must love our neighbour as ourselves. It is an important text to ponder. If we do not really love ourselves, then we will not love our neighbour rightly. Do you understand how beautiful and precious you are in God's eyes? If important people in your life have not loved you, then you may feel you are unworthy. But at the centre of your heart, you "look" like God—you are beautiful. Ask the Lord Jesus to help you understand how much you are loved.

**Lord Jesus, may I imitate you in my care
for my brothers and sisters.**

Ephesians 4.32–5.8 • Psalm 1 • Luke 13.10-17

Be kind to one another, tenderhearted, forgiving one another, as God in Christ has forgiven you.
Ephesians 4.32

Jesus is kind

God is kind, compassionate and forgiving. We show ourselves to be God's children when we, too, are kind, compassionate and willing to forgive, and when we put aside all self-interest and clothe ourselves with what is good and right and true. Jesus gives us the example in the gospel. He is kind. His first thought on seeing a woman crippled with infirmity is to reach out and heal her. In contrast with the Pharisees, who are quick to criticize and condemn, Jesus' heart is filled with compassion. He knows anger only with those whose hearts are hardened, whose vision is narrowed to self. This is all God asks of us. Let us be kind to one another.

Where do we go from here?

To be kind: it's such a small thing, but a precious gift that bestows dignity and love on another person. An act of kindness tells the other that they are special and loved. Take an opportunity today to recognize another's need and to be kind. How many times? Seventy times seventy.

My Jesus, teach me kindness and gentleness.

Ephesians 2.19-22 • Psalm 19 • Luke 6.12-19

N ow during those days [Jesus] went out to the mountain to pray; and he spent the night in prayer to God.
Luke 6.12

....

The prayer of Jesus

Jesus is frequently portrayed as being at prayer in the gospels. One can only imagine the depths of intimacy that passed between him and his heavenly Father. Jesus prayed as he taught us to pray: for his Father's honour first of all; then for himself, that he would have wisdom and strength to do God's will.

Let us not imagine that answered prayer always brings unmixed results. After spending an entire night in prayer, Jesus chose as a friend someone who later betrayed him. It was not a mistake, not an accident. God's plan is not dependent on success. In the garden, Jesus prayed for deliverance. Instead he was given an angel to strengthen him. And so it is with us. Prayer is always answered, even when we do not understand.

Where do we go from here?

Pray always and do not grow weary or discouraged. God hears our prayers and God answers, though often the answer comes in a guise we do not recognize. God knows the depth of our need and the needs of those around us. God is faithful. Ask God to teach you how to pray for yourself and for others. Listen to God's word within.

**My Father, I place my life in your hands.
Do with me as you will.**

Ephesians 6.1-9 • Psalm 145 • Luke 13.22-30

The Lord is faithful in all his words,
and gracious in all his deeds.
Psalm 145.13

God's fidelity

God is faithful, and true to his word. All our sin and sorrow cannot cancel God's eternal plan to share divine life with us. We were made for the happiness that only God can give. Yet we have a choice. Do we accept God's gift? In today's gospel, Jesus issues a warning: Do not take God for granted. God's ways are far beyond our own; God is our Father, strong and true. God loves us; we belong to him. Do you recognize God's presence with you?

Where do we go from here?

God is faithful, true to God's word. We may fail; we often do. But God will never fail us. Pray for the guidance of the Holy Spirit to walk in the ways of the Lord. Jesus tells us this is a prayer that is always answered. What more do we need?

**God, keep me faithful, and never permit me
to be separated from you.**

Ephesians 6.10-20 • Psalm 144 • Luke 13.31-35

"Listen, I am casting out demons and performing cures today and tomorrow, and on the third day I finish my work."
Luke 13.32

....

The work of Jesus

What is the work of Jesus? At first glance, we see him teaching, preaching and healing. Looking deeper, we see the instructions and cures as a clear manifestation of the Father. We see ourselves revealed, as well, as a work of Jesus in process. Jesus' work was accomplished fully in his death, resurrection, ascension and the sending of the Spirit to us. Here is the revelation once and for all of God's infinite love for humanity: he laid down his life for us. And by rising again, Jesus showed the power of love: love triumphs. It can never be overcome by evil.

Where do we go from here?

St. Paul tells us we complete the work of Christ. What is our work? It is simply to believe in Jesus, in his love and his mercy, and to follow his example, which means to daily lay down our lives for our brothers and our sisters. We lay down our lives for others through a day filled with small deeds of service and signs of our love: a smile, a helping hand and the gift of allowing others to help us.

My Jesus, help me to believe, and teach me to understand.

Philippians 1.1-11 • Psalm 111 • Luke 14.1-6

" **I** s it lawful to cure people on the sabbath, or not?"
Luke 14.3

....

Curing on the sabbath

It is significant that Jesus worked many of his miracles on the sabbath, the day set aside especially for the honour and worship of God. By choosing the sabbath, Jesus portrayed his Father as a God of mercy and compassion. True worship of God is manifest in loving. Jesus was also drawing attention to himself as the beloved Son of God, God in person. It is significant as well that the Pharisees and teachers of the Law rejected his message. As leaders, they understood Jesus' claims all too clearly, and refused them. By denying his goodness, they revealed the evil in their own hearts. And so, in the end, by condemning Jesus, they condemned themselves.

Where do we go from here?

What steps do you think you need to take to direct your future in the way most conducive to a life of virtue and godliness? Read and reflect on the Scriptures daily. Read some of the sabbath texts in the gospels. What is Jesus teaching? In what ways can you put his teaching into practice? Make a list of specific and concrete suggestions. We need to consecrate time that belongs to God alone.

My God, remove from me my hard heart.

Revelation 7.2-4, 9-14 • Psalm 24.1-2, 3-4, 5-61-3 • Matthew 5.1-12

A fter this I looked, and there was a great multitude that no one could count, from every nation, from all tribes and peoples and languages, standing before the throne and before the Lamb ....

Revelation 7.9-10

Salvation belongs to God

What a beautiful word picture the book of Revelation paints of the saints in heaven. A great multitude, beyond counting, from all the corners of the earth is standing before the throne of God in joyful worship and praise. On earth they followed Jesus, and now they are united with him in heaven. Today we celebrate them in the feast of All Saints. Living the Beatitudes, today's gospel selection, is the key to eternal life. Each one of them creates an empty space in us that God can fill. Each time we celebrate the Eucharist, we are united to the worship of the saints. They intercede for us.

Where do we go from here?

Reflect on the text of Matthew 5.1-12. What do the Beatitudes mean to you? Which of them most attracts you? Take one Beatitude at a time to reflect upon, and try to understand how it could be formative in your life.

Blessed are they who hear your word and keep it.

Lamentations 3.17-26 • Psalm 103 • I Corinthians 15.51-57 • Matthew 11.25-30 or John 12.23-26

T he steadfast love of the Lord never ceases,
his mercies never come to an end;
they are new every morning;
great is your faithfulness.

Lamentations 3.22-23

Communion of saints

Following on the feast of All Saints on November 1, we have the commemoration of all the faithful departed. There is no disconnect, but rather continuity. The saints have arrived, the holy souls are waiting, and we are on our way. We are reminded of this union each time the Creed is proclaimed: "I believe in the communion of saints." We grieve for our loved ones who have left us, but the separation is only temporary. What joy to be reunited, and with them, to praise God eternally!

Where do we go from here?

This is a good day to reflect on mercy. How many times have you received mercy from God? How many times have you received mercy from a brother or sister? Have you extended mercy? Is there someone in your life whom you are not forgiving? Pray to the Holy Spirit to increase your love and your ability to forgive. Is it hard for you to forgive? Try praying the Our Father with sincerity. As we forgive, we will be forgiven.

Eternal rest grant to those who have gone before us, O Lord.

Philippians 2.1-4 • Psalm 131 • Luke 14.12-14

O Lord, my heart is not lifted up,
my eyes are not raised too high;
I do not occupy myself with things
too great and too marvellous for me.

Psalm 131.1

God's challenge

Today we are invited to examine our attitudes. In writing to the Philippians, Paul exhorts them to be "of a single mind, one in love, one in heart." When we pray over a Scripture passage, we are not reflecting on a message given only to the early Christians; it is spoken to us today.

In the gospel, Jesus uses a parable to describe a familiar situation. A meal is a shared experience, but are we too selective in choosing those whom we are willing to invite? The word of God continues to challenge our attitudes and the choices we make to live the gospel. Let us daily accept the challenge.

Where do we go from here?

Take a risk in trying to get to know an acquaintance who would not be your first choice for a friend. Look for their good qualities. Perhaps invite them to dinner. You may be surprised at the treasure you find. Think about the people you disdain. Ask yourself what it is about them you dislike. Try to get to know them. Reflect on today's gospel. Is this the challenge it is offering? What do you think Jesus is saying to you in this gospel?

**Create in me a clean heart, O God; and put a new
and right spirit within me. (Psalm 51.10)**

Philippians 2.5-11 • Psalm 22 • Luke 14.15-24

"**B**lessed is anyone who will eat bread in the kingdom of God!"
Luke 14.15

End times

In November, the liturgical year looks toward the end times, the fullness of life in God's kingdom. God desires that all people be saved and enjoy the fullness of eternal life in heaven. God continually seeks and invites each person to know and receive God's infinite love poured out each day. However, many are distracted by the attractions of this passing world, and they look for the fulfillment of the deepest longings of their hearts in things and places that cannot give this fullness. As sharers in God's great plan of love, we can be intercessors for our brothers and sisters. Will we accept this invitation from the heart of our loving God?

Where do we go from here?

By our baptism we are called to the banquet of the Body and Blood of the Lord. Partaking of the Eucharist prepares us for the eternal banquet. Truly blessed are we who will eat bread in the kingdom of God. Take time after Mass to sit quietly with Jesus within you, thanking him for the grace of the Eucharist, and listening for direction and strength for the day.

**Thank you, Lord, for the gift of your Body and Blood
that we receive each day.**

Philippians 2.12-18 • Psalm 27 • Luke 14.25-33

"Whoever does not carry the cross and follow me cannot be my disciple."
Luke 14.27

Follow me

Jesus invites us to decide upon our priorities in life. He has promised us true happiness, peace and joy. But this comes at a price. He was utterly honest with his disciples when he said that it would cost them dearly to follow after him. To gain life with Christ, we must be willing to give him everything. This means choosing love over hate, generosity over greed, selflessness over selfishness. How can we do this? It is the love of God that compels us to place him first in our lives. The sacrifices we make are a mere shadow of his great sacrifice for us: the shedding of Jesus' blood, poured out for our redemption.

Where do we go from here?

People often speak of prioritizing their lives. It is a good idea to take a look at what is most important for us to get done in a day. List your priorities for today. Are God and the things of God at the top of the list? Have you provided any time to be still before God in prayer? Do you ask God for help when faced with a difficult situation? When someone is being difficult, do you pray for them? These are interesting questions whose answers are telling. Your priorities tell you where your life is focused.

**Lord, may your love for me transform my life
so that I may truly desire nothing more than life with you.
Help me to joyfully embrace my cross for your sake.**

Philippians 3.3-8 • Psalm 105 • Luke 15.1-10

O, give thanks to the Lord, call on his name,
make known his deeds among the peoples. …
Glory in his holy name;
let the hearts of those who seek the Lord rejoice.   *Psalm 105.1, 3*

God's abundant mercy

In the first reading today, Paul wishes us to be aware of his history. He was a zealous observer of the law to the point of persecuting the Church of God. He would appear to be an unlikely candidate for an apostolic ministry, but this was the mission to which he was called. Paul gloried in God's holy name; how richly we have been blessed by his labours and his writings!

In the gospel, two parables highlight the mercy of God. The good shepherd rescues the lost sheep and restores it to the flock. In our relationship with God, nothing is insignificant. The silver coin lost by the woman in the parable may have had little value in itself, but to her it was important. So, too, we are precious in God's sight. Give thanks to the Lord!

Where do we go from here?

In today's gospel we have the example of Jesus' patient love in seeking the lost sheep. God pursues us when we wander away. Jesus is the visible sign of God's loving desire that we be saved. Then we have the widow who gave all she had, which was very little, for God's glory; and Jesus says she gave more than anyone else. Let us risk giving our whole life to God and let God change it into a coin of great price.

**God, I know you love a cheerful giver.
Let me give freely today.**

Philippians 3.17-21; 4.1 • Psalm 122 • Luke 16.1-8

Brothers and sisters, join in imitating me, and observe those who live according to the example you have in us.
Philippians 3.17

Jesus, our model

Christ is our model and standard; we are to be like Christ in living our earthly lives. St. Paul invites us to imitate him in becoming Christ-like. We need to continue faithfully pursuing the goal of being united to Jesus, and not grow weary. Let us follow St. Paul's example and that of others who follow Jesus. If we follow his example, St. Paul tells us, we may also become examples to others. Like a chain reaction, those who imitate us will be followed by others as well. Our imitating and following will then spread to create a world of people who are like Christ.

Where do we go from here?

Let us be part of the chain, united in love with our brothers and sisters in Jesus. The gospels give us a word picture of how to follow Jesus. We never make the journey alone. We are surrounded by a countless number of brothers and sisters journeying to the kingdom, walking with Jesus. We support one another by prayer. It is only in heaven that we will meet some of the people who have prayed for us. Meditate on the spiritual bond that unites us to so many brothers and sisters.

**Lord God, may I be a bold witness of your love
and mercy to all, especially to the poor, the weak,
the lonely and the outcast.**

Philippians 4.10-19 • Psalm 112 • Luke 16.9-15

"Whoever is faithful in a very little is faithful also in much ...."

Luke 16.10

Faithfulness

To be faithful in small things is an expression of trust and love. The more we trust God and rely on God's providential care for us, the more we can give to others through our acts of love. Our growth in the life of faith is precisely this continual turning over of our trust to God, in good times and in bad.

When performed with love, every action, no matter how small, expresses our desire to be united to Jesus, to be faithful to his word. Our greatest accomplishments are those that are done in conformity to God's will. God knows our hearts. Our faithfulness is our response to God's abundant blessings.

Where do we go from here?

Do you feel like an unlikely candidate to witness to Jesus? Jesus had an uncanny knack of choosing unlikely followers. God sees our hearts. God knows what we are capable of doing for God's glory. God knows us better than we know ourselves. Saints are ordinary people who took God seriously. Be honest about your motives, and seek what God desires for you. God will do the rest.

O Lord, give me the grace to trust in you and to be faithful in all I do.

Ezekiel 47.1-2, 8-9, 12 • Psalm 46 • 1 Corinthians 3.9-11, 16-17 • John 2.13-22

Then he brought me back to the entrance of the temple; there, water was flowing from below the threshold of the temple toward the east ....   *Ezekiel 47.1*

Cleansing water

Today's readings overflow with imagery and depth of meaning. Three themes emerge: water, temple and baptism. In the vision of Ezekiel, we have a vibrant picture of water flowing freely and abundantly from under the threshold of the temple. We can picture a river cascading into the sea, bringing life to all living creatures in it and to the vegetation and trees that line its banks.

St. Paul asks the Corinthians, "Do you not know that you are God's temple and that God's Spirit dwells in you? ... For God's temple is holy, and you are that temple."

We become God's dwelling place through the cleansing waters of baptism, received in the temple of the Church. We are cleansed and purified; the grace of the sacrament remains with us always.

Where do we go from here?

I am the temple of God. It is good to think of this grace as a very personal reality. God—Father, Son and Holy Spirit—dwells in me. If I take time to be quiet before this mystery, I will experience the movement of the God-life within, cleansing and sanctifying me. I am called to dwell with God in the inner chamber of my heart, which is God's temple. Wherever I am, whatever I do, I am the temple of God.

God, help me to realize more fully the gift and spiritual power of my baptism.

Titus 1.1-9 • Psalm 24 • Luke 17.1-6

" I f you had faith the size of a mustard seed, you could say to this mulberry tree, 'Be uprooted and planted in the sea,' and it would obey you."
Luke 17.6

Quality of faith

Just before this gospel verse, Jesus speaks about forgiveness. Forgiveness is a reconciling force in our relationships with God and with one another. At times, we find it hard to believe that we have been forgiven and that our hearts are capable of forgiving. And when we are burdened with troubles, we struggle to believe that God—or anybody—cares. Our faith, nourished by God's words, will grow within us and become our strength to uproot the darkness in our hearts that hinders our flourishing in wisdom and grace. Faith helps us to understand and accept God's purpose in our lives and God's abiding presence with us. Jesus has faith in us: he called us to be his disciples.

Where do we go from here?

Pray to understand how precious you are in the sight of God. Pray to know God's loving mercy and forgiveness in your life. It is only when we can see the beauty of our own hearts, despite our weaknesses, that we are truly able to see the beauty of another's heart in their weakness, and love them. When we know our need for forgiveness, we are readily willing to offer forgiveness to others. To "know" is equated with an existential and experiential understanding of our need as well as our goodness: this is something to think about.

Lord, help us to see the faith you gave us and to live by it.

Tuesday | NOVEMBER 11

Titus 2.1-8, 11-14 • Psalm 37 • Luke 17.7-10

Take delight in the Lord,
and he will give you the desires of your heart.   *Psalm 37.3, 4*

Delight in the Lord

Today's psalm is one of great hope and trust in the face of life's struggles. The whole psalm is worth our reflection; the few verses given
us in today's liturgy provide a ray of its richness. Perhaps these words
sound a little idealistic and naïve, suggesting that simply turning to
God will eliminate all the problems, injustices and pain in our lives.
We experience evil that seems overwhelmingly powerful and destructive in many areas of life, both at a personal and a global level. But evil
does not have the last word! We are called to trust in the Lord and to
do good in even the most insignificant events and choices of each day.
Our hearts can then patiently wait in peace for the gradual but sure
unfolding of God's triumph over evil through the saving work of Jesus'
suffering, death and resurrection. This is our deepest heart's desire.

Where do we go from here?

Turning to the Lord in our need gives us strength and hope in
times of darkness. God is with us and the Holy Spirit is our guide
and teacher—light and understanding will come. Do not allow the
events of life to move you along without considering, in the light
of the Holy Spirit, what a particular event means and how God
is using it for good. Spend some time in silent prayer, asking for
understanding and perseverance in seeking God's will.

**Loving God, give me a trusting heart
to meet the people and events of each day.**

Titus 3.1-7 • Psalm 23 • Luke 17.11-19

Ten lepers approached him … they called out, saying, "Jesus, Master, have mercy on us!" When he saw them, he said to them, "Go and show yourselves to the priests." … Then one of them … turned back, praising God with a loud voice. … Jesus asked, "Were not ten made clean? But the other nine, where are they?"

Luke 17.12-15,17

Gratitude

The reading today from Titus speaks of the gratuitous gift of salvation. God saves us, not because we deserve it, but because of God's mercy. This gift comes to us through Jesus' total surrender of himself, a manifestation of the Father's complete and unconditional kindness and love for us. The gospel speaks of the one who "turned back praising God with a loud voice." Where do you stand in terms of living out of an attitude of thankfulness?

Where do we go from here?

Can I identify with the one leper who returned and gave thanks? Am I with the nine whom Jesus could not find? How do I live my gratefulness in my relationships with God, with family and friends, and at work? It is good to practise saying "thank you." A grateful heart is a happy and prayerful heart.

Jesus, I offer you a grateful heart.

Philemon 7-20 • Psalm 146 • Luke 17.20-25

"The days are coming when you will long to see one of the days of the Son of Man, and you will not see it."   *Luke 17.22*

You are not alone

Sometimes in life, we experience an unexpected crisis that weighs us down emotionally and spiritually. We seek God's help to take away the pain, to heal our wounds and to fix our situation. No matter how hard we pray, nothing seems to change. We feel abandoned. At times like this, "we long to see one of the days of the Son of Man." But God does not forsake us. The last line of the poem "Footprints in the Sand" is a reminder for us all: "'I do not understand why when I needed you most you would leave me.' The Lord replied, 'When you see only one set of footprints, it was then that I carried you.'"

Where do we go from here?

There are times when Jesus stands behind us and holds us close. We cannot see him, but we are secure in his arms. During such times, remember that you are facing in the same direction as Jesus—try to see as he sees. God's perspective is so different from ours. We prepare our hearts through the practice of choosing to see our life and its circumstances with God's view. Our freedom to choose is a powerful tool that God has given us. Finding God in everything—joy or sorrow, hardship or weakness—is a choice guided by the Holy Spirit and undergirded by grace.

Merciful God, look with pity on those who are carrying heavy burdens in life. Strengthen them and give them peace of heart and mind.

2 John 4-9 • Psalm 119 • Luke 17.26-37

"Those who try to make their life secure will lose it, but those who lose their life will keep it."
Luke 17.33

To lose our life

There are times when we feel insecure. We want to make sure that we will be all right no matter what happens. We want to be prepared for any event that comes into our daily lives. There is nothing wrong with this if we do not rely on ourselves alone but place our trust in God, who is our hope.

If our concerns are solely about material things, and we do not reflect on the shortness of this life and how we are just "passing through" this world, God's coming is going to take us by surprise. We will not be ready; we will lose our life. But if we are willing to give our life away in good deeds to help our brothers and sisters, then we will truly keep it. How am I giving my life away?

Where do we go from here?

The paradox of the gospel juxtaposes losing and finding: if I lose my life I will find it. If I cling to my life, I will lose it. Living in the Lord is about living with open hands! Receive all life's gifts with open hands. We are stewards of them, not owners. We do not belong to ourselves; we belong to the Lord. What would a day look like if you saw yourself as a steward and not an owner?

**Lord, show me how you want me to
"give my life away" today.**

3 John 5-8 • Psalm 112 • Luke 18.1-8

"There was a judge who neither feared God nor had respect for people. In that city there was a widow who kept coming to him and saying, 'Grant me justice against my opponent.'"

Luke 18.2-3

....

Persevere in prayer

Prayer draws us close to God and deepens our intimate relationship with God. God knows how weak and sinful we are. That is why Jesus told this parable to remind us not to lose heart in our prayer. God will always be there, but we may not experience this according to our expectations. We are asked to have faith, believing that our prayers will be granted according to God's will and in God's time. If this non-believing judge granted the widow the justice she claimed, how much more, then, will be granted by our heavenly Father, who loves us and will never abandon us. Never give up on praying to God, whatever situation you may be in, and trust that God listens and will respond.

Where do we go from here?

How many of us have regretted a word or action or wished that life had taken a different turn? We have all recited such a litany at one time or another, but our regret changes nothing. We need to learn from these experiences, forgive ourselves and move on—this will bring peace. Each decision to move on in trust is a resurrection moment that brings us into new life.

Lord God, I am weak and will falter in my journey to holiness, but I know that you are there to sustain me in moments of doubt and fatigue.

Proverbs 31.10-13, 16-18, 20, 26, 28-31 • Psalm 128 •
1 Thessalonians 5.1-6 • Matthew 25.14-30

Y ou are all children of light and children of the day; we are not
of the night or of darkness.

1 Thessalonians 5.5

....

God's coming

Today is the last Sunday of the liturgical year, and the Church directs
our attention to the final judgment. Endings are a good time to reflect on the fragility of life. St. Paul tells us that the Lord will come
like a thief in the night, a complete surprise. Everything seems so
secure, but that will be shattered. But the followers of Christ, those
who know the Lord, do not need to worry, because we are children of
light and the day. The children of the light are prepared for the coming of the Lord. Do you feel prepared for the coming of the Lord? If
the answer is no, what do you need to do? He is coming.

Where do we go from here?

As the liturgical year draws to a close, this is a good time to think
about your spiritual journey over this past year. What goals did
you set? What has your heart desired from God? How have you
grown in your faith? How do you want to deepen your love, faith
and trust in Jesus and live in the Holy Spirit? It's worth thinking
about: there is nothing more important than our union with God
and a living faith.

**Lord, I desire to be a child of the light and the day;
renew my spirit.**

Revelation 1.1-4; 2.1-5 • Psalm 1 • Luke 18.35-43

"What do you want me to do for you?" He said, "Lord, let me see again."
Luke 18.41

What do I want Jesus to do?

What do I really want Jesus to do for me today? The blind man asked that he might see again. Are there some aspects in my life in which I need new sight? Perhaps, over the course of the years, I have lost sight of something worthy, or there is a certain truth about my existence that needs re-vision. Maybe I need to see again the beauty and holiness of life: to know God's presence in my wife or my husband, my children or my parents, my brothers or my sisters, my friends or my co-workers. Genesis 1.31 says, "God saw everything that he had made, and indeed, it was very good." God is always good, and life is good. This is the truth that I need Jesus to help me see anew every day.

Where do we go from here?

What do I ask God for? What is top on my list of wants? Our desires move us to actions. Take time to honestly discern which desires motivate you. It is so easy to go through life, pushed by inner drives. To live life unintentionally is not helpful for spiritual growth. It is good to take stock of the direction of your life to see if perhaps you have been blind or have lost sight of any important values. God needs to be the centre and foundation of all we do so that we may grow in holiness.

Loving God, help me to see my worth in your sight, and to see my neighbour in the light of your love.

Revelation 3.1-6, 14-22 • Psalm 15 • Luke 19.1-10

O Lord, who may abide in your tent?
Who may dwell on your holy hill?
Those who walk blamelessly, and do what is right,
and speak the truth from their heart ....   *Psalm 15.1, 2*

. . . .

A listening heart

We can be so preoccupied with our own concerns and interests that we listen to the words of Scripture without really hearing them. Mary is our model of someone who did hear the word of God and was attentive to it. In all the events of her life, she was open and responsive to whatever was asked of her. "She treasured all these things and pondered them in her heart."

In the gospel, we find the familiar story of Zacchaeus. We may be amused by the sight of this little man scrambling down from the sycamore tree, but Zacchaeus was completely earnest. He was not deterred by human respect; he wanted to see Jesus and was not going to be held back by the complaints of others. His heart was now able to listen.

Where do we go from here?

Are we willing to look a little foolish in order to follow Jesus? Zacchaeus was focused on Jesus, and did not notice anything else. Keeping focused is an important element of the spiritual life. Plan each day so that time for being with God is provided: for prayer, for reading the Scripture and for silent listening. Our friendships deepen by taking time to be with the other person, learning about him or her, sharing stories, talking and listening to one another. Friendship with God needs all the same elements.

**Give me, O God, a listening heart,
that I may hear and heed your holy word.**

Revelation 4.1-11 • Psalm 150 • Luke 19.11-28

" I tell you, to all those who have, more will be given; but from those who have nothing, even what they have will be taken away."
Luke 19.26

....

God's ways

These words of Jesus make us cry out, "That's not fair!" When some have more than enough, why should they be given more, while others have nothing? Perhaps we can reflect on this puzzling parable from a different angle: the perspective of faith. The gift of faith is truly that—a gift! But, like all gifts, it calls for receptivity and a response. This response must be freely given. God does not force faith upon us or take away our freedom. God longs to give us more and more, so let us keep our "talent" of faith alive and growing, through lives lived in love and service each day.

Where do we go from here?

As we meet the circumstances and challenges of each day, do we not feel enriched, "gifted," when we respond with faith and generosity? The gift of faith grows and multiplies as we allow it to guide our lives. But if we put our faith in our pocket, only to be pulled out at church next Sunday, it will shrivel up, and we could lose even what we think we have. Let us be thankful for the wonderful gift of faith that nurtures and sustains our lives each day.

Increase my faith, dear Lord. May I keep it alive and growing through a generous response to you and in service of my brothers and sisters. Amen.

Revelation 5.1-10 • Psalm 149 • Luke 19.41-44

A s he came near and saw the city, he wept over it ....
Luke 19.41

Jesus wept

In these few sentences, Jesus gives us a picture of the loving, compassionate and merciful heart of God, his Father. Jesus knows what makes for peace; yet he sees the blindness and indifference in the hearts of his people for all that God wants to bestow on them. And so he sheds tears of compassionate love as he views the city of Jerusalem. There are crosses to bear in daily living. We need faith, trust, hope and love on life's journey. Even today in our dear, suffering, confused world, our Jesus yearns for the happiness and blessedness of all God's beloved children. Jesus desires us to share with him this concern and care for the happiness and blessedness of each one God has created.

Where do we go from here?

In the Spirit we share a bond with all who are in God. We can do so much through prayer. We can touch those near us and those on the other side of the continent. The power of prayer is unlimited. Take on the task, in union with Jesus, of intercession for the outpouring of the Holy Spirit. Set aside some time during the day to centre yourself, enter into God's presence and send the saving Spirit of God forth through your desire. Seek to be in union with the prayer of Jesus on the cross. In your heart—and in God's love—carry the needs of nations, the poor and oppressed, of your family, friends and all who cross your path today.

Jesus, make me an intercessor for the needs of the world.

Revelation 10.8-11 • Psalm 119 • Luke 19.45-48

H appy are those whose way is blameless,
who walk in the law of the Lord.
Psalm 119.1

Consecrated to the Lord

Today we recall the tradition that Mary's parents presented their young daughter to God in the Temple, and dedicated her life in the service to the Lord. Mary knew in her heart that dedication to the Lord demanded unselfish surrender, which is one of the great acts of love. She faithfully followed and meditated on the word of God. She was always open to what the Lord asked of her, and ready to respond to the challenges of love. Another characteristic of Mary that makes her a remarkable woman is her "presence." The gospels tell us very little of her accomplishments beyond the mere fact that "she was there." Like Mary, who walks in God's ways, may we be there for our brothers and sisters in sorrow, in joy, in sickness and in death.

Where do we go from here?

This is a good day to recall your own baptism when you were consecrated to God and to God's service. Think about the meaning of baptism: the power of God's grace at work in this sacrament. At baptism you receive all you need to live your Christian life. Look up what the *Catechism of the Catholic Church* says about baptism. Are you using the full spiritual power you received at baptism? Or have you grown hazy about God's gifts present within you? We can hold God to all his promises.

**Lord, grant me a generous heart in serving you.
Fortified in the Holy Spirit, may I be open and
always ready to respond to new challenges.**

Revelation 11.4-12 • Psalm 144 • Luke 20.27-40

"Those who belong to this age marry and are given in marriage; but those who are considered worthy of a place in that age and in the resurrection from the dead neither marry nor are given in marriage. Indeed they cannot die anymore ...."   *Luke 20.34-36*

Trust in the resurrection

Pondering over Luke's story, I recalled one stanza from a style of Japanese poetry called Renku: "Drifting into deep sleep/ I trust in resurrection." After the sleep of death, we believe we awaken to life everlasting. Jesus confounded the Sadducees, who did not believe in the resurrection. He referred to Moses and the burning bush. Long after Abraham, Isaac and Jacob died, God said, "I am the God of Abraham and the God of Isaac and the God of Jacob." These words imply that God is the God of the living, not the dead. Today we commemorate St. Cecilia, martyred for her faith. She surrendered her mortal life to gain life immortal. She trusted in the resurrection of the body and life everlasting.

Where do we go from here?

As we near the end of another year, it is a good time to reflect on the end of our life: the moment we will see Jesus and enter into God. The moment of our death reflects how we have lived our life. If we have walked in love with God during our lifetime, then death is not a traumatic wrench but is like passing over a final threshold. Jesus has put all our enemies—even death—under our feet. I will die one day. How can I live better now?

Lord, into your hands I commend my spirit.

Ezekiel 34.11-12, 15-17 • Psalm 23 • 1 Corinthians 15.20-26, 28 • Matthew 25.31-46

"Truly I tell you, just as you did it to one of the least of these who are members of my family, you did it to me!" *Matthew 25.40*

Enter into the kingdom

Jesus' criterion for entering the kingdom of heaven is love. Whatever we do for the least among us, Jesus tells us, we do it to him. St. John of the Cross writes, "In the evening of life, we will be judged on love." We all know that we will be judged when we die. At that time, many things will no longer matter: whether we have been rich or poor, educated or uneducated. What will matter is how we showed love to those around us. How compassionate were we when faced with others' needs? Did we give ourselves without counting the cost? Jesus, our king, asks that we open our eyes to the needs of those around us, and respond with compassion and love.

Where do we go from here?

The feast of Christ the King, which we celebrate today, puts before us the second coming of Jesus in glory. The gospel tells us that our deeds judge us. Jesus sits silently in judgment; our hearts give testimony to where we are destined. The second great commandment of loving as Jesus loved is the key to eternal life. Are you proactive in living the command of love? How can loving service become a more realized part of your life?

Lord, touch me with your compassion and help me to consider the needs of others, especially the weak, poor, downtrodden and voiceless.

Revelation 14.1-3, 4-5 • Psalm 24 • Luke 21.1-4

"Truly I tell you, this poor widow has put in more than all of them; for all of them have contributed out of their abundance, but she out of her poverty has put in all she had to live on."

Luke 21.3-4

Giving all

What could possibly motivate a person to give all that she has despite her poverty? Sacrifice is only possible when love is present. Only love could move a person to give away everything without thinking of herself. To be selfless and totally empty of self is what God desires from us, so that God can dwell in us. Only in this state can he fill us with his love. Only with hearts full of God's love can we love others. God's love that fills our hearts cannot be contained, but necessarily overflows in love to others.

Where do we go from here?

How can you emulate the example of the poor widow? This is another Scripture passage that is important to reflect on. We listen to and ponder the word of God so that we may be changed. Risk putting yourself, the gift of your time and your service into God's treasury without conditions.

**Let your love, O Lord, dwell in my heart
so that I may love others as you love me.**

Revelation 14.14-19 • Psalm 96 • Luke 21.5-11

S ing to the Lord, bless his name;
tell of his salvation from day to day.
Psalm 96.2

Sing a new song

This short passage sums up the Christian life. As we become more aware of God's goodness, our hearts are grateful and we burst into song. As we try to live in God's goodness, our lives become songs of praise to the Lord. As we reach out to others in need, to help them or just to be there for them, we proclaim God's salvation. Jesus showed us the power of God to save. God's gift of salvation is at work within us, through our participation in the mission of Jesus. Likewise, in the goodness and kindness of others, we experience God's saving help, and our life is a song of praise to the glory of God's name.

Where do we go from here?

St. Augustine says to sing a new song. When we sing not only with our voice but with our spirit, then we are singing a new song to God. We sing when we are happy and when things are going well. When we hear others singing, we know all is well for them. The psalmist tells us that our singing witnesses to God's saving work in our lives. Focus your life in God and sing the new song. When you are living in God, you can always sing a new song. It is stronger than life's adversities.

**Jesus, help me to receive your gift of salvation
each day and to sing a new song of praise.**

Revelation 15.1-4 • Psalm 98 • Luke 21.12-19

"So make up your minds not to prepare your defence in advance; for I will give you words and a wisdom that none of your opponents will be able to withstand or contradict. ... By your endurance you will gain your souls."

Luke 21.14-15, 19

Given words and wisdom

Have you ever been faced with an encounter that filled you with dread, and you were paralyzed with fear, not knowing how to respond to the situation? Then, in the midst of the discussion, did you find yourself speaking words you had not thought of in advance—the very words that were needed to break an impasse or bring clarity and healing? That was the Holy Spirit in action! Luke isn't recommending a careless approach to the responsibilities and choices that make up each day. With lives deeply rooted in faithful prayer and with hearts open to hear God's voice, our efforts to prepare for our day will be guided by the strong but gentle voice of the Holy Spirit. The Spirit will speak and act through us in ways we could never have imagined.

Where do we go from here?

Trusting the movement of the Holy Spirit can be a scary thing. We like to be in control. The problem with this is that we are really not in control. Do you think you can control your life? If not, what is controlling your life? You can decide who will be in control, and your best bet is God. God has already won the victory. Move over and let go of being in the driver's seat! Wonderful things can happen then, and you can relax.

Holy Spirit of light and love, surprise me with your word today! Give me a listening and responsive heart, especially in challenging encounters.

Revelation 18.1-2, 21-23; 19.1-3, 9 • Psalm 100 • Luke 21.20-28

E nter his gates with thanksgiving,
and his courts with praise.
Give thanks to him, bless his name.

Psalm 100.4

....

Bless his name

St. Augustine says we are Easter people and Alleluia should be our song. Alleluia means "Praise God." Praise for the ancient Hebrew is very close to our word "thanks." Praising God fills our lives with God's presence and reminds us of God's greatness and faithfulness. Acknowledging God's presence makes us grateful and thankful for all the good things God has done for us. But it is not easy to say Alleluia all the time. Do you find God in problems as well as in joy?

Where do we go from here?

When we are grumpy and out of sorts, we are not always ready for good news. Jesus brings good news! Let Jesus' good news be the basis of your living, and surrender grumpy days. Of course, there will be hard days, but that does not mean they have to produce grumpiness. Alleluia should also be our song for the problem times of life. God can bring good out of every circumstance. Do you believe it? If you let the joy of the Lord enter into your heart, then you are good news for others.

Lord God, I praise and thank you for the countless blessings you have given me. May your good news be the building block of my life.

Revelation 20.1-4, 11-15; 21.1-2 • Psalm 84 • Luke 21.29-33

And I saw the dead, great and small, standing before the throne, and books were opened. Also another book was opened, the book of life. And the dead were judged according to their works, as recorded in the books.

Revelation 20.12

Map of life

What a powerful end-of-the-year reading is given to us today: a vision of the Last Judgment, all the dead standing before the throne of God while the Book of Life is read. Jesus is not there as a stern judge. We will be judged by our works, by the way we lived our life, and by the way we loved. How we live our lives is shaping us now for the new heaven and the new earth, where God will dwell with us and we will be God's people for all eternity. God himself will wipe away the tears from our eyes, and we will all dwell together in joy. "Death will be no more; mourning and crying and pain will be no more, for the first things have passed away" (Revelation 21.4).

Where do we go from here?

Heaven is not only won by great deeds, but by the smallest acts of kindness. If we fill our lives with small acts of kindness and loving care for our brothers and sisters, eternal life is ours. And even now, living a free and selfless life brings happiness. Look to Jesus; his example gives us a map for our lives. The Scriptures give a detailed game plan. Engage the Scriptures: study them, pray over them and listen to them at the liturgy.

Amen. We await the new heaven and the new earth.

Revelation 22.1-7 • Psalm 95 • Luke 21.34-36

O that today you would listen to his voice!
Do not harden your hearts …
Psalm 95.7

Hear the voice of the Lord

When we begin an Advent season, our thoughts lead us to Christ's coming among us in human form. We no longer have his physical presence, but he assures us, "I am with you always; yes, to the end of time." Time: how elusive it is! It moves forward, day after day. We can do nothing to control it, but with its graces and challenges, it is ours to use. Though we might feel that we lack love and generosity, we can take heart from these words of St. Teresa Benedicta of the Cross (Edith Stein): "At the end of the day, just take everything exactly as it is, put it in God's hands and leave it with him. Then you will be able to rest in him, really rest, and start the next day as a new life."

Where do we go from here?

Begin your day by taking a few minutes to listen to God's voice and to pray for the guidance of the Holy Spirit for the day. Time keeps moving on; days and years pass by, but God is eternal and does not pay much attention to time. We have been given an eternal moment to work in: "today" in the eternal "now." Use this moment of time well. Let it be God-centred; it lasts for eternity. Now is really the only time we have.

Lord, help me to use well your gift of time.

Isaiah 63.16-17; 64.1, 3-8 • Psalm 80 • I Corinthians 1.3-9 •
Mark 13.31-37

"**B**eware, keep alert; for you do not know when the time will come."
Mark 13.33

Be alert

Life on this earth is relatively short, so we must always be alert and careful in what we do, how we live and how we speak. We must be aware of the fact that it is only by the gratuitous grace of our Saviour, Jesus Christ, that we can accomplish any good work for our neighbours or families, or offer advice in words of comfort or praise. The gospel of today calls us to be alert and watchful. May the light of God's face be your guide as you strive for salvation, and be your peace as you rest in the will of the Father in heaven.

Where do we go from here?

Beware, keep alert, keep awake and be watchful. Liturgically, we are commemorating the coming of God and looking forward to the second coming at the end of time. "Prepare" is a key word throughout the Advent season: we hear it in the message of the prophets and as a solemn warning on the lips of John the Baptist and Jesus. Prepare! God comes to us every day. This contemporary coming is the important one, because if we do not prepare for Jesus' coming into our lives today, we will not be ready to receive him when he comes in glory. Prepare! Let the word echo throughout your Advent!

Jesus, help me to live Advent in a spirit of joyful hope and conscious preparation.

Isaiah 2.1-5 • Psalm 122 • Matthew 8.5-11, 13

"**L**ord, I am not worthy to have you come under my roof; but only speak the word, and my servant will be healed."
Matthew 8.6-8

I do believe

We should ask to grow in our faith every day. Often when Jesus performed miracles, he did so in response to the faith of those who asked. "Do you believe that I can do this for you?" The centurion was a pagan, and he evidently had witnessed the power of Jesus. He did not hesitate to ask for a favour. He believed that Jesus could cure his servant. How astonishing and humbling is this story for us! Do we really believe that God is in charge of our world? Do we continue to witness to Jesus? Our fidelity can be a light for those who are searching for truth. May we be a light that will show whoever we meet that Jesus is the way to eternal life and happiness.

Where do we go from here?

The message of Isaiah again points to the messianic kingdom. For those who walk in God's ways, there will be peace. When Jesus returns, all nations will be at peace. Let us go to the mountain of God, where God is to be found, and we will be taught what we are to do. The mountain of God is our time of prayer, set aside for God that we may be taught God's ways. Take time to pray over the text of Isaiah 2.1-5. What does it mean to you to climb the mountain of the Lord? What does it mean to walk in the light of the Lord? Write down your reflections.

**Lord, I do believe you can work wonders in me
and through me.**

Isaiah 11.1-10 • Psalm 72 • Luke 10.21-24

" I thank you, Father, Lord of heaven and earth, because you have hidden these things from the wise and the intelligent and have revealed them to infants ...."
Luke 10.21

God among us

Today if we were to see Jesus face to face, live with him, eat with him and walk with him, would we be any different from what we are now? Today's gospel reminds us that knowledge and cleverness are not the criteria we need for communication with our heavenly Father. We need to know Jesus: his life, his teaching. We need to have a childlike heart—not a childish one, but one that is simple and pure. Jesus will show us the way to the Father, if we but trust in him and his Spirit of Love. Following Jesus will be our path to the Father and to eternal happiness.

Where do we go from here?

Isaiah is the special prophet for Advent. In beautiful word pictures, he tells us about the Messiah, his attributes and the fulfillment of time. The messiah will judge with righteousness, not by appearance, but in truth. At his coming, all creation will be at peace. We will no longer hurt or destroy one another, because we will all know the Lord. It is knowledge of God that will change the world. Let us begin now to know the Lord, and to be established in an inner peace that will ripple out into our world. We will plant the seed of the kingdom.

Lord, I rejoice in your presence and ask you to pour out your love on all your children.

Isaiah 25.6-10 • Psalm 23 • Matthew 15.29-37

Great crowds came to him, bringing with them the lame, the maimed, the blind, the mute, and many others. They put them at his feet, and he cured them. *Matthew 15.30*

....

Go up to the mountain

Jesus loved to go to the mountain to be alone with his Father, to be with his apostles, to teach and probably just to enjoy the beauty around him. Isaiah tells us, "On this mountain … the Lord God will wipe away all tears"—there will be feasting, and death will be destroyed forever. What a consoling message for God's people. The gospel says that Jesus went up the mountain. There he healed many and was moved with pity and love toward those who had followed him and fasted for three days. Jesus still opens blind eyes, heals wounded hearts and feeds us daily with himself as our strength and hope. If we follow him by living what he taught, we, too, will praise and glorify him on the holy mountain of his glory.

Where do we go from here?

The Advent readings taken from the prophet Isaiah are among the most comforting readings in the Old Testament. We are preparing for the birth of Jesus, God among us. During Advent, we celebrate the three comings of Jesus: as a baby at Bethlehem, his coming to each of us, and his coming in glory at the end of time. The prophet Isaiah prepares us for the second coming of the Son of Man in glory. Take time to ponder the liturgical readings of Advent. They point to a mystery much broader than a babe in a manger. What do you think?

Lord, heal me that I may follow you with freedom and love.

Isaiah 26.1-6 • Psalm 118 • Matthew 7.21, 24-27

"**N**ot everyone who says to me, 'Lord, Lord,' will enter the kingdom of heaven, but only the one who does the will of my Father in heaven."

Matthew 7.21

....

Come, Lord

Preparing for the coming of the Lord involves a real internal conversion. Attending the liturgy, giving alms and saying "Lord, Lord," without showing justice or giving of self in our actions and intentions to our neighbours or family, draws a zero in the sight of God. We must be sincere and loving from our hearts, and follow the word of God in order to draw near to our Saviour. The gospel tells us to build our lives on the rock of God's word. We must act on God's word, not merely listen and then go and do what we want.

Where do we go from here?

Christ is the rock upon which we build. Isaiah tells us, "Those of steadfast mind you keep in peace—in peace because they trust in you" (26.3). Keeping our eyes fixed on Jesus with steadfast minds and hearts, and trusting in his love and the gift of his Spirit become our rock-like security in all the changes of life. Pray using the image of Christ as a rock, and think of the ways you need to be strengthened, along with the ways you already have been strengthened. Ask God for what you need.

Lord, give me a steadfast heart and a willing spirit.

Isaiah 29.17-24 • Psalm 27 • Matthew 9.27-31

"**D**o you believe that I am able to do this?" They said to him, "Yes, Lord." Then he touched their eyes and said, "According to your faith let it be done to you."

Matthew 9.27-29

....

I see

Did you ever pick up a familiar book and receive a new insight about the text as you were reading? You were able to see it in a new way. This is seeing in the way that God wants us to see God's word in Scripture. We often dismiss what we routinely hear or experience. Yet, sometimes we are struck in a new way by something very familiar so that we actually take it in, because we opened our minds and listened. Can it be that the two blind men in the gospel could see because their faith opened their eyes? If that is true, is it possible that our faith in Jesus can open our eyes to things we do not understand?

Where do we go from here?

Today's reading from Isaiah concentrates on newness and restoration. This is the wonderful message of Advent. God is among us, our sins are forgiven, and we will have joy and new life. All creation will be renewed: "Shall not Lebanon in a very little while become a fruitful field, and the fruitful field be regarded as a forest?" (Isaiah 29.17). Isaiah goes on to say that the blind will see and the deaf will hear. Advent is a time of joy. How do you want to be renewed during this time of Advent? Hold this before the Lord.

Jesus, we ask you to open our eyes blinded by selfish desires, and open our ears to the cries of the poor.

Isaiah 30.19-21, 23-26 • Psalm 147 • Matthew 9.35–10.1, 5, 6-8

When he saw the crowds, he had compassion for them, because they were harassed and helpless, like sheep without a shepherd.

Matthew 9.36

Be compassionate

Advent is a time when we open our hearts. We long for the compassion of Jesus to touch us, as well as all our brothers and sisters everywhere who suffer from violence and war, so that our wounds and blindness may be healed. We long for his touch and his smile to light up the dark places of our earth, so that all may welcome his coming with joyful and grateful hearts.

Jesus never passed by anyone who needed his compassion and mercy. He healed all who sought a cure from their pain. He gave his disciples the power to do as he did, to go and seek out all who were lost or abandoned, and to cure them.

Where do we go from here?

By baptism you have been called to be a disciple of Jesus, to do as Jesus did. You are called to proclaim the gospel of joy and hope, and, yes, to open the eyes of the blind and to untie those who are bound. Quite a job description: ask the Lord how you are to do this. The answer may be a surprise. God will give the gifts needed for your task.

**Lord, open my heart to serve in whatever way
you want me to.**

Isaiah 40.1-5, 9-11 • Psalm 85 • 2 Peter 3.8-14 • Mark 1.1-8

" The one who is more powerful than I is coming after me; I am not worthy to stoop down and untie the thong of his sandals."
Mark 1.7

To prepare the way of the Lord

It is amazing that God waits for our repentance. God is patient with us, for with God, one day is as a thousand years, and God does not wish anyone to be lost. But the day of the Lord will come like a thief in the night. Will we be ready? Will we be found without blemish and at peace? The cry of the Baptist still sounds, calling all to repentance: "Prepare a way in your heart for your God." Let the voice of John the Baptist ring in your ears and hearts. "Prepare a way for the Lord." Repent with a sincere heart, and seek God's face.

Where do we go from here?

Amid all of this we hear a voice crying, "Comfort, O comfort my people…" (Isaiah 40.1). What good news this is for us! For from the desert of this world, the voices of the poor that call for justice will be heard. This is the work of the Messiah. He has come in Jesus, but until he comes again, we are his hands to clothe the naked, to find homes for the homeless, to feed the hungry and to spread the kingdom. Stretch out your arms to all in need.

Lord, fill my heart with a spirit of repentance, that I may follow you in compassionate love.

347

Genesis 3.9-15, 20 • Psalm 98 • Ephesians 1.3-6, 11-12 • Luke 1.26-38

But the Lord God called to the man, and said to him, "Where are you?" He said, "I heard the sound of you in the garden, and I was afraid, because I was naked; and I hid myself." He said, "Who told you that you were naked? Have you eaten from the tree of which I commanded you not to eat?"

Genesis 3.9-11

Where are you?

What a wonderful passage this is from the book of Genesis, chosen specially by the Church for this feast. The passage details the sin of our first parents.

When we sin, God calls to us, "Where are you?" And if we hear the voice of the Lord, our first reaction is to be afraid and ashamed. When we sin, we are naked and vulnerable, so we hide behind denials and illusions. Mary was chosen because there was an open emptiness in her that God could fill with God's grace. And God did this in an abundant measure.

Where do we go from here?

"Where are you?" Are you listening to the voice of God? Take the question to prayer; sit in silence in the presence of God's question. Let it reverberate within until you hear the answer. Where are you? Meditate on chapter 3 of Genesis.

Lord, empty my heart of all but your transforming Word. Help me to be receptive.

Isaiah 40.1-11 • Psalm 96 • Matthew 18.12-14

H e will feed his flock like a shepherd;
he will gather the lambs in his arms,
and carry them in his bosom,
and gently lead the mother sheep.

Isaiah 40.11

Gentle shepherd

The gospel tells us that Jesus is the good shepherd who seeks the lost sheep and finds it. Jesus was sent from the Father to gather sinners and the lost into the kingdom of heaven. God wants us all to be saved. The prophet Isaiah gives us such a tender image of the shepherd: he gathers the lambs in his arms, close to his heart. This is an image of the tender, loving mercy of our God. From the moment we sinned, God has sought us. Take time in the presence of the Blessed Sacrament and thank God for the gift of salvation.

Where do we go from here?

Have you strayed away from the faith, or does God seem far from you? God is always near; we simply lose our focus and do not hear God's gentle whisper. Pray the simple prayer of Advent: "Come, Lord Jesus." Throughout the day, repeat these words in your heart, and truly desire that Jesus find you. When he does, ask him what you are to do.

Lord Jesus, be merciful to me, a sinner.

Isaiah 40.25-31 • Psalm 103 • Matthew 11.28-30

" Come to me, all you that are weary and are carrying heavy burdens and I will give you rest."
Matthew 11.28

Come to me

When two animals are yoked together, they share the weight of the job. The same thing happens when we share Jesus' yoke, except that Jesus bears the heaviest part of the burden. God became human so that we could rise from the terrible yoke of sin, and be free and joyful in God's presence. The prophet Isaiah explains it this way: "Those who wait for the Lord shall renew their strength, they shall mount up with wings like eagles, they shall run and not be weary, they shall walk and not faint" (Isaiah 40.31). In the grace of the Lord, we can run in the same joyful freedom whether we are three or 83.

Where do we go from here?

Seek to be joyful in the Lord in your prayer and in all your tasks and service for the Lord. Do you find yourself grumbling because of all you have to do or because someone has asked you a favour? Instead, thank God for your work and the strength you have to help. When someone asks a favour, do it with a smile. Thank God you have the gift of love to give. The blessing will be yours.

Lord, help me to give with a joyful heart and not to grow weary, but to run in your ways.

Isaiah 41.13-20 • Psalm 145 • Matthew 11.11-15

For I, the Lord your God, hold your right hand;
it is I who say to you, "Do not fear, I will help you."
Isaiah 41.13

I will help you

Fear not! God is with us and his help will never fail. Our God is gracious and merciful, ready to give when we ask. God created us for himself and pours out grace upon us to fill us with his presence and keep us in his love. God will make the wilderness of our hearts a place of flowing water and beautiful growth. Step out in faith to give yourself into God's hands; trust the loving presence and guidance of the Holy Spirit. Take the risk to "let go and let God" take charge of your life. God is the good shepherd who will unfailingly bring us home.

Where do we go from here?

God loves us greatly. God has given freely to us the abundance of his presence and life. Let us freely give of ourselves to others in loving service. God loves a cheerful giver. Is there something you can do today for a brother or sister?

Jesus, give me a loving and generous heart.

Zechariah 2.10-13 or Revelation 11.19; 12.1, 3-6, 10 • Judith 13 •
Luke 1.39-47

S ing and rejoice, O daughter Zion! For lo, I will come and dwell
in your midst, says the Lord.
Zechariah 2.10

....

Mary, our mother

Our Lady of Guadalupe, whose feast we celebrate today, carries Jesus
in her womb. Mary's soul was made ready for receiving Jesus through
the grace of her Immaculate Conception. She speaks to Juan Diego
with such loving tenderness, a tenderness she bestows on all her children. She is our mother who cares for us deeply and desires that we
receive the salvation that is ours in her Son. This is cause for great
rejoicing—God is among us.

Where do we go from here?

The Holy Spirit prepares us for the coming of Jesus. God is not
stinting in grace. We need only open our hearts to receive it. Living in the Spirit gives unity and harmony to our lives. Are you
living earnestly in the Spirit? This is a day-to-day decision. Begin
each day with a sincere gift of yourself to God and renew that
gift frequently throughout the day. Make God a part of your daily
routine. A quiet inner prayer before important decisions will bring
enlightenment.

**Jesus, send your Spirit into my heart,
and I shall be renewed.**

Sirach 48.1-4, 9-11 • Psalm 80 • Matthew 17.10-13

R estore us, O Lord God of hosts;
let your face shine, that we may be saved.
Psalm 80.19

Let your face shine upon us

The Church's prayers during Advent are a great longing for the restoration that Jesus brings. We celebrate the memorial of his first coming, and earnestly desire his second coming in glory. Jesus came to St. Lucy, whose feast day is today; she gave her life to him completely and was strengthened in the Holy Spirit to lay down her life for Jesus, as he did for her. His glory shone upon her as she entered into the presence of her bridegroom.

Where do we go from here?

Enter whole-heartedly into the earnest longing of the Church during this season. Ask to receive a new restoration in the Holy Spirit, a new fervour to seek the Lord and to follow in his ways. Come, Lord Jesus.

**Jesus, fill my heart with longing for you
and fervour in my service for your sake.**

Isaiah 61.1-2, 10-11 • Luke 1 • 1 Thessalonians 5.16-24 •
John 1.6-8, 19-28

There was a man sent from God, whose name was John. He came as a witness to testify to the light, so that all might believe through him. He himself was not the light, but he came to testify to the light.

John 1.6-8

··

Rejoice in the Lord

Rejoice, rejoice in the Lord always! Release your spirit and let it be free to seek the will of the Father. For God desires our salvation and has clothed us in the mantle of justice and peace like a person adorned with jewels. Do not be afraid to proclaim Christ to the world, for in his Spirit is the strength of God, and he will preserve you in soul and body, and keep you from every kind of evil. Pray always to discern the path of truth and purity of heart to which you are called in Christ Jesus. John the Baptist knew his place in the plan of the Father. He did not claim to be what he was not, but bent in humility and gave God the rightful place. Can we claim to do the same?

Where do we go from here?

In today's second reading, St. Paul exhorts us to rejoice in the Lord and to pray unceasingly. The theme of joy continually appears and reappears during the Advent season. What is this joy? It is a fruit of the Holy Spirit. Joy is deeper than any sorrow, and it can sustain us in the most difficult of circumstances. If we keep the Lord in our minds and hearts all during the day, we will know joy.

Lord, let me find joy in your Holy Spirit.

Numbers 24.2-7, 15-17 • Psalm 25 • Matthew 21.23-27

M ake me to know your ways, O Lord;
teach me your paths.
Lead me in your truth, and teach me,
for you are the God of my salvation;
for you I wait all day long.
Psalm 25.4-5

....

The power of prayer

In prayer God makes known his ways and the path we are to follow. God helps us each step of the way. Prayer opens our hearts to receive God's grace. It is in God's company that we find calmness and peace. God is present to us and ready to teach us as we wait upon him in prayerful listening for the direction of the Holy Spirit dwelling in our hearts.

Where do we go from here?

To pray unceasingly, we set aside times for silent listening to God and for reading the Scripture, perhaps in the early morning before the day begins. From your time of prayer, take away a word or thought to hold in your heart. Frequently return to the thought or phrase throughout the day, and for a moment, inwardly pause to become conscious of your inner word. This is unceasing prayer, a way of being in the presence of God all day long, even during the busiest of days.

Lord, teach me your ways and lead me in the way of truth.

Zephaniah 3.1-2, 9-13 • Psalm 34 • Matthew 21.28-32

A h, soiled, defiled, oppressing city!
It has listened to no voice; it has accepted no correction.
It has not trusted in the Lord;
it has not drawn near to its God.

Zephaniah 3.1-2

Repent and listen to the Lord

The prophets sometimes spoke strong words of doom to the people. God spoke through his prophets this way in order to wake up God's people and call them back. The list of grievances in today's reading is interesting. The people have not listened, have not been willing to be corrected, have not trusted or drawn near to God. God is calling God's people to awareness of what they are doing so that they may change. This list applies to me today. Do I listen? Am I willing to be corrected? Do I trust the Lord, and am I seeking to draw near to God?

Where do we go from here?

A good test for whether I am listening to the Lord and willing to be corrected is my willingness to listen to my neighbour and receive correction. Can I put my anxiety into God's hands? Ask Jesus to show you how to trust in his guidance and walk in his ways. Reflect on what ways you are seeking to draw near to God. Besides your own times of prayer, shared prayer with your family or a group can be very beneficial for spiritual growth.

**Lord, fill my heart with loving trust
and help me to walk in your ways.**

Genesis 49.2, 8-10 • Psalm 72 • Matthew 1.1-17

For he delivers the needy when they call,
the poor and those who have no helper.
He has pity on the weak and the needy,
and saves the lives of the needy.

Psalm 72.12-13

....

He hears the cry of the poor

Jesus in his humanity is the image of God made visible. The Old Testament writers give a word picture of God in anthropological language so Israel can understand and can be in relationship with God. In the Old Testament, God hears the cry of the poor, cares for the needy, heals the lame and the blind, and frees the captive and those who are oppressed. God is a righteous God of loving tenderness. Jesus comes preaching the good news of love and freedom; he loves the poor and outcast, and heals many who are brought to him.

Where do we go from here?

This is the God who calls each of us to holiness. Why are we sometimes afraid of a God who loves us so tenderly? The loving mercy of God for us is shown especially in the gospel of Luke. Take time to read Luke's gospel slowly; study it, and pray over it. The vulnerable babe of Bethlehem reveals the lengths to which God was willing to go for love of us. Are we willing to imitate that generous gift of self-giving?

**My Jesus, what have you not given for me?
Help me to give all I am in return.**

Jeremiah 23.5-8 • Psalm 72 • Matthew 1.18-24

As Jesus passed along the Sea of Galilee, he saw Simon and his brother Andrew casting a net into the sea—for they were fishermen. ... And immediately they left their nets and followed him.

Mark 1.16,18, 20

....

Follow Jesus

Jesus sees them in the midst of their work and immediately calls them. They follow immediately. This sense of immediacy is astounding and presents a paradigm for what our response to God needs to be. We do not start by saying "yes" with such alacrity. We grow into it by day-to-day choices. St. Thomas of Aquinas says virtue is easy. What he is talking about is virtue acquired by practice. We fail, but we persevere until, with practice and the grace of God, we gain facility. It is like a craftsman learning his trade: it comes through practice and experience. Strategic planning is also helpful in growing in virtue and responding to the Lord with immediacy.

Where do we go from here?

Do you have a strategy for your spiritual growth? Reflect on your life, where you are now, and where you need to go. In order to make the plan work, what choices do you need to put into place? Then begin! Our failures never count with God. God sees our perseverance and how many times we get up and begin again. The grace of God strengthens our feeble efforts, and through grace, we will be victorious. Count on it.

**Jesus, give me strength and the gift of endurance
to seek and do your will.**

Judges 13.2-7, 24-25 • Psalm 71 • Luke 1.5-25

B e to me a rock of refuge,
a strong fortress, to save me,
for you are my rock and my fortress.
… For you, O Lord, are my hope. *Psalm 71.3, 5*

God our refuge

Advent focuses on the coming gift of salvation. Every year we relive the mystery of God's gift of re-creation as we retell the story of Jesus. The Church does this so that we have the opportunity to enter into that story and make it our own. With each new year, we are meant to receive the grace of redemption more profoundly, to become one with Jesus in the Father's will. Our participation in the liturgical seasons has the power to transform us and make us holy. God's loving mercy gives us the cycle of seasons to clothe ourselves more deeply in the grace at work within us. God is our rock of refuge and our strong fortress to save us in all circumstances.

Where do we go from here?

Let us worship in spirit and in truth, standing before the altar in open and joyful receptivity to the grace of the Eucharist. Jesus is uniquely present in four ways in the Eucharist: in the sacrament, in the priest, in the proclamation of the Word and in the Assembly. His presence is salvific. When we gather for liturgy, we are the Body of Christ, and when the Word is proclaimed, it is truly Jesus speaking to us with the power to change us. Be aware of the presence of Jesus in the liturgy; take time to study and learn more about this great mystery. Read the Vatican II document on the liturgy, Constitution on the Sacred Liturgy *(Sacrosanctum Concilium)*.

My Jesus, I place all my trust in you.

Isaiah 7.10-14; 8.10 • Psalm 24 • Luke 1.26-38

The angel said to her, "Do not be afraid, Mary, for you have found favour with God."
Luke 1.30

My strength is sufficient

St. Luke recounts the moment when God became human. Mary was the receptacle to receive our salvation. It is always so comforting for us to hear the words "do not be afraid": "Don't worry. I am with you and have great power to keep you safe and to do what I have promised." Mary believed the words of the angel. We also need to believe that God's promises to us will be fulfilled.

Where do we go from here?

Do you find yourself facing many troubles and anxieties? So many of the circumstances of life are beyond our control, but Jesus has promised that his grace is sufficient for us. Offer your anxiety to the Lord, and renew your offering each time your mind is filled with fear and worry. Jesus has promised that his strength is greater than our weakness and troubles.

Jesus, receive the troubled thoughts of my heart and give me your peace.

2 Samuel 7.1-5, 8-12, 14, 16 • Psalm 89 • Romans 16.25-27 •
Luke 1.26-38

"**Y**ou will conceive in your womb and bear a son, and you will name him Jesus."

Luke 1.31

God-with-us

It was God's initiative that allowed the great King David to build a temple for God's glory, and it was to be built when God ordained, not David. Even before David, God led the people step by step to the Promised Land, always guiding them, always merciful toward their failings.

God chose the time for the Son to become human and to be born as one of us. Not in a palace, not of a queen, but of an ordinary Jewish girl in a poor, unknown town. Prepared from her birth, this simple woman was graced by the Trinity to be the mother of God's Son. Like the great David, Mary said "yes" to the revelation of the angel, and behold, our God came among us.

Where do we go from here?

"Do not be afraid." In the Old and New Testaments, God continually speaks these words to individuals he chooses for a mission. We need this assurance from God, because the task often seems too large and we are so small. God likes to work with the poor and needy, because they know their need of God's strength. No mission was greater than Mary's—she trusted God and said "yes." We may ask the Lord, "How is what you are asking possible?" Like Mary, let us trust in God's grace and say "yes."

Lord, open my heart to receive your Word.

Monday | **DECEMBER 22**

I Samuel 1.24-28 • I Samuel 2 • Luke 1.46-56

And Mary said, "My soul magnifies the Lord, and my spirit rejoices in God my Savior, for he has looked with favour on the lowliness of his servant. Surely, from now on all generations will call me blessed …."

Luke 1.46-48

Magnify the Lord

Christmas is drawing nearer, and the liturgy puts the example of Mary before us to prepare for this beautiful feast. In her we see God's plan of salvation at work: how God chooses the lowly, and how God does wonderful things in them. Mary recognized her lowliness, but by God's grace she became great. Mary bore our salvation. She is our model for discipleship. Her lowliness mirrors that of her Son, Jesus, who did not cling to divinity but was willing to be born in a stable, surrounded by animals and welcomed into the loving arms of Mary and Joseph.

Where do we go from here?

My soul magnifies the Lord. We can all sing this hymn with Mary. The Magnificat belongs to all God's children, because God works wonders in us every day! Like Mary, we are to be "Word bearers." The word of God conceived in Mary's womb through the power of the Holy Spirit is also conceived in us spiritually through the Holy Spirit. Reflect on the Annunciation scene in Luke and apply it to your spiritual life. Where are the parallels?

Lord, prepare my heart for the feast of Christmas.

Malachi 3.1-4; 4.5-6 • Psalm 25 • Luke 1.57-66

See, I am sending my messenger to prepare the way before me, and the Lord whom you seek will suddenly come to his temple.
Malachi 3.1

....

Refiner's fire

Who can endure the day of his coming? Are we ready for the coming of the Lord? The first reading, from Malachi, speaks of the coming of the Messiah, and Israel needs to be purified and ready for his coming. The Church uses this challenging reading as Christmas draws near and Jesus the Messiah will be among us. To follow Jesus, to be united in him with the Father in the Spirit, calls for deep purity of heart, a cleansing and regeneration. It is not always easy, but grace supports us, and the fruit is eternal life.

Where do we go from here?

The refiner's fire burns off all the dross from gold; and fuller's soap is like lye in its ability to cleanse. Being purified and being cleansed of all our impurity and dross do not sound like very pleasant experiences. Yet, God knows that each of us is a precious gold vessel that contains the divine life. The Holy Spirit purifies us gradually, and only to the extent that we can bear. Trust God and say, "Yes, with the grace of God, I can endure the day of his coming." Spiritual growth is a wonderful adventure that ends in glory.

Here I am, Lord. Take me.

2 Samuel 7.1-5, 8-12, 16 • Psalm 89 • Luke 1.67-79

T hen his father Zechariah was filled with the Holy Spirit and spoke this prophecy: "Blessed be the Lord God of Israel ….
Luke 1.67

Tomorrow

The day before Christmas, the Church's liturgy puts before us the canticle of Zechariah. Zechariah and Elizabeth had waited faithfully for the coming of the Messiah. Elizabeth gave birth to the one who would announce his coming. Zechariah acknowledges and sings a hymn of praise for all of Israel. The time of waiting is over and salvation has begun. All the descendants of Abraham have received the gift of salvation. God's mercy will take human form and live among us.

Where do we go from here?

Invite Jesus into your life in a new and deeper way, so that your time of waiting will be over and the gift of salvation will be intensified in you. God's mercy will accompany you throughout life until Jesus comes to escort you into eternal life. This is not an impossible fairy tale; it is our faith. Never stop inviting Jesus to lead you to new levels of holiness.

**Jesus, all my hope is in you.
Lead me into the glory of the Father.**

Isaiah 9.2-4, 6-7 • Psalm 96 • Titus 2.11-14 • Luke 2.1-16

T he angel said to them, "… I am bringing you good news of great joy for all the people: to you is born this day in the city of David a Saviour, who is the Messiah, the Lord."

Luke 2.10-11

....

A Saviour is born for us

The readings for the Midnight Mass of Christmas are bursting with joy over the good news. Isaiah can hardly contain himself: the people who walked in darkness have seen a great light … he is named Wonderful Counsellor, Mighty God, Everlasting Father, Prince of Peace (9.2-4, 6-7). St. Paul's letter to Titus says, "The grace of God has appeared, bringing salvation to all" (Titus 2.11-14), teaching us to live in a new way and giving us the power to do so. Then, in the gospel, the angels announce to the shepherds, "Do not be afraid … to you is born this day … a Saviour." To you, the outcasts of society, the poor, a saviour has been born. In God's loving providence, the first to hear the good news are the poor. The good news is for all, and we hear it again on this night and thrill with joy.

Where do we go from here?

The liturgy of the Masses of Christmas is so rich. Take time to read and ponder the readings of all three Masses. May the joy of Christmas be in your mind and in your heart. Share the good news with others; it is too good to keep it a secret!

Jesus, may the blessings and joy of Christmas spread throughout the whole world, bringing peace.

Friday | **DECEMBER 26**

Acts 6.8-10; 7.54-59 • Psalm 31 • Matthew 10.17-22

S tephen, full of grace and power, did great wonders and signs among the people. ... "Look," he said, "I see the heavens opened and the Son of Man standing at the right hand of God!"

Acts 6.8, 7.56

....

Receive my spirit

The day after Christmas, which celebrated God's great love, the story of Stephen brings us to the foot of the cross. St. Luke, who wrote both the gospel that bears his name and the Acts of the Apostles, tells the story of Stephen as a mirror image of Jesus' death. What an abrupt passage from the Christmas story to the story of Stephen; we are faced with the price of Jesus' coming among us and the cost of discipleship. Stephen sees "the heavens opened and the Son of Man standing at the right hand of God." Jesus was born, died, rose again and ascended to his Father. Stephen's vision tells us to have hope. We will see the Lord.

Where do we go from here?

The feast of Christmas is a little Easter celebration. It tells the beginning of Jesus' story against the background of God's salvific work, and Easter completes the story of Jesus against the same background. Reflect on the story of Stephen in the Acts of the Apostles. What do you receive from it? What virtues and values can you put into place in your life in understanding the Lord's teaching in this passage?

**Be with me, Lord, and help me to face
all the challenges of life with love.**

I John 1.1-4 • Psalm 97 • John 20.2-8

So she ran and went to Simon Peter and the other disciple, the one whom Jesus loved, and said to them, "They have taken the Lord out of the tomb, and we do not know where they have laid him."

John 20.2

....

Seeking the Lord

Mary ran to the disciples to tell them Jesus was gone. Her great love impelled her to seek help as soon as possible to find the body of Jesus. Mary runs again, this time with joy, to tell them that she has seen the Lord and that he has risen. The image of Mary running is a wonderful picture of how we should seek Jesus—with eagerness and joy. Christian joy is a fruit of the Spirit, much deeper and stronger than life's suffering and troubles.

Where do we go from here?

Think about the mystery of Christian joy. In our deepest centre, we can have joy and peace in the midst of pain and turmoil by fixing ourselves with trust in God's provident care. The apostle John, whose feast we celebrate today, was not martyred, but he knew much suffering and tribulation; yet his heart was always fixed in Jesus. As an old man, he continued to preach about the love of God and neighbour as the only way to walk in the Spirit.

Jesus, fill me with the joy of your Spirit.

Genesis 15.1-6; 17.3-5, 15-16; 21.1-7 • Psalm 105 •
Hebrews 11.8, 11-12, 17-19 • Luke 2.22-40

The child grew and became strong, filled with wisdom; and the favour of God was upon him.
Luke 2.40

The family

Today we celebrate the feast of the Holy Family of Jesus, Mary and Joseph. Jesus, the Son of God, grew up in a loving family. He grew in human knowledge and experience. Jesus, the Son of God, wanted to experience all that we experience, with the exception of sin, so that we might return with him to the Father. The ordinariness of the life of the Holy Family, with its sorrows and joys, is a model and sign of hope for all families.

Where do we go from here?

Let us pray for the holiness of family life. Pray for the strengthening of family life in our society and throughout the world. We need also to pray for families in crisis and for children who are not surrounded by loving families. Most important of all, ask the Holy Family to allow your family to grow in wisdom and love. Mary and Joseph, in their obedience to God and in their loving relationship to one another, teach each of us how to act in all the circumstances of life.

**Lord, please strengthen family life in our society,
and shelter children with the love of their parents.**

1 John 2.3-11 • Psalm 96 • Luke 2.22-35

N ow by this we may be sure that we know him, if we obey his commandments. … but whoever obeys his word, truly in this person the love of God has reached perfection.

1 John 2.3, 5

....

Imitate Jesus

We have reached perfection when we obey God's words. And how do we know we are obeying God's words? If we are walking as Jesus walked. The gospels map out our way to God. Jesus is the way, and if our life has taken on Jesus' attitudes and deeds, then we are being obedient to God's commands. In our journey, God's grace strengthens our feeble efforts. Just as Mary did at the Annunciation, we receive power from on high to walk in the ways of God.

Where do we go from here?

Our obedience perfects us in God's love. We can then become a channel of God's love to others through the power of the Holy Spirit. The Holy Spirit accompanies us on our journey of faith; we never journey alone. We are never alone in facing hard decisions or getting through impossible situations. Place all your confidence in God's promise. God is with you.

Jesus, fill my heart with trust in all your promises, and renew me in your love each day.

I John 2.12-17 • Psalm 96 • Luke 2.36-40

And the world and its desire are passing away, but those who do the will of God live forever.
I John 2.17

....

God is with us

We are coming to the end of another year. Time passes so quickly and the years mount up. The passing of time, with its births and deaths and the cycle of life and changing events, give us a sense of what St. John means by the world "passing away." We want to cling to good moments, but cannot. It is our imperfect world that will pass away. All that is good and beautiful and true will remain. The Advent readings promise us a new heaven and a new earth. What that will be, we cannot imagine. We do know that all things will be filled with the glory of God, and we shall be like God.

Where do we go from here?

Everything that is of God will remain. The promise is that those who do the will of God will live forever. What are the qualities in your life that are eternal? Be specific and list them in your journal. What qualities will not last for eternity? What do you want to do? Love is eternal. Those who love and do the deeds of love are eternal. Jesus coming as a babe in Bethlehem brought a new creation. You also are a new creation. Walk into the new year clothed in God's love, and end this year with a promise of fidelity and a hope of abundant grace. Amen.

**Lord, help me to embrace what is eternal
and to live my life in your will.**

I John 2.18-21 • Psalm 96 • John 1.1-18

But you have been anointed by the Holy One, and all of you have knowledge.

I John 2.20

....

Power to be children of God

What is the anointing of the Holy One? It is the Holy Spirit. The Holy Spirit was Jesus' gift to us when he returned to the Father. He promised that the Spirit would teach and help us understand all Jesus taught and did.

The abiding presence of the Holy Spirit in our hearts is why St. John says, "[A]ll of you have knowledge." We carry within us the inestimable treasure of God's life that gives us the power to be children of God.

Where do we go from here?

God tells us we have the knowledge within us to follow Jesus in faithful love. Jesus has given us the Holy Spirit as our guide. Studying our faith and understanding what the words of the Scripture mean help us to use the wonderful gifts of the Holy Spirit. We need both head and heart knowledge to follow the Lord. We study our faith so that it may pass into our hearts. We reach out to what we love. Love, the heart, activates the way we live our faith.

Teach me your ways, O Lord.

Participating Monasteries

Canada

Precious Blood Monastery, Regina, Saskatchewan
Precious Blood Monastery, Hamilton, Ontario
Precious Blood Monastery, London, Ontario

Contributors:

Sister Eileen Mary, RPB, London
Sister Theresia Elder, RPB, Regina
Sister Marie Arsenault, RPB, Hamilton
Sister Joyce Beneteau, RPB, Hamilton
Sister Gisele Goguen, RPB, Hamilton
Sister Mary Jane MacPherson, RPB, Hamilton
Sr. Moira McClafferty, RPB, Hamilton
Sister Margaret Nadeau, RPB, Hamilton
Sister Arlene Bondoc, RPB, London
Sister Claire Jamboy, RPB, London
Sister Linda Thompson, RPB, London
Sister Jeaneth Villegas, RPB, London

Dominican Queen of Peace Monastery, Squamish, British Columbia

Contributors:

Sister Claire Marie, op
Sister Mary Angela, op
Sister Mary Regina, op
Sister Jean Marie, op
Sister Mary Bernadette, op

Participating Monasteries

United States

Dominican Monastery, Benicasa, Delaware

Contributor:
Sr. Mary Emmanuella Handlos, op

Corpus Christi Monastery, Menlo Park, California

Contributor:
Sister Mary of the Sacred Heart, op

Monastery of the Blessed Sacrament, Farmington Hills, Michigan

Contributors:
Sr. Faustina Marie, op
Sr. Dominic Marie, op

Monastery of the Infant Jesus, Lufkin, Texas

Contributors:
Sister Mary John, op
Sister Mary Jeremiah, op
Sister Mary Thomas, op
Sister Mary Margaret, op

Monastery of Our Lady of the Rosary, Summit, New Jersey

Contributors:
Sister Maria Teresa, op

Participating Monasteries

Ireland

St. Catherine of Siena Monastery

Contributors:

Sister Fiona, op

Sister Margaret, op

Sister Ann Marie, op

Sister Clare Marie, op

Sister Mairead, op

Sister Niamh, op

Sister Regina, op

Sister Mary Emmanuel, op

Sister Mary Kathleen, op

Sister Paula Mary, op

Sister Mary Breda, op

Notes

Books to Enrich Your Spirit

The Garden Way of the Cross

By Fr. Thomas Stanley
Illustrations by Louise Tessier

Rather than make figurative plaques for the walls of
a parish church, artist Louise Tessier created ceramic
tiles that focus on botanical imagery drawn from Fr.
Thomas Stanley's reflections. Collected in this book are
the stunning images of each of these stations along with
prayerful meditations and the plant's symbolic relation to
the station. Through these vibrant images and evocative
reflections we go on a botanical journey through Jesus'
life-giving death and resurrection.

144pp PB 978-2-89646-407-4 $18.95

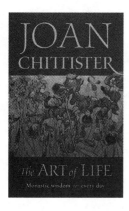

The Art of Life

By Sr. Joan Chittister, OSB

The best of ourselves - that's what Sr. Joan Chittister wants
each of us to become. Through brief daily reflections, the
bestselling author looks to great works of art for inspiration,
bringing the monastic perspective to the brushstrokes of
masters like Van Gogh, Cezanne, Millet, and more. This
stirring and inspiring collection is full of the wisdom, wit,
encouragement, and advice that have made Sr. Joan one of
the great spiritual writers of our time.

128pp PB 978-2-89646-537-8 $19.95

NOVALIS
www.novalis.ca

Books to Enrich Your Spirit

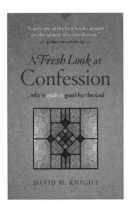

A Fresh Look at Confession:
Why it Really Is Good for the Soul
By Fr. David M. Knight

A Fresh Look at Confession is unlike anything you may have read about the sacrament. Fr. Knight speaks about the heart of Confession, its meaning and mystery, and why it is so necessary for authentic followers of Christ. This is deep theology, explained in clear language. But it's also much more: Father Knight's moving, intensely personal account of his own journey as a sinner takes readers beyond theory and into the awe-inspiring reality of our complete redemption in Jesus.

128pp PB 978-2-89646-574-3 $14.95

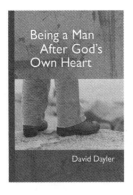

Being a Man After God's Own Heart
By David Dayler

Through gripping accounts and stimulating reflection questions, *Being a Man After God's Own Heart* challenges men to consider the lives of biblical and historic figures to see how they answered God's call to do extraordinary things. Whether on their own or in small groups, this book will help men discover real ways to integrate faith with everyday life.

112pp PB 978-2-89646-489-0 $11.95

Cornerstones of Faith:
Reconciliation, Eucharist and Stewardship
By Cardinal Thomas Collins

Regular celebration of the Sacrament of Reconciliation changes the way we relate to those around us. The Eucharist nourishes and sustains us as disciples of Jesus. Through these Sacraments, we experience what Collins refers to as "a profound inner conversion that leads us to live in a spirit of generosity, which is most fully revealed in the sharing of time and talent" and are compelled to be good stewards of God's gifts to us.

Cornerstones of Faith offers accessible reflections with tangible exercises to help readers live their faith every day. Questions at the end of each chapter make this an excellent resource for both personal reflection and parish discussion groups.

112pp PB 978-2-89646-531-6 $12.95

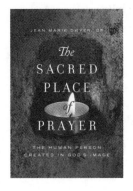

The Sacred Place of Prayer:
The Human Person Created in God's Image
By Sr. Jean Marie Dwyer, OP

Learning to be a person of prayer introduces new and wonderful elements into our life. Grow in wonder and awe of the divine presence of God in your life through a life of prayer. Let Sr. Dwyer, a monastic and woman of deep prayer, help you learn the fundamentals of prayer and find ways to make it a central part of your daily life.

164pp PB 978-2-89646-318-3 $16.95

NOVALIS
www.novalis.ca

Books to Enrich Your Spirit

Aspects of the Heart:
The Many Paths to a Good Life
By Sr. Joan Chittister, OSB

Sr. Joan Chittister brings us fifty different ways to explore the role that our hearts can play in our spirituality and humanity. With the wisdom of an attentive sage, Chittister writes brief, two-page contemplations to help us unlock our hearts and the spiritual depths within.

112pp HC 978-2-89646-538-5 $14.95

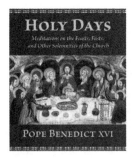

Holy Days:
Meditations on the Feasts, Fasts and Other Solemnities of the Church Year
By Pope Benedict XVI

Beginning with Advent and concluding with the feast of Christ the King, *Holy Days* presents selected homilies that the Pope has pronounced over the course of the liturgical year in Rome. Organized by season and feast days, with brief introductions, this short volume will be a welcome companion for those journeying through the liturgical year.

96pp PB 978-2-89646-529-3 $12.95

NOVALIS
www.novalis.ca